TREASURES OF
Tennessee & Kentucky

Tennessee State Capitol Building, Nashville
Photo by Brent Moore

Kentucky State Capitol Building, Frankfort
Photo by Erin Pettigrew

by Damon Neal

a part of the Morgan & Chase Treasure Series
www.treasuresof.com

MORGAN & CHASE PUBLISHING INC.

Morgan & Chase Publishing, Inc.
531 Parsons Drive, Medford, Oregon 97501
(888) 557-9328
www.treasuresof.com

Printed and bound by Taylor Specialty Books–Dallas TX
First edition 2008
ISBN: 978-1-933989-17-4

THE
TREASURE
SERIES

I gratefully acknowledge the contributions
of the many people involved in the writing and production of this book.
Their tireless dedication to this endeavour has been inspirational.
–William Faubion, Publisher

The Morgan & Chase Publishing Home Team

Operations Department:
V.P. of Operations–Cindy Tilley Faubion
Travel Writer Liaison–Anne Boydston
Shipping & Receiving–Virginia Arias
Human Resources Coordinator–Heather Allen
Customer Service Relations–Elizabeth Taylor, Vikki West
IT Engineer–Ray Ackerman
Receptionist–Samara Sharp

Production Department:
Office Manager–Sue Buda
Editor/Writer–Robyn Sutherland
House Writer–Prairie Smallwood
Proof Editor–Clarice Rodriguez
Photo Coordinator–Wendy L. Gay
Photo Editor–Mary Murdock
Graphic Design Team–C.S. Rowan, Jesse Gifford, Jacob Kristof

Administrative Department:
CFO–Emily Wilkie
Accounting Assistants–David Grundvig, Tiffany Myers
Website Designer–Molly Bermea
Website Software Developer–Ben Ford

Contributing Writers:
Mary Beth Lee, Dave Fox, Mark Allen Deruiter, Cynthia Garcia, LaShonda Sims, Jamie McCartney, John Holtzman, Rick Martin, Alexis McKenna, Amber Dusk, Carol Bevis, Catherine Perez, CJ White, Dusty Alexander, Jamee Rae, Jeanie Erwin, Jennifer Buckner, Karuna Glomb, Kate Zdrojewski, Kevin Monk, Lisa Morris, Marek Alday, Mary Knepp, Mary Sandlin, Maya Moore, Patricia Smith, Paul Hadella, Robert J. Benjamin, Sandy McLain, Sarah Brown, Susan Vaughn, Timothy Smith, Todd Wels, Tamara Cornett

Special Recognition to:
Casey Faubion, April Higginbotham, Gregory Scott, Megan Glomb, Eric Molinsky, Marie Manson, William M. Evans, Gene Mitts

This book is dedicated to Kentucky and Tennessee's most amazing resource, the people who live there.

Foreword

Welcome to *Treasures of Tennessee and Kentucky*. This book is a resource that can guide you to some of the most inviting places in Tennessee and Kentucky, states filled with rich histories and natural diversity. From the Great Smoky Mountains to the breathtaking Bluegrass region, Kentucky and Tennessee offer stunning views and pleasant subtropical climates. Both states are known for their inventive and talented people. They have created the Kentucky Derby, fascinating museums, multitudes of shopping opportunities and the most flavorful cuisine to be found anywhere in the world.

While visiting Kentucky and Tennessee, you should partake in the enlightening cultural heritage of both states. Take a moment to visit some of the interesting and moving sites throughout both states. Everything from Mammoth Cave Natural Park, to the Tennessee River, to the Red River Gorge, these two states have it all. If you enjoy outdoor recreation Tennessee and Kentucky are filled with bountiful activities. There are endless hiking trails just waiting to be explored, plus rivers and waterways that are ideal for fishing, boating and rafting. Kentucky and Tennessee have unmatched natural features that will have you reaching for your camera before you can even think of making an itinerary. Both states are places of great diversity, with admirable collections of restaurants, art galleries, bed-and-breakfasts, and exciting shopping opportunities.

In preparing *Treasures of Kentucky and Tennessee*, we talked to literally thousands of business people about their products and their passions. We walked along the Appalachian Trail as we reflected on the incredible history of these two interesting states. We visited community theatres and hundreds of attractions such as zoos, museums and an abundant array of cultural celebrations. You are holding the result of our efforts in your hands. The *Treasures of Tennessee and Kentucky* is a 341-page compilation of the best places in Kentucky and Tennessee to eat, shop, play, explore, learn and relax. We had the privilege of seeing all the great people and places this book is about. All you have to do now is enjoy the result of our efforts.

—**Cindy Tilley Faubion**

STATE OF TENNESSEE

PHIL BREDESEN
GOVERNOR

Dear Readers:

As Governor of the great State of Tennessee, I would like to thank you for taking interest in our state. The following photos, facts, and stories help paint a picture of the Tennessee Treasures that make this such a special place to live.

I truly feel honored to serve as Governor of this state and am equally honored to live here as a citizen. Tennessee has a little something for everyone. We have a diverse landscape of rolling mountains, expansive farmlands, and beautiful lakes and streams. We also enjoy a wonderful mixture of urban and rural character that provides opportunities for most any lifestyle. Our southern hospitality and strong workforce and economy make Tennessee one of the best places in the country to settle down to start a family or build a career.

While I am confident this book will demonstrate many of these positive attributes of Tennessee, I want to encourage you to visit for yourself. We will be glad to welcome you, and I know you will be glad you came.

Warmest regards,

Phil Bredesen

PB/jee

Table of Contents: Tennessee

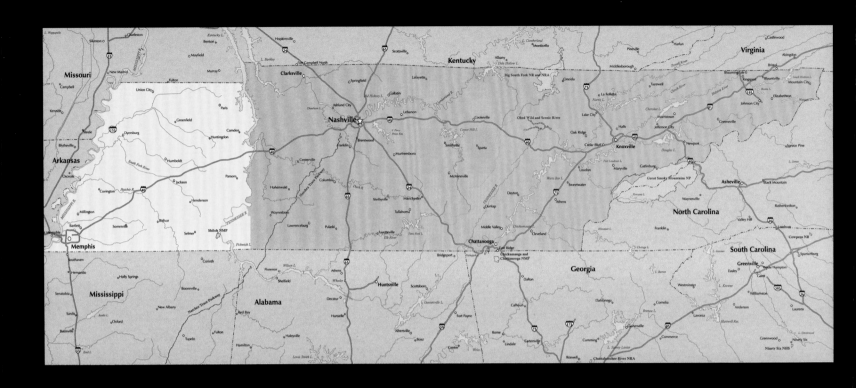

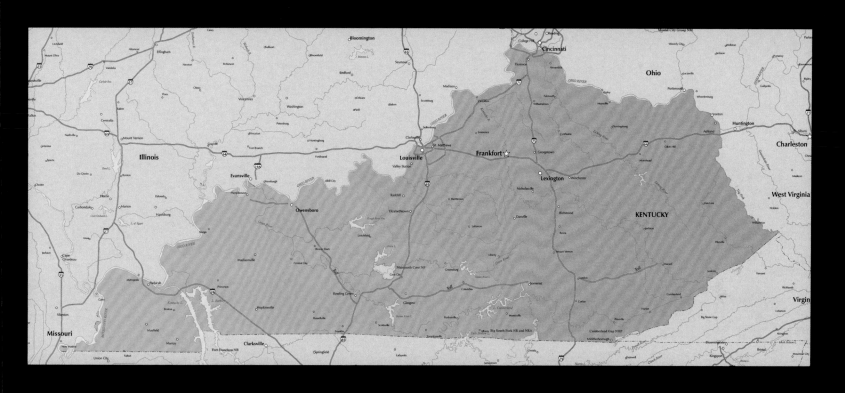

How to use this book

The *Treasures of Tennessee & Kentucky* is divided by region and category. Categories range from special treasures to wines, with headings such as accommodations, attractions, galleries, museums, restaurants and shopping in between. In the index, all of the Treasures are listed alphabetically by name. We have provided contact information for every Treasure in the book. They are the places and businesses we encourage you to visit during your future travels through Kentucky & Tennessee.

We sincerely hope you find this book to be both beautiful and useful.

Memphis, TN

West Tennessee

Agape Child & Family Services

Love is the driving force behind Agape Child & Family Services. Established in 1970, Agape has been providing children and families with healthy homes for more than 37 years. This Christian-based, nonprofit organization offers services including foster care, pregnancy counseling and adoption, in coordination with the Adoption Center of the MidSouth. Agape's three offices in Memphis and Jackson serve the entire West Tennessee, Mississippi and Arkansas region with Christ-centered services, education and advocacy. The organization's accomplishments have been widely recognized. In 2001, Agape launched the Families in Touch (FIT) program, which provides support services to homeless pregnant mothers and their children so they can remain in their own homes. Due to an astounding 87 percent success rate, the program's service capacity has nearly doubled since its inception. Agape's Counseling Center (ACC) is the largest faith-based counseling center in the Mid South, providing marriage and family counseling services. Together, Agape's Board of Directors, employees and generous volunteers run one of the most distinguished nonprofits of its kind. By 2010, Agape aims to be the premier voice for children, adults, and families, serving more than 50,000 people annually. Despite the growth and success of Agape Child & Family Services, it remains forever committed to preserving relationships, transforming lives and building loving communities.

111 Racine Street, Memphis TN
(901) 323-3600
www.agapemeanslove.org

Walker Auctions

Since 1979, the folks at Walker Auctions have conducted more than 2,000 auctions specializing in two main areas: fundraising auctions for charities throughout the United States and Canada, and real estate and estate auctions performed throughout the mid-South. Each year, these talented auctioneers help charities raise more than $10,000,000. The Walkers are known for conducting benefit auctions in a fun-filled manner and providing profitable consultation before the auction. Many groups consider them the leading benefit auctioneers in the country. Their credentials testify to this as well. Lance Walker was selected by the National Auctioneers Association (NAA) to co-write and teach the Benefit Auctioneer Specialist Program for other auctioneers, while Terri Walker has been selected as first runner-up twice in the NAA International Auctioneers Contest. Members of the NAA recently elected Lance to their board of directors, and Terri recently completed a term as chair of the Tennessee Auctioneers Commission. In the Memphis area, the couple enjoys helping people who need to sell real estate quickly. People settling estates, or home owners who are facing divorce, job transfer or any other circumstance can count on the services of Walker Auctions. The Walkers' son Conner has recently joined the family business as well. Mid-Southerners have learned that when you need a fast talker, you need Lance, Terri or Conner Walker. Walker Auctions is located in Memphis just off I-240.

6363 Poplar Avenue, Suite 317, Memphis TN (901) 384-9992 *www.walkerauctions.com*

The Peabody Hotel

A Memphis landmark in the heart of downtown, The Peabody Hotel Memphis has long been the South's Grand Hotel. Since the completion of a major renovation in 2005, it has even more claim to the title. Each of the hotel's 464 rooms and suites were remodeled and redecorated. The historic ballrooms and public spaces, such as the famous Grand Lobby, have been carefully restored. Guests can now enjoy the luxury they've come to expect from this icon with a fresh new gleam. In addition to its deluxe guest rooms, the hotel offers a variety of specialty suites. Peabody Suites feature reception parlors that fit up to 15 guests. Romeo and Juliet Suites offer exquisite loft bedrooms with spiral staircases and a reception parlor accommodating up to 30 guests. Celebrity Suites include a king bedroom, wet bar, refrigerator, formal dining room and small parlor. For the ultimate in accommodations, the Presidential Suite provides the largest parlor. One of the hotel's main attractions is The Peabody Marching Ducks, who live on the roof and spend their days in the Grand Lobby fountain. Every morning at 11 and evening at 5 the ducks march to and from the fountain to the strains of John Philip Sousa's *King Cotton March*. The Peabody offers three restaurants, including Chez Philippe, the only Mobil Four-Star restaurant in the mid-South. Enjoy grand accommodations and meet the lovable ducks at The Peabody Hotel.

149 Union Avenue, Memphis TN
(901) 529-4000
www.peabodymemphis.com

Oakslea Place

Oakslea Place

Oakslea Place is a Jackson bed and breakfast that is rich in history, in charm and in architectural integrity. It's also haunted, in a harmless sort of way, according to owner Ric Testani and some of his guests. Ric Testani purchased the 1860 home in 2004 and, after a complete renovation, took in his first guests in 2005. This Southern plantation is one of the oldest homes in Madison County. Tunnels running underneath the house hid Confederate soldiers during the Civil War. The walls of Oakslea Place feature hand-painted murals depicting the home's exterior and hand-painted designs that repeat like wallpaper. Guests choose from four suites. Two are doubles, perfect for families or guests seeking more space. The Scarlett Suite offers a separate area that brides appreciate for hair and makeup application on their wedding day. The Ashley Suite features panoramic views of the enchanting garden. Guests love the grounds, which feature an abundance of flowering plants and make photogenic backdrops for wedding pictures. The banquet facilities can accommodate parties as large as 200 people, while the Viola and Tara Rooms each seat up to 40 people and can be equipped for business functions. The Webster Library is a lovely space for intimate, informal gatherings. Guests usually take breakfast in the home's centrally located Breakfast Room or in one of the cafés. Whether or not you hear footsteps or see an apparition, you can be certain that in all ways Oakslea Place is romantic and other-worldly. Prepare to be charmed at Oakslea Place, one of Jackson's most beloved landmarks.

1210 N Highland Avenue, Jackson TN
(731) 554-1760
www.oakslea.com

Oakslea Place Restaurants

Culinary delights await around every corner at the 9,000-square-foot Oakslea Place, a Jackson mansion that now operates as a bed-and-breakfast. Choosing where to eat might prove to be your toughest challenge, because there are four extraordinary restaurants. Owner Ric Testani opened the bed-and-breakfast and its four separate restaurants in 2005. Each restaurant occupies a special place in this beautifully preserved 1860 home. Guests enjoy specially prepared meals in the Breakfast Room, located in the center of the house. The Rhett Café beckons for a mid-afternoon pick-me-up. The café's large windows and outdoor seating options make this a desirable spot to enjoy the gardens along with a shot of espresso, cappuccino, latte or flavored coffee. The Plantation Tearoom offers still more views. Floor to ceiling windows and an intimate setting attract bed and breakfast guests, or you can book the space for a private function. You can make a reservation in advance for dinner in the more formal Viola Room, where the owner himself prepares gourmet cuisine such as his signature pasta dishes. The Viola Room also can be reserved for meetings and special functions. Oakslea Place is more than a pretty, historic face. Visit the Oakslea Place Restaurants for versatile dining options in a grand mansion of magnificent proportions.

1210 N Highland Avenue, Jackson TN
(731) 554-1760
www.oakslea.com

The Inn at Hunt Phelan

In 1990, when Bill Day moved into a home that has been in his family for more than 175 years, it was, as he says, in "wrecking ball condition." After 14 years of painstaking restoration based on the plans of original architect, Robert Mills, the Inn at Hunt Phelan once again reflects its antebellum elegance. Amazing attention to detail, down to replicating the original drapery fabric, has earned Hunt Phelan a national design award from the American Society of Interior Designers as well as more than 20 local and national restoration awards. This bed-and-breakfast features 12 sumptuous guest rooms that showcase antique furnishings and authentic fabrics. The spacious bathrooms create the spa-like ambience of an upscale hotel. The inn's restaurant, called Dinner in the Mansion, is one of Memphis' few four-star establishments. It serves up exquisite French Creole cuisine by Chef Stephen Hassinger in elegantly ornate dining rooms. The Veranda Grill offers cocktails, conversation and bistro fare either inside or on the patio. The beautifully landscaped grounds, New Orleans-style patio and large fountain with a stage gazebo create the ideal setting for a wedding or other special occasion. The mansion also features banquet rooms. Placed on the National Register of Historic Places in 1970, the inn has hosted three past American presidents and even (long ago) the president of the Confederacy. Come experience rich history and old-fashioned Southern hospitality at the Inn at Hunt Phelan.

533 Beale Street, Memphis TN
(901) 525-8225
www.huntphelan.com

Talbot Heirs Guesthouse

For travelers weary of one-size-fits-all hotel chains, the Talbot Heirs Guesthouse offers a sophisticated sanctuary. Tucked away in the Gayoso Peabody District of downtown Memphis, Talbot Heirs combines over-the-top personal service, private surroundings and a convenient location. Owners Tom and Sandy Franck assure your comfort with spacious suites that feature several styles of décor, from traditional to trendy. Standard features include CD players, cable television and full kitchens with coffee makers, toasters and dinnerware. Business travelers appreciate the complimentary high-speed Internet access, dual phone lines with voice mail, and a first floor business center that includes copiers, mail service and a drop point for overnight delivery service. Just minutes from Beale Street, Peabody Place, the Mississippi River and the business district, the guesthouse is within easy walking distance of just about anything you could want, including theaters, sports venues, museums, newsstands and restaurants. The *New York Times* calls the guesthouse "one of the city's best secrets," and many actors and celebrities, including Hal Holbrook, have stayed here. Whether you travel for business or pleasure, enhance your time in Memphis by staying at the Talbot Heirs Guesthouse.

99 S 2nd Street, Memphis TN
(901) 527-9772 or (800) 955-3956
www.talbotheirs.com

Old English Inn

The exclusive styling of the Old English Inn in Jackson charms all who visit. Chip Coughlin reopened the inn in 2004 after a complete restoration, which included the addition of stained glass windows and antique English furnishings. From the English garden landscaping to the Tudor architecture, the charms of an English country home surround the guests. Each of the 103 rooms and suites has the air of a private residence. Canopy beds, fireplaces and patios are some of the luxurious options. If you stay in the Presidential Suite, you will be in a room that President Gerald Ford once occupied. Each room offers high-speed Internet access. The inn may have an English appearance, but the on-site World Champion Cajun Cookers Bar-B-Que is decidedly Southern. Chef Darrell Hicks serves steak, chicken and seafood in addition to his award-winning barbecue. "You start with the best ingredients and you end with the best product," he says. The inn serves a complimentary Belgian waffle breakfast as well as a Sunday buffet that draws about 500 patrons each week. Five conference rooms can accommodate everything from a small reception to a large seminar. Catering services are available. Guests appreciate the outdoor pool and free admission to Gold's Gym, located next door. The inn is close to many area attractions, including golf and the Rockabilly Hall of Fame. For a combination of Southern and English charm, come to the Old English Inn.

2267 N Highland Avenue, Jackson TN
(731) 668-1571
www.oldenglishinn.com

Pickwick Cabin Rentals

When you visit Pickwick Lake, Pickwick Cabin Rentals can provide you a place to stay that meets your requirements, whatever they may be. Pickwick Cabin Rentals is the premier provider of vacation cabins at the lake, and its high standards ensure your satisfaction. If you prefer the outdoors, you can stay in a secluded cabin tucked amid trees and greenery. For water-lovers, Pickwick has lakefront cabins where aquatic activities are steps from your door. You can also book one of the cabins that are set back but have open views of the shimmering lake. Another choice is the Aqua Villas next to the Aqua Lake Harbor overlooking Pickwick Lake. Here, you have access to pools, tennis courts, playgrounds and boat rentals. All Pickwick rentals are fully furnished with towels, linens, barbecue grills and kitchenware. Near the lake you can golf, take in the annual boat races and fishing derbies, or visit the Shiloh National Military Park, home of the 1862 Civil War battle. To reserve your cabin for your great escape, contact owner Beverly Rushing or one of her talented staff members at Pickwick Cabin Rentals.

25 Bluebird Road, Counce TN
(731) 689-0400 or (800) 848-8177
www.pickwicklakecabins.com

Highland Place
Bed and Breakfast Inn

You'll see rainbows in the hallway when the light streams through the leaded panels at Highland Place Bed and Breakfast Inn. It's just one of the lovely details that makes staying at this 1911 Colonial Revival mansion such a pleasure. Art lovers especially find kindred spirits in innkeepers Bill and Cindy Pflaum. Pieces from their extensive art collection add Native American tones throughout the home. The four guest rooms are quite different from each other, though equal in luxury. The Louis Room, named for the family that built the mansion nearly a century ago, features a large Plantation bedroom ensemble with armoire, side tables and an elegant queen bed. The fireplace and four-poster bed in the Hamilton Room make it ideal for a romantic getaway. If you're feeling stressed, a long soak in the Butler Suite's claw-foot tub may be just what you need. Wall's Atrium, a three-room suite, is big on charm, thanks to a skylight, adobe-style log fireplace and tile mural. Breakfast is a festive affair, featuring freshly ground coffee, fresh fruits and whatever goodies Cindy is making from scratch. Your hosts will also serve a complete five-course dinner if you make prior arrangements. The beauty is in the details at Highland Place Bed & Breakfast Inn. Plan a visit to see for yourself.

519 N Highland Avenue, Jackson TN
(731) 427-1472 or (877) 614-6305
www.highlandplace.com

Animal Photography by Peggy Foster

Peggy Foster has a patient and non-threatening presence that animals respond to immediately. She also has an artist's knack for capturing their personality on film. For over 16 years, Peggy has photographed the endearing looks and soulful eyes of our four-legged companions. Her portfolio reminds us of the many reasons why we love our pets. She prefers to create *environmental portraiture* at the client's home whenever possible, since pets tend to be more relaxed in their own surroundings. "Their comfort level will definitely show in their expressions," she adds. Her work has appeared in many horse and dog magazines, on billboards and even in a Disney movie. While Peggy generally works with cats, dogs and horses, she has also photographed birds and even a lizard or two. For pet portraits that you will treasure forever, contact Animal Photography by Peggy Foster.

Memphis TN
(901) 324-7695
www.gotpets.net

Wags & Whiskers

Betty Kay spent a lot of time at dog shows with her three Portuguese Water Dogs before she opened her shop in Memphis, Wags & Whiskers. When she wasn't following the competition, she was visiting vendors to stock up on products that weren't available in her hometown. Today, pet owners will find an array of specialty items for dogs and cats at Betty's store, including toys and healthful foods. You can also purchase what you need to dress your pet warmly or to make him or her look like a rock star, because Wags & Whiskers carries pet clothing. Attending to pets with special needs is something that Betty takes seriously. She carries treats for dogs with diabetes, joint problems and allergies. She also offers cat litter for cats with health problems. Working with local rescue organizations and sponsoring adoption days at her store are other ways in which Betty tries to make a difference. A sight that all Memphis-area animal lovers must see is the Wags & Whiskers version of an Easter Parade that files in front of the store each year. It features pets decked out in their finest spring attire. Proceeds support local pet charities. Drop by Wags & Whiskers, where you are always welcome to bring your pet into the shop with you.

5101 Sanderlin Avenue, Suite 104-A, Memphis TN
(901) 761-6064
www.wagswhiskers.com

Memphis Drum Shop

Whether they're looking to bash out heavy metal beats or back up gospel music, every drummer from the beginner to the professional will be pleased with the service and supplies at Memphis Drum Shop. This store offers acoustic drums from all the major brands, such as Yamaha, Pearl and DW. If you're looking for state-of-the-art Roland and Yamaha digital drums, you'll find them here too. "We do not position ourselves as just a pro shop," says owner Jim Pettit. "We are community-oriented; I want to be here for that local drummer." Pettit adds that his passions are "drums, music and people." The store's staff consists of friendly, knowledgeable drummers ready to offer top-notch advice. Professional drummers give classes at the shop, which also offers clinics and concerts that feature popular local drummers as well as famous international drummers and music ensembles. Memphis Drum Shop's Vintage Vault, with its historical exhibits of snares, drum kits and cymbals, is a tourist destination, and the shop's T-shirts turn up all over the world. Every year, the shop hosts a Jazz for St. Jude benefit concert for St. Jude's Children's Hospital. Famous jazz drummer Peter Erskine once said, "If you can play a simple beat and play it well, all the other stuff will come together as it is supposed to." Find your way to the beat with a visit to Memphis Drum Shop, a store for drummers by drummers.

878 S Cooper Street, Memphis TN
(901) 276-2328
www.memphisdrumshop.com

Eclectica Scrapbooks & Stamps

If you have a passion for scrapbooking, you will get a little giddy at Eclectica, a source for Reminisce, Colorbok, Daisy D's and many other popular suppliers. Many people travel on faith to this store just north of the Wolfchase Mall, having heard that its selection of scrapbook supplies and rubber stamps rivals that of any store in the Mid-South. After driving two or three hours in some cases, they step anxiously through the door to take it all in. Owner Rhonda Feiler never tires of seeing their reaction, a look on their faces that says they have found heaven. Rhonda, an avid scrapbooker herself, decided to open Eclectica because other stores weren't feeding her hunger for the latest innovative supplies. She says that her mission is to make the world a more beautiful place, one scrapbook page at a time. If you are new to the hobby, Eclectica offers classes with a schedule that changes monthly so that everyone can eventually get in on the fun. The creative staff offers instruction in stamping and card making as well as scrapbooking workshops. Wild & Wacky Sales bring folks hurrying through the door every Wednesday to see what items have been discounted for that day only. For a selection of scrapbook supplies that won't disappoint, try Eclectica.

2965 N Germantown Parkway, #104, Memphis TN
(901) 377-0730
www.eclecticamemphis.com

The Quilting Barn

The Quilting Barn, located on historic Depot Square in Arlington, opened for business December 1, 2005. Owners Lynda Hoskins and Shelia Medlin describe themselves as sisters by love and partners by choice. With a mission to carry on the tradition of handmade quilts, they found the perfect building (originally constructed in the 1800s) to house the Quilting Barn. They offer lots of quality fabric to choose from and many classes designed to teach even the most inexperienced of seamstresses the age-old arts of hand-piecing and quilting. For those who want to speed up the process, classes are also offered in piecing and quilting by sewing machine. Lynda and Shelia were blessed by their dad, now in his 80s, with the gift of a long-arm Gammill Quilting Machine. The sisters offer quilting services for those customers who like to piece their quilt tops but prefer to have them machine-quilted. Check out the Quilting Barn's website for directions to this wonderful destination in old-town Arlington.

12019 Walker Street, Arlington TN
(901) 867-4824
www.arlingtonquiltingbarn.com

Klassy Katz

If Toni Katz's career had followed the path laid out by her education, she might be reviewing the quality of the Memphis water supply right now. Instead, she is fostering the art of quilting at her fabric shop, Klassy Katz. About a year after opening the business, Toni won a Bernina sewing machine dealership, becoming one of only two Bernina dealers in the Memphis area. Klassy Katz now devotes an entire section to displaying the machines and to a large teaching area. Teaching, after all, is what got Toni into this business. After receiving her degree in water resource management, she became a stay-at-home mom who earned money by teaching people how to sew. Maybe some day she'll get to use her college degree, but right now she's having too much fun teaching classes in how to make clothing, embroidery software and quilting to think about it. Klassy Katz is also the exclusive Nolting quilting machine dealer for the Memphis area, and the only location in the city offering independent patterns for making clothes. With its wide array of fashion fabrics, two classrooms and an expert staff to teach people how to use the latest sewing machines, it is the place to go for all your quilt and fashion-making needs. Toni invites you to drop by.

2958 Elmore Park Road, Bartlett TN
(901) 213-0099
www.klassykatzquilts.com

Yarbrough's Music

For over 32 years, Yarbrough's Music has fostered camaraderie among local musicians through Tuesday night bluegrass jams and a full-service music store. Phil and Mary Yarbrough and family have been doing their part to preserve roots music, first in a small coffee shop in Raleigh, then at the music store, which opened in 1973. The Yarbroughs describe a jam session as a place "where the pickin's free and the jam is sweet." It's a place where musicians from seven to 70, whether professional or brand-new to their instruments, can come together for the fun of making new friends and the love of the music. Guests are treated to the sounds of banjos, guitars and keyboards as well as mandolins, drums and fiddles. Musicians of all ages and backgrounds marvel at the products and services available at the store. In addition to musical instruments, audio, lighting and video needs can all be met here with a selection that includes 500 of the most popular product lines in each category. You'll soon find that the only thing the Yarbrough family loves as much as music is good customer service. The family offers repair and rental services, plus music education, courtesy of Yarbrough's Music University, where you can learn any style of guitar, banjo, mandolin, drums or dulcimer. No matter what level you're at, Yarbrough's Music can take you on the next step. Visit the experts today and let them put you in tune with your musical dreams.

6122 Macon Road, Memphis TN
(901) 761-0414
www.yarbroughsmusic.com

Lane Music

If you took lessons at some stodgy music school when you were young, you probably wish for something different for your child. In Memphis, the cool choice is the Lane Music Rock School, offered through the metro area's full-line music store. The Rock School meets weekly for 90 minutes, and leads students to the goal of performing live and recording a CD of the gig. You can count on Lane Music not only for this exciting approach to music instruction but for a huge selection of instruments as well. You'll find everything from pianos, guitars and stringed instruments to clarinets, saxophones and other band instruments. Realizing that not everyone aspires to become a rock star, Lane Music helps music students achieve their goals on any instrument it sells in the store. About 500 students per week receive instruction in the school. Lane Music has earned recognition as an Inner Circle Kawai piano dealership, Kawai's most prestigious award. A sister store, Memphis Music, is a full-line Yamaha dealership offering pianos that include digital Clavinovas and Disklaviers. Both stores provide a comfortable setting for customers to try out any of the instruments. Musicians of every level also enjoy browsing the nice selection of instructional books and songbooks at both locations. Hit all the right notes at Lane Music.

9309 Poplar Avenue, Germantown TN
(901) 755-5025
www.lanemusic.com
5237 Poplar Avenue, Memphis TN (Memphis Music)
(901) 937-8484
www.memphispiano.com

Fiddler's Green Music Shop

Fiddler's Green Music Shop is Memphis' only all-acoustic music store. Owner Clay Levit has created a listening room where traditional and folk musicians can enjoy playing the instruments, in contrast to the noisy environment in many electric guitar stores. Fiddler's Green offers the largest selection of Breedlove guitars in Memphis and also showcases beautifully handmade Altman mandolins, which sound woody and aged even when new. Clay is also the only dealer in the city to handle Blueridge guitars, a brand greatly favored by bluegrass pickers. Want to learn to play an instrument? The shop's accomplished teachers offer lessons in various styles of play, and instruction books and videos are available as well. Fiddler's Green repairs all types of instruments and stocks the largest selection of strings in the area. A guitar player himself since age 11, Clay also used to be an organic farmer. When he and his wife moved to the city, she encouraged him to follow his heart, and Fiddler's Green is the result. Clay actively promotes acoustic music by sponsoring the Mid-South Celtic Arts Alliance and the Memphis Symphony and supporting local bluegrass music associations. Whether you're looking for a fine instrument, new strings, instrument repairs or just a place to network and noodle with other musicians, Fiddler's Green Music Shop is the place to go.

5101 Sanderlin Avenue, Suite 104-B, Memphis TN
(901) 684-2227
www.fiddlersgreenmusicshop.com

Yarn to Go

Yarn to Go has all the needles, yarn, patterns and supplies knitters need to keep themselves in stitches. Elizabeth Crockett opened the Memphis business after a 14-year retirement. At first, she sold yarn from her home, but the sheer volume of calls she was getting convinced her to open her own store. Today, that store offers everything a knitter needs. Bins of yarn line the walls of two full rooms. Ninety percent of the yarn is imported, much of it from Italy. The large assortment includes the very popular eyelash yarn and ribbon yarn used in many modern knitting projects. Another room in the store is dedicated to patterns that will fire your fancy and keep those knitting needles clicking for years to come. You'll also find knitting needles in many sizes and price ranges. Even if you're not looking to buy anything, you're welcome to come in, sit down and knit. Elizabeth says most of her customers find knitting very therapeutic. "You can lose your mind in a pattern and ball of yarn and not think about another thing," she says. Knitters stopping in will find staff and customers interested in sharing ideas and answering questions. Elizabeth teaches classes for every skill level at the shop. Prepare for your next knitting project with a visit to Yarn to Go.

2883 Poplar Avenue, Memphis TN
(901) 454-4118 or (866) 383-5918
www.yarn2go.com

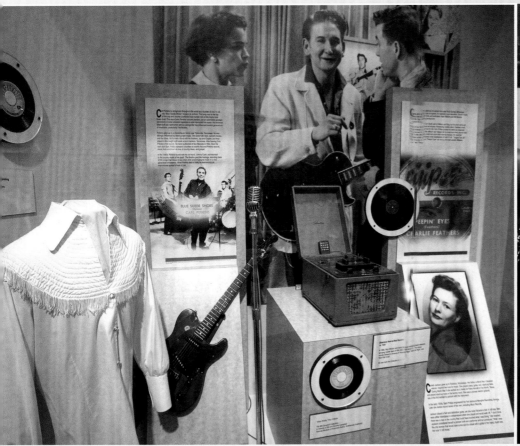

Memphis Rock 'n' Soul Museum

The Memphis Rock 'n' Soul Museum celebrates the history of rock 'n' roll and soul music. In 1996, the Smithsonian Institution developed a traveling exhibition entitled *Rock 'n' Soul: Social Crossroads* to mark its 150th anniversary. Following the completion of the exhibition, a group of Memphis visionaries raised the funds to acquire musical memorabilia and to complete the installation and construction of a museum that would permanently house the exhibition. The museum tells of the musical legends of all races, born rich or poor, who overcame obstacles to create a sound that changed the culture of the world. The Rock 'n' Soul's MP3 audio guide allows visitors to tour at their own pace and contains more than 300 minutes of information as well as more than 100 songs recorded in and around Memphis from the 1930s to the 1970s. The seven galleries showcase more than 30 instruments and 40 costumes and tell the story of the music that influenced the culture and life of the world from the mid 20th century to today. Expect to find it all here, from 1930s sharecropper's porch music and 1940s Beale Street blues to details about the lives of Elvis Presley, Johnny Cash, Jerry Lee Lewis and B.B. King. Come experience the magic of the Memphis Rock 'n' Soul Museum. It's now located in the FedExForum at the corner of legendary Highway 61 (the Blues Highway) and world-famous Beale Street.

191 Beale Street, Suite 100, Memphis TN (901) 205-2533

Graceland

Heartbreak Hotel

Mud Island River Park

Whether you're traveling two miles or 200, Mud Island River Park is a worthy destination. This piece of Americana, one of 11 parks operated by the Riverfront Development Corporation, encompasses acres of fun and education right across from downtown Memphis. History buffs, put on your walking shoes and prepare for tales of the Mighty Mississippi. Admittance to the park is free, but purchase of the Mud Island Savings Package gains you entry to the Mississippi River Museum, a ride on the Monorail, and a guided Riverwalk Tour. A full-size 1870s steamboat replica, an 1860s gunboat replica and myriad Civil War artifacts will leave you awestruck. The RiverWalk, five city blocks long, provides a detailed scale model of the Lower Mississippi River from Cairo, Illinois all the way down to the Gulf of Mexico. For active enjoyment, you can rent a pedal boat, canoe, kayak or a bike. Pack a picnic lunch and sprawl on the green. Several concession stands, located throughout the park, offer hot dogs, ice cream and other delicious snacks. If you ride the one-third of a mile Skyway, you'll get a birds-eye view of the park. On the second Friday of each month April through October, Mud Island offers a full-service camping trip. Tents, entertainment and marshmallows are provided. The only thing you'll need to bring is your sleeping bag. Space is limited, so make your reservations early. At Mud Island, you can run, ride, row, relax and rejoice in the natural beauty. How you spend your hours at Mud Island River Park is up to you.

125 N Front Street, Memphis TN (901) 576-7241 *www.mudisland.com*

Casey Jones Village

All aboard for Casey Jones Village. Nestled between the mighty Mississippi and the rolling Tennessee River lies West Tennessee, one of the three Grand Divisions in the state. Steeped in a rich heritage and dotted by communities with distinct personalities and nuances, West Tennessee is a rural landscape that is peaceful, eclectic and just waiting to be explored. Located in the center of the division is the historic town of Jackson. Jackson's landmark treasure is the charming Casey Jones Village, one of Tennessee's top 10 travel attractions, who's namesake is Jackson's own Casey Jones, America's railroad legend. His original 1890s home now houses the Historic Casey Jones Home & Railroad Museum. Discover the life, legend and song of Casey Jones on this must-see stop. Voted Jackson's best restaurant the last three years in a row, Brooks Shaw's Old Country Store is located on the Village Square and features the world famous Old Country Store restaurant with three delicious Southern buffets daily, a beautiful 1890s Ice Cream Parlor & Fudge Shoppe, a delightful Gift and Confectionery Shoppe and the Old Country Store To Go. All are accented with a private collection of over 15,000 antiques on display. Located only seconds off I-40, exit 80A, Jackson and Casey Jones Village are indeed the Best Whistlestop between Memphis and Nashville. For more information visit the Casey Jones Village website or call. Y'all come!

Jackson TN
(800) 748-9588
www.caseyjones.com

The Shops of Saddle Creek

The Shops of Saddle Creek was the first shopping center in the nation designed as a lifestyle center. Opened in 1987, the center combines an open-air, town square setting with a classic brick-face design, complete with elegant water fountains and a blend of upscale local and national boutique tenants. These elements come together to provide shoppers with a shopping experience unlike any other in the greater Memphis area. For more than 20 years, The Shops of Saddle Creek has continued to be the destination of choice for shoppers seeking a convenient and unique shopping center due to its excellent location and exciting tenant mix. The property consists of three separate components: Saddle Creek North, Saddle Creek South and Saddle Creek West, located at the intersection of Poplar Avenue and West Farmington in the heart of Germantown. Widely regarded as one of the premier shopping destinations in the Mid-South, The Shops of Saddle Creek boasts an impressive tenant roster which includes some of the most sought-after tenants, such as The Apple Store, Chico's, Coach, Coldwater Creek, J. Crew, J. Jill, Talbots, Talbots Mens, Sharper Image, Williams-Sonoma and more. The shopping center has consistently attracted tenants that have their exclusive metropolitan Memphis location at Saddle Creek. The property's successful history has established The Shops of Saddle Creek as the premier shopping destination in Memphis.

7615 W Farmington Boulevard, Germantown TN (Saddle Creek North)
2055 West Street, Germantown TN (Saddle Creek South)
7509 Poplar Avenue, Germantown TN (Saddle Creek West)
(901) 761-7604
www.shopsofsaddlecreek.com

The AutoZone Liberty Bowl

In 1959, Ambrose F. "Bud" Dudley fulfilled his dream of hosting a college football game in his hometown of Philadelphia when he founded the Liberty Bowl. Philadelphia houses the Liberty Bell, and Memphis is now home to the bowl game, which stands on the same principles as the Liberty Bell and the Declaration of Independence—American patriotism and liberty. After five years in Philadelphia and one year in Atlantic City, Dudley moved the Liberty Bowl to Memphis in 1965. Since that time, the AutoZone Liberty Bowl has flourished and become one of the great community and sporting events in Tennessee. The game is the seventh oldest college bowl game and is one of college football's tradition-rich games. Many of college football's greatest players, coaches and teams have participated in the bowl. Adding to the game's uniqueness is the fact that it is the only bowl game in the country that features a charitable organization in its official logo and in every aspect of its operation. Memphis-based St. Jude Children's Research Hospital is the bowl's longtime charitable partner. The mission of the AutoZone Liberty Bowl has been reached in dramatic proportions over the past four decades. That mission is to showcase Memphis to the world, generate significant economic impact for the community, host phenomenal activities and events and stay true to the Red, White and Blue patriotic theme of Liberty.

Memphis TN
(901) 795-7700
www.libertybowl.org

Memphis Botanic Garden

If you're looking for a perfect place to stop and smell the roses, visit the Memphis Botanic Garden. This tranquil spot is one of the South's finest horticultural attractions. The garden encompasses more than 96 acres of sweeping vistas, lakes and woodlands. Owned by the City of Memphis, the garden is like a piece of famous jewelry, worth more than the sum of its parts. Contained within it are 23 specialty gardens. These include a world-class aquatic garden, a 6,000-square-foot horticultural center housed in four separate buildings and an iris garden that began with a gift of 2,000 iris bulbs to the city. The Ann Heard Stokes Butterfly Garden features plantings designed to attract butterflies. The Japanese Garden of Tranquility is a beach garden and is home to Canada geese, turtles and koi. It boasts a red Oriental bridge that is one of the most photographed sites in Memphis. The Little Garden Club Sensory Garden is specially designed to be accessible to those in wheelchairs or who have limited vision. The main building displays works by local artists. A regularly scheduled summer concert series showcases the talents of top musicians. The garden is an arts center and a focal point for civic and fraternal groups. It hosts educational programs and provides support for the city's 84 plant societies and garden clubs. A trip to the Memphis Botanic Garden is good for the soul.

750 Cherry Road, Memphis TN
(901) 576-4122
www.memphisbotanicgarden.com

Germantown Festival

Grab your pup and start training now for the annual Running of the Weenies race. The race is one of the most anticipated activities at the Germantown Festival. More than one hundred dachshunds come from all over to enter the competition, which has become a well-known tradition. Germantown has been hosting the festival for more than 35 years, and it is most definitely an event not to be missed. Held the weekend after Labor Day, the festival is the last hurrah of summer and gives the community a chance to reconnect.

Each year, hundreds of arts and crafts exhibitors set up shop to showcase their talent. Festival goers enjoy wandering through the booths that feature everything from woodcarving to handmade clothing. Children's rides, car exhibits and concession booths serving tasty treats will keep you amused for hours on end. Add live music on the Festival's entertainment stage and you've got yourself a full day of family fun. The Germantown Festival provides an opportunity for local groups to raise funds for community activities and also helps finance college scholarships for selected high school seniors in the community. Whether you're a native or an out-of-towner, get ready for a fun-filled weekend a the Germantown Festival.

7701 Poplar Pike, Germantown TN
(901) 757-9212

Tennessee River Museum

Whether this is your first visit to Hardin County or you are a lifelong resident, the Tennessee River Museum is sure to entertain and educate you with the artifacts, displays and memorabilia of the area surrounding the Tennessee River. The river divides the state, creating two distinct geological zones with a variety of fossil specimens. See examples of those fascinating fossils, including the first insect fossil found in North America, naturally preserved in amber. The area's rich archeological history is on display, including an assortment of pottery, arrowheads, ceremonial objects and the famed Shiloh Effigy Pipe, made of red stone and carved in the shape of a kneeling man. Learn about the struggles of a Cherokee nation group that passed through Savannah as it traveled west on the Trail of Tears. Civil War buffs should check out the display depicting the Battle of Shiloh, fought on grounds near the town. One exhibit focuses on the area's history of steamboats, and another shows visitors how the musseling industry used fresh water mussel shells in the manufacture of buttons. Visit the Tennessee River Museum to learn more about the rich history of the Tennessee Valley.

495 Main Street, Savannah TN
(731) 925-8181 or (800) 552-FUNN (3866)
www.tourhardincounty.org/trm.htm

The Children's Museum of Memphis

Since the award-winning Children's Museum of Memphis opened in 1990, millions of visitors have walked through the doors. Five galleries house exhibits designed to spark the imagination, encourage exploration and appeal to the senses. Cityscape Gallery lets kids shop for groceries, climb a real fire engine and become a dentist. See how your body works in the Growing Healthy Gallery. Kids can hear their own heartbeat amplified, climb through a giant heart and ride a bicycle on Mars. Take to the air in the Going Places Gallery, where children experience a flight simulator, a wind tunnel, a hot air balloon and a real airplane cockpit. The Art Smart Gallery allows kids to explore visual arts by painting, sculpting and creating computer animations. Children can learn the performing arts and become stars by singing to a karaoke machine or by dressing in costumes and using props on stage. The WaterWorks Gallery contains a 50-foot model of the mighty Mississippi River, and kids can learn how water works as the flow turns a water wheel. Playscape Park welcomes children from birth to age four to a separate area that is safe but stimulating. You can hold your child's birthday party at the museum or even schedule a wedding reception. Bring the whole family to the Children's Museum of Memphis and create memories to last a lifetime.

2525 Central Avenue, Memphis TN
(901) 458-2678
www.cmom.com

Memphis Zoo

Do you long to gaze into the eye of an elephant, hear the cry of a bald eagle and admire an endangered panda bear—all in one day, if possible? Tour the world through the animal kingdom at the Memphis Zoo. One of the most diverse zoos in the nation, it is home to more than 3,500 animals in state-of-the-art environments with magnificent architecture. It began as a home for abandoned and special needs animals, including a black bear who was a former baseball mascot, and the original MGM roaring lion. Today it is on the way to becoming a national landmark. The zoo updates its facilities constantly, adding new entertainment and educational venues each year. A progressive leader in ecological preservation and education, the zoo musters an impressive calendar of educational programs for all ages. Learn about the nocturnal habits of bears during the Northwest Passage Snooze, or visit giant pandas Ya Ya and Le Le in the China exhibit. Take a trip to the heart of midtown Memphis to visit the Memphis Zoo and enjoy nature's masterworks.

2000 Prentiss Place, Memphis TN (901) 276-WILD (9453)
www.memphiszoo.org

The Memphis Redbirds at AutoZone Park

Photo by Allison Rhoades

AutoZone Park, located in the heart of downtown Memphis, is more that just a ballpark. It has been a symbol for the city of Memphis for nearly a decade, the centerpiece of Downtown Memphis' revitalization. The ballpark opened to a sellout crowd on April 1, 2000 as the Memphis Redbirds took on their parent club, the St. Louis Cardinals, in a thrilling exhibition game. More than 5,000,000 fans have passed through the turnstiles at AutoZone Park since that day. Year in and year out, the Memphis Redbirds are among the top teams in attendance in all of Minor League Baseball. Simply put, the fans love this place, and it's not just the baseball that draws them. They come for the special barbecue nachos, entertainment from the RedHots and Rockey, and the unique atmosphere—a relaxing oasis of baseball and fun amidst the hustle and bustle of downtown. The Memphis Redbirds are a not-for-profit organization that returns every penny to the community through AutoZone Park and its two youth baseball programs: RBI (Returning Baseball to the Inner City) and STRIPES (Sports Teams Returning in the Public Education System). A beautiful sight for baseball fans and non-fans alike, AutoZone Park hosts the hometown Memphis Redbirds from April through September, and is the site for community events year-round including concerts, races, and corporate and charity functions. For ticket information, call or visit the website.

175 Toyota Plaza, Memphis TN
(901) 721-6000
www.memphisredbirds.com

Fire Museum of Memphis

You'll feel the burn — literally — at the Fire Museum of Memphis. A special room in the museum, located between Main and Second Streets, shows visitors what it's like to be in a living room that catches fire, complete with the quickly rising temperature. This room, along with exhibits on combustion and smoke detection, is among the ways the museum demonstrates fire safety to both adults and children. The museum's location at a fire station built in 1910 and used

until the 1960s will delight history buffs, as will the large collections. The museum displays fire department badges from around the world, as well as a variety of firefighting equipment from the past century. Toy collectors will want to check out the exhibit of more than 900 firefighting-themed toys. The museum also pays tribute to fallen firefighters with a memorial. A gift shop provides visitors with the chance to bring a little bit of firefighting history home with them. Come to the Fire Museum of Memphis, where exhibits that entertain and inform will appeal to visitors of all ages.

118 Adams Avenue, Memphis TN
(901) 320-5650
www.firemuseum.com

Biblical Resource Center & Museum

Since 1997, Chairman and CEO Don Bassett and his wife, Museum Director Nancy Bassett, have welcomed 1,000 visitors a month to view artifacts and replicas associated with the Bible at the Biblical Resource Center & Museum in Collierville. Don holds a master's degree in biblical studies from Harding University Graduate School of Religion and has 35 years experience in the ministry. Popular museum stops include a Bible learning lab designed for kids and a reference library filled with books and videos on the archaeology and geography of the biblical world. A permanent hands-on exhibit entitled the Bible's Journey details how the Bible became the written word of God. Learn about God's book through artifacts excavated from Bible Lands as well as such replicas as the Egyptian Rosetta Stone and the Persian Cyrus Cylinder. An annual

simulated archaeology dig teaches proper excavation of a site. Participants discover items that have been buried for them, then clean and catalogue their findings, just like they would on a genuine dig. The museum offers study trips, group tours, lectures and presentations. The setting is non-denominational. Admission is free. Make a close examination of the living word of God at the Biblical Resource Center and Museum.

140 E Mulberry Street, Collierville TN
(901) 854-9578
www.biblical-museum.org

The Grapevine

Come and sit awhile at The Grapevine in Arlington Historical Depot Square, just minutes from Memphis. This quaint tea room and gift shop offers an inviting atmosphere that beckons both locals and visitors alike. Pour a spot of tea and order from a menu rich in delightfully prepared items. Try the cheese tea biscuits, heavenly chicken salad sandwich or the special pimento cheese sandwich. All offerings are made fresh daily on the premises. The fun begins when you order dessert. Mama's Pudding is the pièce de résistance, but any one of the Homemade Desserts to Die For on the menu will put a smile on your face. Combine a delicious meal with a little browsing on the side. The gift shop features antiques, lamps and home décor. If you're looking for a small token to bring away with you, consider a piece of handmade jewelry, a vintage bookmark, a china tea set or an heirloom candle. One of the handmade greeting cards might just catch your eye. Owner Sheryl Wooley loves to organize little girl tea parties as well as bridal luncheons and baby showers. Have your private party at The Grapvine, regardless of the occasion. Once a quarter, The Grapevine holds a special event of its own. These include a Valentine's candlelight dinner, a Mother's Day brunch and murder mystery dinners. Let The Grapevine whisk you away to a time when life was a little slower, a little gentler, and when a little conversation was just the thing.

6284 Chester Street, Arlington TN
(901) 867-9292
www.grapevinetearoom.net

MO's Edge CoffeeHouse

Home of the Avalanche—the world famous, highly addictive, double espresso milkshake—MO's Edge CoffeeHouse is a place for individuals and small groups to enjoy some of the best coffee and espresso drinks in the world. You can read or write, enjoy live music or perform it. Call ahead for a light buffet or special orders. The coffeehouse is located on the edge of the University of Memphis campus. Centrally located, MO's Edge is a venue for local and touring musicians to woodshed (practice) and share new music. Live music six nights a week includes blues, rock, jazz, folk, pop and more. Parking is free. Monday Open Mic brings out local and traveling artists and candidates for Wednesday Songwriter Scout Night. Play a game of cards, the jukebox or 40 games on the mega-touch video. Take advantage of free hi-speed wireless Internet. Check out new music on the website. Classic and cutting-edge Memphis photographs, original music and other Memphis treasures are always available. Enjoy independent film screenings and movies with surround-sound in the den. If you're looking for local flavor in a smoke-free venue with espresso and coffee, sodas, desserts and snacks, MO's Edge is a relaxing place to visit. Enjoy the garden in good weather where you can stop to smell the roses or smoke. MO's Edge CoffeeHouse—a Memphis Original with an Edge.

3521 Walker Avenue, Memphis TN
(901) 324-7892
www.mosedge.com

Dinstuhl's Fine Candy

Chocoholics unite at Dinstuhl's Fine Candy in Memphis, where delectable sweets such as chocolate pecan fudge, cashew crunch and chocolate-covered strawberries please the eye as well as the sweet tooth. For five generations, the Dinstuhl family has combined the finest ingredients to create its special treats. These ingredients include fresh butter, cream, sugar and real chocolate. Small batches are blended by hand, the method used by founder Charles Martin Dinstuhl, Sr. when he first opened the doors in 1902. The candy kitchen now occupies more than 11,000 square feet, up from the original 400. According to President Rebecca Dinstuhl, maintaining the values and ideals of the family's ancestors keeps the company viable. The modern manufacturing facility lets Dinstuhl's meet high demand while maintaining high quality. In the future, the company hopes to go national with select items. Several years ago, Dinstuhl's candies were certified as kosher by the Vaad (rabbinical council) of Memphis. Rabbi Jacob Greenblatt supervised the koshering of the candy plant. The sumptuous candies have recently made their way to Super Bowl XL, the NBA playoffs in Miami and Los Angeles and the Kentucky Derby, where they are fit for the Queen. Visit Dinstuhl's Fine Candy in Memphis and help yourself to a little piece of heaven.

5280 Pleasant View Road, Memphis TN
(901) 377-2639
www.dinstuhls.com

Bob Richards Jewelers

Bob Richards has been in the jewelry business his entire life. It never occurred to him to pursue any other profession. Richards spent many years in the family jewelry store established by his father in 1927. After attending watchmaking school, he repaired watches for six stores in the largest premier jewelry chain in Memphis. He attended Rolex technical training in New York in 1977 and 1980 for his Rolex certification. Bob Richards Jewelers opened in Memphis in 1984 and moved to its present location in 1999. The family business includes Bob's wife, Polly, and his two brothers, Jerry and Ron, doing repair and custom design. Bob's son, Anthony, represents the family's third generation in the business. In 2003, the store was selected as an independent Official Rolex Jeweler, a distinction afforded to few jewelers. The process required to become a Rolex dealer is a slow one; potential dealers are scrutinized before they enter into the relationship. Rolex is just one of the luxury watch and jewelry lines offered by Bob Richards Jewelers. "We shop hundreds of vendors to find special pieces, then I look at each piece from a repairman's view," Richards explains. "I refuse to buy light-weight, poor quality pieces that will cause problems for my clients. We want items purchased here to last a lifetime." Richards grows his company as his father did more than 80 years ago, staying educated in the world of jewelry and always offering good value for your dollar, personal attention and the skill to service your cherished items. Bob Richards Jewelers lives up to its slogan: The Only Jeweler You'll Ever Need.

7730 Wolf River Boulevard, Suite 103, Germantown TN
(901) 751-8052
www.bobrichardsjewelers.com

Mednikow Jewelers

For more than 115 years, fine jewelry has been the lifeblood of the Mednikow family. At Mednikow Jewelers, the family upholds the Memphis tradition begun by Jacob Mednikow, who first set up shop here in 1891. The Russian word *mednikow* means coppersmith, and Jacob brought the family trade of fine metalwork with him from the Old Country. The family tradition of excellence continues to drive its members, and today fourth-generation Jay Mednikow serves as the company's president. Every bit as important as family tradition is the store's family of employees, who are devoted to giving you the best jewelry buying experience possible. "All members of the sales staff are trained gemologists," says owner Bob Mednikow. Mednikow Jewelers' employees operate in accordance with the standards of the American Gem Society, guaranteeing a high level of ethics and integrity. More than half the jewelry sold here is made in the firm's own workshops. "By establishing our own manufacturing arm, we have assured our customers a continuing emphasis on quality," Bob says. You'll also find some of the finest designer jewelry lines in the world, including those of Mikimoto, David Yurman and John Hardy. The store carries watches from Rolex, Patek Philippe and Cartier. Come experience sterling service and world-class jewelry at Mednikow Jewelers.

474 Perkins Extended, Memphis TN (901) 767-2100 *www.mednikow.com*

Lansky Bros.

When you think of Memphis, you think of the origins of rock and roll and the blues—and musicians need clothes. In 1946, a family-owned surplus store opened on Beale Street, the place to be for aspiring musicians. The 1950s brought even more musicians, and Lansky Bros. made the decision to switch into high-fashion menswear. The Lanskys began shopping fashion shows around the country to find unique clothing for musicians. Bernard Lansky took great pride in dressing his windows to attract customers. One day, he noticed someone peering into the window. He invited the young man in, but the youth politely refused and said, "When I get rich, I'm going to buy you out." Bernard responded, "Don't buy me out. Just buy from me." The young man was Elvis Presley, and Bernard Lansky became clothier to the king. Elvis looked to Bernard for his distinctive fashions throughout his life. Notable outfits include the gold lamé suit that Elvis wore for his first performance on the Ed Sullivan show. Elvis's business drew in folks such as B.B. King, Johnny Cash, Isaac Hayes and many more. Lansky Bros. recently celebrated its 60th anniversary. Now with three generations in the business, the Lansky family has five shops in the lobby of the Peabody Hotel. Lansky at the Peabody is a fine men's shop featuring sportswear and the Clothier to the King brand. Lansky 126 is a contemporary premium denim boutique for men and women. Lansky Lucky Duck is a gift shop, Lansky Essentials is a newsstand and Lansky Logowear provides Peabody Hotel apparel. You'll want to stop by soon.

149 Union Avenue, Memphis TN
(901) 529-9070
www.lansky126.com

Shelton Clothiers

Before Shelton Clothiers opened its doors in 2005, well-dressed Memphis businessmen usually went to East Memphis to do their shopping. Shelton Clothiers provides a downtown alternative for fine men's apparel while making a style statement all its own. From its hardwood floors to its large mirrored fitting area with leather seating, the store has the feel of a well-appointed executive lounge. Part of the Shelton strategy is to focus on designers that are hard to find locally, such as John H. Daniel Custom Tailors, S. Cohen, XMI and Tallia. Shelton Clothiers also offers clothing affordable enough for the businessman just starting to climb the ladder to the top. Owner Tom Shelton cites the continued revitalization of the downtown area as his main reason for locating his shop in the heart of the city. "Downtown is just more fun," he says, "and there's more to do here after you shop." Ever since his family closed its men's store outside of Chicago in 1986, Tom had been preparing himself to strike out on his own. He went to school at the University of Memphis and earned a degree in business management. Then he learned every detail of the industry while working 15 years in sales and management at an upscale men's shop in East Memphis. Let Tom dress you in professional style at Shelton Clothiers.

147 S Main Street, Memphis TN (901) 522-9995
www.sheltonclothiers.com

Accent Jewelers

How do they do it? Customers of Accent Jewelers have been asking themselves this question for more than 30 years. The owners would be happy, in fact, to explain how they keep the prices of their jewelry low. Indeed, with very few exceptions, they guarantee that jewelry you purchase from them will appraise for double the price you paid, or they will refund your money. They can also explain how they can afford to pay so nicely for the jewelry and silver that you no longer need. It all has to do with keeping overhead low and being satisfied with making a profit rather than a killing. Known by a different name when it first opened, Accent Jewelers has since changed addresses within White Station Tower, expanded, and changed ownership. Through all these transitions, business standards have always remained high. The company is committed to providing outstanding craftsmanship, excellent value, and above all, a level of personal service that keeps customers coming back. Accent Jewelers is known in Memphis and surrounding areas as the largest volume buyer of Antique and Estate jewelry, factory closeouts and store liquidation jewelry merchandise. That's why you'll find a large selection of one-of-a-kind jewelry at prices much lower than most retail stores. Try Accent Jewelers for repairs, appraisals and cash jewelry loans, too. Join the legion of satisfied customers who have made this business their jeweler of choice.

**5050 Poplar Avenue, Suite 127,
Memphis TN 38157
(901) 682-8036**
www.accentjewelers.com

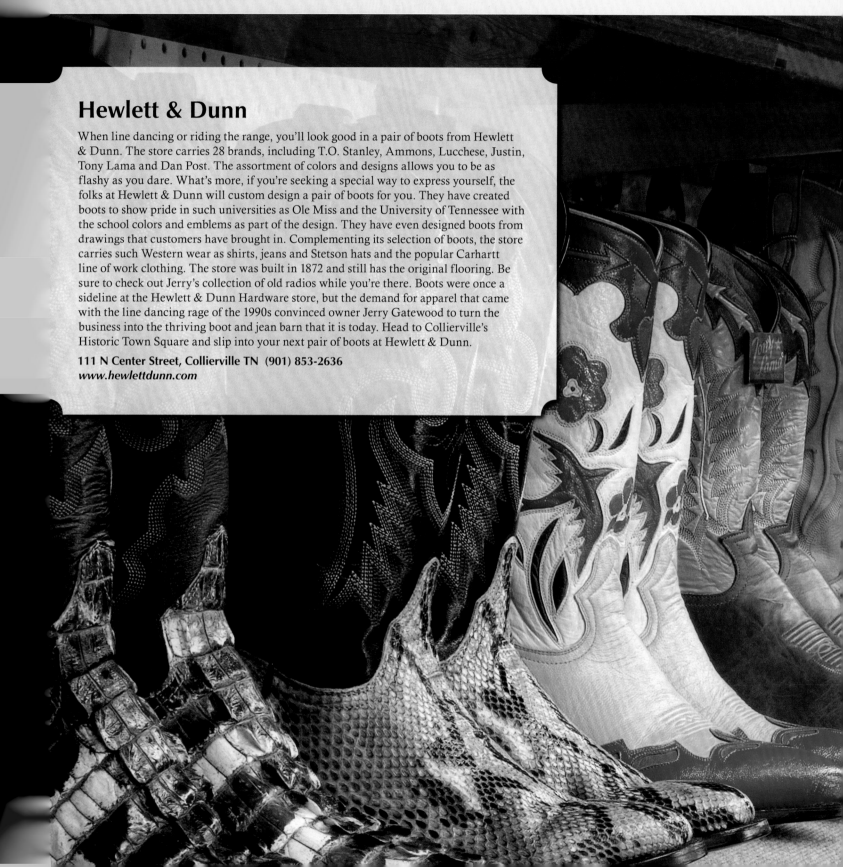

Hewlett & Dunn

When line dancing or riding the range, you'll look good in a pair of boots from Hewlett & Dunn. The store carries 28 brands, including T.O. Stanley, Ammons, Lucchese, Justin, Tony Lama and Dan Post. The assortment of colors and designs allows you to be as flashy as you dare. What's more, if you're seeking a special way to express yourself, the folks at Hewlett & Dunn will custom design a pair of boots for you. They have created boots to show pride in such universities as Ole Miss and the University of Tennessee with the school colors and emblems as part of the design. They have even designed boots from drawings that customers have brought in. Complementing its selection of boots, the store carries such Western wear as shirts, jeans and Stetson hats and the popular Carhartt line of work clothing. The store was built in 1872 and still has the original flooring. Be sure to check out Jerry's collection of old radios while you're there. Boots were once a sideline at the Hewlett & Dunn Hardware store, but the demand for apparel that came with the line dancing rage of the 1990s convinced owner Jerry Gatewood to turn the business into the thriving boot and jean barn that it is today. Head to Collierville's Historic Town Square and slip into your next pair of boots at Hewlett & Dunn.

111 N Center Street, Collierville TN (901) 853-2636
www.hewlettdunn.com

What's Hot

Vicki Olson and her aunt and partner, Sherry Courtenay, have taken the guesswork out of fashion at their terrific and trendy shop, What's Hot. This Germantown favorite opened more

than 15 years ago and has since become a first-stop on the area's shopping circuit. What's Hot offers patrons a hip, lively and fun-filled environment where they can shop for the latest in contemporary fashions. With an eye toward quality, Vicki and Sherry scour the country to find the latest women's styles for each season, as well as all the bells, whistles and bows that make an outfit complete. The shop's appealing interior, exemplary service and up-to-the-minute styles all come together to create a memorable shopping experience. In addition, you'll find handbags and accessories from well-known designer lines such as Brighton, exciting gifts and home accessories, plus a selection of Memphis Music CDs showcasing local talent. Skip the crowded chain stores and enjoy a shopping excursion that sizzles at What's Hot.

**7685 Farmington Boulevard #105, Germantown TN
(901) 755-4179**

Taylor Lane Totes & Bags

It's as if the purses, totes and diaper bags that Angela Brenner designs are highly contagious. Young customers report that their college roommates have ordered her bags for themselves after seeing those of their friends. Moms ditch their plain diaper bags after seeing the trendy ones their neighbors are carrying. A work-at-home mom, Angela began Taylor Lane Totes & Bags, her web-based business, in 2003, and it quickly caught attention worldwide. Angela combines

style with function to give women on the go a reason to look forward to toting their stuff around town. "I love what I do," says Angela, and it shows in her trademark bright colors and cheerful patterns. Feedback from customers has been overwhelmingly positive. "I can't stop buying your purses," exclaimed one satisfied customer. Another thanked Angela for providing a solution whenever she needs a baby shower gift. "The diaper bags are so adorable," she said. Take a look at the products at Taylor Lane Totes & Bags and prepare to start a style revolution among your friends.

www.taylorlanetotesandbags.com

Très Chic

At trendy Très Chic, owner Angela Bisceglia manages to blend the sophistication of an upscale boutique with the kind of Southern hospitality that makes everybody feel at home. The shop caters to women from 30 to 60 years old who want cutting-edge, hot-off-the-runway style. Store manager Sherry Saxon's fashion savvy, plus her 25 years of retail sales experience, guides Très Chic clientele to just the right items to accentuate their individual personalities and achieve a unique look. The boutique features many specialty lines of clothing to delight even the most discriminating shopper. It also offers an extensive selection of accessories, finishing touches that can help you create a signature look. Instead of the same jewelry lines you might find at many other retail stores, at Très Chic you'll find pieces that have been designed locally as well as pieces from New York designers. Customers come here to shop and quickly discover that Très Chic is also a fun place to socialize. Friendships sometimes form between clients. Husbands and friends can enjoy a sitting room, while you take advantage of the boutique's roomy, tastefully decorated fitting rooms. Come browse cutting-edge fashion and let your inner fashionista strut her stuff at Très Chic, where you will be treated like the special woman you are.

**9155 Poplar Avenue, Suite 13,
Germantown TN
(901) 756-1281**

Coming Attractions

Coming Attractions has been a leader in women's fashion since opening in the heart of Memphis in 1981. As its name suggests, styles that will be catching the eye this season are the focus. Characteristically, the fashions you'll find at Coming Attractions are comfortable enough to be worn over and over again. Brands such as CP shades from California, Mycra Pac, Babette and Lauren Vidal are as easy to wear as they are stylish. For styles with an artistic bent, browse one-of-a-kind jackets from Joshi and Memphis native Joyce Wilkerson featuring handwoven woolens and beautiful silk/cotton blends. The store also features hand-designed jewelry by Jeanne Jones, created especially to accent the clothing collection at Coming Attractions. Clients attribute the store's lasting popularity to its reputation as a gathering place where friends come together to find the clothes they love to live in. Make it your favorite place to shop for comfortable style.

597 Erin Drive, Memphis TN
(901) 685-8655

Doris McLendon's Jewelry

Doris McLendon travels to jewelry markets in New York, Switzerland, Hong Kong and Las Vegas to find cutting-edge jewelry designs for her Germantown shop. High-end designer jewelry, combined with antique and estate jewelry, gives a distinctive quality to Doris McLendon's Jewelry that sets it apart from other area shops. Although Doris opened her shop in 2002, her experience reaches back to her days as a junior high school teacher in Mississippi. After working part-time for a jeweler during one summer, her natural affinity for jewelry surfaced, and she never returned to teaching. In 1989, Doris moved to Memphis with her family. After holding

positions as a manager and buyer for other jewelers, she opened her own jewelry store in 1992, sharing a lease with five others. Her present shop serves a prestigious area with discerning clientele. She chooses her selection with her clients' tastes in mind and carries many top designer lines. She also offers pre-owned Rolex watches (not affiliated with Rolex Watch USA) and performs repairs on watches and jewelry as well as on silver flatware and hollowware. The store earned the Germantown Chamber of Commerce Small Business of the Year award in 2005, an honor Doris credits to her exceptional employees, who eagerly share their expertise with customers. For jewelry that makes a statement, come to Doris McLendon's Jewelry and Expect to be Impressed.

9387 Poplar Avenue, Germantown TN
(901) 758-8605
www.dorismclendon.com

Photo by Henry Dunay

Masterpiece Jewelers

Masterpiece Jewelers specializes in diamonds and estate jewelry. Its expansive inventory of estate pieces means customers often find pieces handcrafted over a century ago. Masterpiece Jewelers also hosts an in-house jewelry artist and welcomes customers who want a one-of-a-kind piece for their special someone. Owner Randolph Reeves understands jewelry. He has built his jewelry store from the ground up. Reeves spent his college years working part-time for experienced local jewelers. He took such a liking to the trade that he chose to concentrate his studies on gemology. As Reeves continued working under other jewelers, word spread that he had the knack essential for success as a jeweler. With the help of referrals and word-of-mouth, he was able to open his own store in 1987. Located in the Oak Hall Building, Masterpiece

Jewelers is well away from the rush of crowded shopping malls, and offers a relaxed and comfortable atmosphere for customers to explore the jewelry selection and make their choice. Masterpiece Jewelers enjoys a reputation for customer service and its customers keep coming back. Stop in to visit Randolph Reeves' dream and you'll see why.

555 Perkins Road Extension #315,
Oak Hall Building, Memphis TN
(901) 681-0501

Photo © 2005 David Katz/Arnold Katz Photography

Edgar Degas, French (1834-1917)
Danseuse Ajustant Son Soulier, 1885
(Dancer Adjusting Her Shoe)
Pastel on Paper
Collection of The Dixon Gallery and Gardens: Bequest of Mr. and Mrs. Hugo Dixon, 1975.6

Mary Cassatt, American (French School) 1845-1926 The Visitor, ca. 1880
Oil on canvas with gouache Collection of The Dixon Gallery and Gardens;
Bequest of Mr. And Mrs. Hugo N. Dixon, 1975.28

The Dixon Gallery and Gardens

Since 1976, the Dixon Gallery and Gardens has been one of the Memphis area's premier art institutions. The Dixon is the legacy of Hugo and Margaret Dixon, philanthropists who bequeathed their home, gardens and collection of French Impressionist paintings for the enjoyment and education of future generations. The Dixon residence is surrounded by 17 acres of woodlands and gardens that reflect the couple's appreciation of nature. The initial Dixon collection of 26 exquisite paintings contains the works of French and American Impressionists, Post-Impressionists and related schools. The collection also includes 18th and 19th century British portraits and landscapes. It has grown to include more than 2,000 works. Major acquisitions have included the Warda Stevens Stout collection of 18th century German porcelain, the Armand Hammer collection of Daumier prints and the Adler pewter collection. Visitors can see works by Edgar Degas, John Singer Sargent, Claude Monet and Paul Cezanne. The Dixon offers public educational programs, including school tours. The gallery relies entirely on member donations to supplement the Dixon bequest and receives no city, state or federal support. Visit the Dixon Gallery and Gardens to view the public legacy of a couple who acquired and preserved magnificent works of art for the future enjoyment of others.

4339 Park Avenue, Memphis TN
(901) 761-5250
www.dixon.org

Lee Gaugh, Glass Artist

Since opening his first studio in his home in 1987, Lee Gaugh has become one of the most respected glass artists in Tennessee. President of the West Tennessee chapter of the Tennessee Association of Craft Artists, he specializes in the restoration and repair of stained-glass windows. His expertise in this area has taken him to the Gulf Coast to repair damage done by Hurricane Katrina. For his own designs, he works in many forms of glass art, including stained, fused and etched glass. His gallery in Jackson's Neely House houses a wide sampling of his jewelry, platters, vases and decorative items. Lee's decision to become a glass artist came to him like a religious calling. While a junior in high school, he visited Washington D.C., where he toured the National Cathedral. Gazing upon the stained glass windows, he knew at once that he wanted to create that kind of glass. During his training, Lee worked in studios and traveled the country studying art and architecture. Currently, he is a teacher as well as a practitioner of the craft, offering group and individual instruction in the various processes of glass art. Call upon Lee Gaugh for repairs or lessons, or visit his gallery to view his designs.

190 E Forest Street, Jackson TN
(731) 695-1916
575 S Royal Street, Jackson TN (gallery)
www.repairchurchwindows.com

Marguerite's Fine Art & the Neely House Artopia

Marguerite's Art Gallery is in the historic New Southern Hotel in downtown Jackson, and the Neely House Artopia is in the railroad district just to the south. In these galleries, you'll find artwork by local and regional artists, including paintings, pottery, sculpture, jewelry, clothing and furniture. When you come in you may find one of the artists at work in the studio or a group of children learning the joy of art. Both galleries are the inspiration of Alicia McEarl. By the age of 14, Alicia was already thinking how wonderful it would be to own a gallery. In 2005, this dream came true as Marguerite's Fine Art. Alicia named the gallery after her grandmother, a well-known local portrait artist, who encouraged the young girl. Alicia herself is an artist whose many commissioned works include murals, pet portraits, pop art, landscapes and still lifes. She loves to paint any surface that will accept paint, including furniture and clothing. Alicia offers classes in rooms behind the main gallery. With the opening of the Neely House Artopia in 2006, Alicia has added another showcase for locally created pottery, glasswork and painting. This old home, opened as a railroad hotel in 1911, is grand enough to house a number of other businesses in addition to the gallery, including a paint-a-piece shop, lady's boutique, bookstore and coffee shop. How many of us can say that we knew what we wanted to do before we even started high school? Alicia's vision continues to unfold at Marguerite's Fine Art and the Neely House Artopia. Stop in, enjoy some conversation and a great cup of coffee.

124 E Baltimore Street, Jackson TN (Marguerite's)
(731) 427-3006
575 S Royal Street, Jackson TN (Neely House)
(866) 795-1566
www.margueritesfineart.com

L Ross Gallery

L Ross Gallery offers a peaceful yet vibrant setting for its extensive collection of abstract works, contemporary canvases and primitive carvings. Whether in rich layered paintings, ancient encaustics, expressive stones, clays or reclaimed objects, the painters and sculptors represented by L Ross Gallery explore their personal connections to the mysteries of life. Owned by Linda Ross, a Memphis art consultant for more than 20 years, the gallery represents a number of established American artists that include Anton Weiss, Sandra Ehrenkranz, Lisa Jennings, Helen Phillips and Brent Funderburk. The recent expansion of the gallery in East Memphis has allowed the addition of many exciting young regional artists, such as Kurt Meer, Ian Lemmonds, David Comstock, Jeni Stallings, Bobby Spillman, Bo Rodda and Lisa Weiss. The newly expanded space also provides the opportunity for designers and architects to work directly with their clients at the gallery. You are welcome to visit L Ross Gallery Tuesday through Saturday.

5040 Sanderlin Avenue, Suite 104, Memphis TN
(901) 767-2200
www.lrossgallery.com

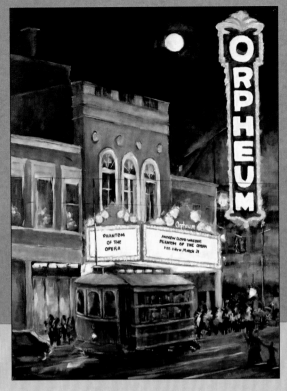

Pointe South Studio

With bold colors and a warm palette, Debbie Richmond captures the defining spirit of every animal she paints, whether it be the powerful movements of a horse, the majesty of a lion or the sweet nature of a Labrador Retriever. "I truly enjoy painting still lifes and landscapes," she says, "but painting animals is my passion." Debbie's paintings have won many awards, both locally and nationally, but her most rewarding accomplishments are when a painting actually brings happy tears to her client's eyes. "When a painting is unveiled and that special expression has been captured in my subjects face and eyes, my clients see for the first time that their beloved pet will live forever through that painting," Debbie says. "It can be a very sweet, emotional moment." Debbie directs Pointe South Studio, a private painting studio that also serves as an artist management organization. You can see Debbie's paintings at Stodghill and James Gallery in Richland, Mississippi; Palladio Gallery and Antiques in Memphis; and in her own personal gallery in the Blue Plate Café and Gallery in downtown Memphis. Find Debbie at Pointe South Studio, or view her inspiring work on your next art tour of Memphis.

3286 Pointe South Cove, Memphis TN
(901) 748-1666
www.DebbieRichmondArt.com

Rivertown Gallery

Rivertown Gallery in downtown Memphis displays the work of local artists in a creative and cooperative environment. The gallery has a reputation in Tennessee and beyond for highlighting the talent of both seasoned and up-and-coming artists. For 10 years, the passion and perseverance of gallery owner Pamela K. Craig has helped artists gain confidence and experience in the art world. While pursuing her dream of showcasing her own work, she has opened the doors of expression for others. Now, with 2,000 square feet of space in Pembroke Square, Craig—also known as PAKC—gathers painters, sculptors, photographers, jewelry makers and other creative people into the growing arts scene in the South Main Arts District. Rivertown Gallery is artist-run, which means that the artists who display double as studio representatives, contributing their time and expertise instead of paying commissions for exhibition space. If you seek original fine art at reasonable prices, the cooperative philosophy of Craig's Rivertown Gallery makes this possible. Craig, who was born in Memphis, is a former Austin, Texas, art teacher. Her works include both seek-and-find abstract art and graphically realistic pieces. To view the work of more than 15 individual imaginations in one place, stop in at Rivertown Gallery. You're likely to meet one or more of the artists in person.

119 S Main Street, Memphis TN (901) 527-7573 *www.rivertowngallery.net*

Bright Light Glass Studio

As the oldest family-owned and operated stained glass studio in the Memphis area, Bright Light Glass Studio has enjoyed working with and for many interesting people. Luminaries such as Elvis Presley, President Ronald Reagan, Senator Curtis Person, Disneyland Florida and others have enjoyed the special attention that Janet and Nick DeStefano afford each and every client. The company's corps of talented people creates exquisite glass pieces that can hang alone or be incorporated into the design of windows and doors. In Memphis, you can see examples of the studio's work at the Peabody Hotel and the Danny Thomas Pavilion. Decorative glass from Bright Light Glass Studio adorns thousands of homes, churches, hotels and businesses across the southern and eastern states and as far away as Puerto Rico. In addition to completing commissions from individuals, businesses and organizations, Bright Light Glass Studio also offers decorating construction and provides companies with original glass art works as well as fine wood doors and carved wood fireplace mantels. Many home and architecture magazines have run lavish full-color articles on the studio and its work. Founded in 1964 by Jack Cain (Janet's father), this is a business that is committed to high quality and personal service. Join the long list of satisfied clients by commissioning Bright Light Glass Studio to create something beautiful and original for you.

5210 Pleasant Road, Suite 1B, Memphis TN
(901) 372-8200
www.brightlightglassstudio.com

diVa Colour Studio

A brighter, shinier hair color can make you feel like a million bucks. Not only does it transform your appearance, it also lifts the spirits and rejuvenates the self-image. When you walk out of the hair salon, you know you look good. After two weeks have gone by, however, you might notice the luster in your hair has faded. Somehow, it looks less natural and feels more brittle. Within two months, you're back in the hairdresser's chair. "The use of color on hair has increased 1,000 percent over the last 20 years," says Ted Cortese, colorist and owner of diVa Colour Studio in East Memphis. "Obviously, there's a great need to keep colored hair looking better, longer." Although it's impossible to prevent fading, Cortese recommends two tricks to help slow the process. First, retain moisture and sparkling highlights by using less heat to blow-dry your hair. Airflow that's too hot will rob hair of its moisture. Use hot air only for the final steps of styling. Second, switch to shampoos, conditioners and other hair-care products especially formulated for color-treated hair. "Another cause of dry, brittle fading is the chemicals used for the process," says Cortese. "New shampoos on the market help solve the problem by using natural fruit-and-grain acids, which, along with natural antioxidants, help remove the damaging effects of the hair-coloring process. The bottom line is the superior technology of some shampoos and conditioners absolutely make hair feel softer and give it more body with an abundance of shine." Come experience the difference at diVa Colour Studio, or visit the online store.

1068 Brookfield Road, Memphis TN
(901) 761-4247
www.divacolourstudio.com

Epic Total Salon

Whether you walk in or make an appointment, the professionals at Epic Total Salon welcome you. These internationally trained stylists, colorists and manicurists work their magic to transform you from ho-hum to fabulous. Feel like a movie star as the staff pampers you from head to toe. Customized haircuts and coloring, manicures and pedicures, makeovers and facials are just a few of the choices you have. Highlight your crowning glory with Elumen by Goldwell exclusive hair products from posh European salons. Indulge yourself with a special service such as waxing or hair weaving. For total wedding day beauty, consult with Epic's onsite bridal consultants. Epic Total Salon has been touched by celebrity. As a promotion for Reese Witherspoon's *Legally Blonde*, MGM paid the tab for anyone willing to go blonde. Takers walked in the salon door as brunettes and left stunningly blonde. Epic has been featured on Fox Network's *Ambush Makeover*, and its staff has worked alongside celebrity stylist Ted Gibson during Fashion Week at the Memphis Botanic Garden. Owner Gregory Fry received the Best of Memphis Award for the salon's neon signage in the 2005 Memphis Flyer contest. Beauty, both inside and out—that's what Epic Total Salon is all about. Whether you prefer fashionable, trendy or traditional, the pros at Epic Total Salon eagerly await your arrival.

712 S Mendenhall Road, Memphis TN (901) 818-5501
www.epictotalsalon.com

Johnson Family Chiropractic Clinic

Johnson Family Chiropractic Clinic is a place where adults and children alike can find relief from pain. State-of-the-art equipment such as thermal scan and surface EMG assists the staff in locating the subluxation, or partial bone dislocation, that is causing your body to hurt. "Find the subluxation, correct it and then leave it alone," said Clarence Gonstead, one of the most important developers of chiropractic. Johnson Family Chiropractic follows his system, which is very precise in application. The only bone adjustments should be those that are necessary to achieve improvement. The benefits of a chiropractic adjustment are many. In addition to reducing swelling and pain, it can increase circulation and eliminate nervous irritation. "The patient's comfort is our primary concern," says Reed Johnson, Doctor of Chiropractic, whose goal is to educate and support patients on the path to optimal health and wellness. Treating the whole person is the clinic's focus. The friendly atmosphere of the office will put you and your child at ease. Make pain a thing of the past with the help of Johnson Family Chiropractic Clinic.

5695 Quince Road, Memphis TN
(901) 767-6727
www.johnsonfamilychiro.com

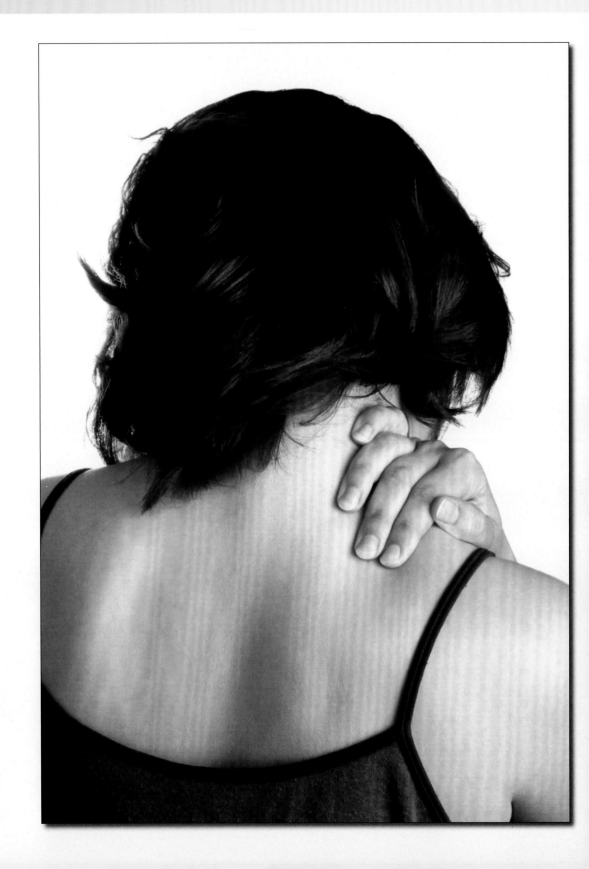

Chiropractic Memphis

As the largest chiropractic group in the Memphis area, with four locations as of August of 2007, Chiropractic Memphis is a prominent wellness leader in the community. These offices boast the latest in high-tech equipment, including the Insight Millenium, a state-of-the art computer scanning system that helps the doctors pinpoint and treat pressure problems on a patient's nervous system. From the moment you step inside, it's clear that these clinics are different. With a modern décor and floor plan, the surroundings are inviting, making what can be an intimidating experience for first-timers seem much less daunting. Doctors Alan Arstikaitis, Dave Kellenberger, Kurt Price and Matt Hayden head up these offices and are very passionate about what they do. The doctors and staff love making a difference in the lives of their patients and gladly take on patients of any age and in any state of health to help them regain their full health potential. "Chiropractic centers around adjustments of the spine," says Dr. Matt Hayden. "The biggest aspect of chiropractic is the natural, drug-free approach and the focus on finding the root of the problem and not just treating the symptoms. Adjustments are used not only to relieve patients' back and neck pain, but are part of a focus on all-around wellness." Put yourself in good hands at Chiropractic Memphis.

Memphis TN
www.chiropractic-memphis.com

Renaissance Day Spa

If you're looking for relaxation, renewal and transformation, Renaissance Day Spa lives up to its name. Shirley Oliver, an aesthetician, co-owns and operates the spa with daughter Jameena Wade, a nail technician and the spa's chief financial officer, and daughter Tisha Lundy, also a nail technician and the company's marketing manager. In addition to maintaining the spa, Shirley has worked as a medical technologist for more than 25 years. Her focus centers on nutrition and wellness, and she attends day spa conferences to keep up with industry trends. Renaissance offers a diverse menu of services designed to rejuvenate you. Options include facials, massages, manicures, pedicures, waxing, lash and brow tinting, body bronzing and back treatments. Renaissance can help you design a spa party for your group of four or more. Bridal parties are popular, as are weddings, birthdays, girls' days out and employee appreciation parties. Spa party services may be customized and can include a healthful catered brunch. Renaissance gift certificates make thoughtful corporate or personal gifts. Spa packages allow you to indulge in the ultimate rejuvenation, inside and out, with an entire day of pampering. Shirley and her family look forward to treating you like family in the relaxing atmosphere of Renaissance Day Spa.

3294 Poplar, Suite 200, Memphis TN, (901) 452-1544, *www.renaissancedayspaofmemphis.com*

French Country Imports

Housed in a row of charming French townhouses in one of East Memphis' finest residential neighborhoods, French Country Imports encourages browsing. You can wander through charming rooms of 18th and 19th century French furniture and accessories covering 5,000 square feet. The shop's roots reach back to Shea Design, an interior design firm founded in 1982 by Lynda Shea, an allied member of the American Society of Interior Designers. Lynda responded to client demand for quality French country furniture by making her first buying trip to France in 1984. Shortly thereafter, she opened French Country Imports. Since then, Lynda and her staff of designers have made close to 50 buying trips, exploring such regions as Provence, Normandy and Alsace and bringing home the best of their finds. Today, Shea Design's staff of six talented designers occupies two upstairs rooms at the store. The firm offers an expansive library of fabric samples and catalogs to give clients the widest array of choices possible. Shea specializes in residential design, but the designers here also have completed corporate and commercial projects. Lynda and her staff invite you to take a stimulating walk through French Country Imports, then consult the design team about the styles that work best in your home.

6225 Old Poplar Pike, Memphis TN (901) 682-2000
www.frenchcountry-imports.com

Architectural Timberworks

Thanks to Architectural Timberworks, beams from old cabins and barns take on a new life inside the homes of discriminating buyers. "From my first hewn log cabin of poplar and white oak built on a family farm in 1980, I've been obsessed with creating natural living environments from heavy timbers," says owner Wade Burrus. He will build an entire log or timber frame home for you, made out of reclaimed wood and reproduction timbers. Wade is also the person to call for a wide range of design work. Fireplace mantles handcrafted with corbels or full timber legs are a specialty, as are timber stairways with railings. What separates Architectural Timberworks from other log home companies? Fine craftsmanship and attention to detail are important elements of this company's success. Of course, quality timbers are essential, too. Nothing can add warmth and grace to a home like vintage wood. Even the reproduction timbers are handcrafted, distressed and custom-aged to give them a magnificent look. Contact Architectural Timberworks to start the ideas flowing for your project.

9656 Memphis-Arlington Road, Lakeland TN
(901) 569-1228
www.burruscompany.com

Source One Flooring & Stone

It's not often that people take the time to write a letter in praise of a job well done, but it happens at Source One Flooring & Stone. Tom Zarta and his son, Tommy are experienced installers of tile, hardwood, carpet and granite tops. If you need a floor, they know how to lay it. About 80 percent of their work is residential and the other 20 percent is commercial. Evidence of their solid skills and success became public when Source One was named the Top Contractor in Memphis in 2006. Clients can trust the expert installation and are amazed by the appearance of the finished counter tops with virtually invisible seams. A recent client thanked Source One for suggesting that they lay the floor tiles on a diagonal. The end result was exactly what the client was looking for. Source One will take the stress and anxiety out of remodeling and other construction projects. The down-home atmosphere, top-notch customer service, skills, experience and quality work will bring you back again and again as new projects come into your life. Source One Flooring & Stone will make you glad you had a task to do.

8400 Wolf Lake Drive, #107, Bartlett TN
(901) 382-7981

Gallery Collection

The kitchen is once again becoming the center of home and hearth, a place where families and friends gather to cook, eat, laugh and love. Gallery Collection can help you design and construct the kitchen of your dreams, from appliances to cabinetry. Manager Chuck Tracy is a certified kitchen designer with more than 38 years of experience in custom kitchen design in the Memphis area. Chuck oversees an expert team of professionals who are dedicated to helping you with every aspect of kitchen design. Because they emphasize a complete kitchen concept, the Gallery Collection's team members are qualified to manage even the most detailed renovation or new construction projects. Comprehensive service and attention to detail save precious time and allow you to enjoy your new kitchen that much sooner. Indulge yourself and your family with a kitchen designed for your needs and lifestyle. Rely on the experts at Gallery Collection.

4646 Poplar Avenue, Suite 128, Memphis TN (901) 761-4600
www.gc-kitchens.com

SEE the Difference Interiors

Diane Gordon could have kept running SEE the Difference Interiors, her successful interior design business, out of her home and private warehouse, but the allure of being part of the revitalization of downtown Memphis was too strong to resist. "Watching the rebuilding and the rebirth of downtown has been exciting," says Diane, whose 2,000-square-foot showroom fits right into the arts district. Its eclectic mix of furniture and décor appeals to creative individuals seeking to make a personal statement with their home design. "I like to mix and match vendors," explains Diane. "I like to be different, and I like my clients to have something different and unexpected and not easily copied." With 3,000 fabric samples, the shop gives customers plenty of options for upholstered furniture. Diane and her design team advise clients to keep things simple and comfortable. "People become overwhelmed and can't see what they really have," she points out. "Your home should be streamlined so it supports your lifestyle." Just before opening the showroom, SEE the Difference Interiors participated in the 2006 Vesta Home Show in downtown Memphis and walked away with half of the awards. No doubt Diane's success at the show contributed to the instant response when her shop opened its doors. Customers poured in from throughout Memphis and Germantown, and from as far away as Little Rock. Head downtown to find creative ideas for your home at SEE the Difference Interiors.

6 West G. E. Patterson Avenue #103, Memphis TN
(901) 522-9696
www.seethedifferenceinteriors.com

Layne Popernik, Realtor

With more than 15 years in the real estate industry, Layne Popernik has garnered most of the highest recognitions in the field. A member of the Multi Million Dollar Club for annual residential sales, she is also an Accredited Buyer Representative, a coveted designation bestowed by the Real Estate Buyer's Agent Council. When serving as a buyer's agent, Layne has the legal obligation to place the interests of the buyer before her own interests and those of the seller. Honesty, integrity and professionalism are the watchwords that have made her successful and respected. In 2005, Layne joined the leading Judy Mac team at Crye-Leike Realtors as Judy McLellan's showing partner. The following year, she put her talents to work for the community as the local Leukemia Lymphoma Society Woman of the Year for 2006. Layne, who lost her mother to cancer several years ago and who has faced the disease herself, was the biggest fundraiser for blood cancer research in Memphis that year. She is thankful that she can continue to live, work and give back to the community. Before her cancer diagnosis, Layne spent several years on fertility drugs trying to become pregnant. Realizing that these were a likely cause of her cancer, Layne and her husband Steve decided to adopt a son and daughter. "Looking back, I think if I hadn't had breast cancer, I wouldn't have my children," she says. Let Layne express her gratitude and enthusiasm for life with professional realty services that represent your interests and serve your community as well.

6525 Quail Hollow Road, Memphis TN (901) 756-8900

The Fashion Academy

First impressions count for a lot. The Fashion Academy can help you put your best foot forward by offering classes that focus on the basics of good grooming, wardrobe selection and personal presentation. A leader in the image industry for 33 years, the Fashion Academy specializes in color analysis. Under the direction of Carolyn Bendall, the Academy not only provides up-to-date comprehensive training for certified image and color consultants worldwide, but also provides corporate seminars, retail sales training, individual consultations, fashion shows and much more. If you're concerned about your image, the Fashion Academy can set you and your staff on the path to success. Fashion Academy image consultants are found in salons and spas across the United States.

226 Front Street, Suite 206, Memphis TN
(901) 384-0724
www.fashionacademy.net

Drew Renshaw, Builder

Drew Renshaw, Builder specializes in creating not just houses, but architectural works of art. Owner Drew Renshaw listens closely to each of his clients to determine their needs and desires and helps them realize their dreams. He and his staff study the time period that the client's house should emulate and pride themselves on using building techniques and materials that mimic methods and resources available during that era. Whether making hewn wood beams with the same tools used nearly 200 years ago or creating brick walls with the methods of the French countryside in the 1700s, Drew Renshaw, Builder is dedicated to authenticity. Sometimes it is an addition to an existing house that needs to look as if it had always been there. Drew Renshaw, Builder is a perfect choice in these situations. The staff ensures that each project results in a warm, timeless residence suited to the family that will be living in it. They gladly work within realistic budget constraints and set forth and meet reasonable time frames in all of their projects. From dramatic, sweeping front entryways to old-style kitchens with modern amenities, Drew and his staff can make your dreams come true. Just take a look at their website to see for yourself.

512 Williamsburg Lane, Memphis TN (901) 864-1726 *www.drewrenshawbuilder.com*

Town Village Audubon Park

Town Village Audubon Park is more than a place to live, it's a lifestyle. You've worked hard all your life and now it's time to enjoy the fruits of your labor. Step inside this gated senior living community and let the security and friendliness surround you. You can be as active or leisurely as you like. Hop aboard the transportation provided or drive your own car. Socialize with neighbors or just spend time alone in your elegant one or two bedroom apartment. The choice is always up to you. With Laurelwood shopping and the Dixon Gallery and Gardens a stone's throw away, you'll never feel isolated. You can walk across the street and engulf yourself in the natural beauty of the Memphis Botanical Garden and Audubon Park. Try signing up for a stimulating educational program and join the lifelong learners club. Stay healthy with a daily dip in the indoor heated pool or chalk up a mile or two on a recumbent bicycle in exercise class. Membership in the cultural guild is available at no extra cost. Through the guild, you'll enjoy outings to the symphony, ballet and local museums. A beauty salon, library and computer lab, card room and craft room are all available to residents. You can invite your family to join you for a delicious, heart-healthy meal in the full-service dining room. Apartments feature fully equipped kitchens, full-sized washers and dryers, spacious closets and walk-in showers for your safety. The well-trained staff is on duty 24 hours a day to meet your needs or in case of an emergency. You don't have to leave your life behind. Bring it with you to Town Village Audubon Park, where life is better than ever.

950 Cherry Road, Memphis TN
(901) 537-0002
www.horizonbay.com/communities

Catholic Schools Office

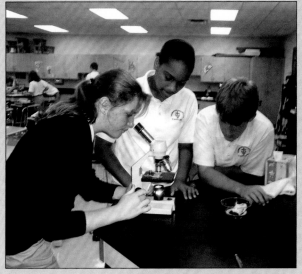

For more than 150 years, educators and administrators in the Diocese of Memphis Ca
Schools have joined together in the shared belief that raising a child involves more tha
academic success. The Catholic Schools seek to nurture and support students while
challenging them to grow intellectually, spiritually and emotionally. Educating the w
child is the mission. Due to the dedicated efforts of principals, teachers, students and
the Diocese has been blessed with record growth. The system now has 28 schools, inc
elementary, middle, high and special education schools. It enjoys the highest enrollm
in 29 years—more than 8,700 students. Administrators attribute the success of the sc
system to its commitment to high standards, superior curricula and assessment meas
Effective communication with families is also key. In 2006, 95 percent of the graduat
high school seniors continued on to college and earned $18,500,000 in scholarships. V
the schools are based on the spirit of Christ and the teachings of the Church, 40 perce
the student body is non-Catholic. All are welcome. Stop by the Catholic Schools Offic
learn more about how you and your child can become a member of this thriving comm

5825 Shelby Oaks Drive, Memphis TN (901) 373-1254
www.cdom.org/schoolsite/schoolshome.htm

Tisha Wright—Realtor

If you're thinking of making Western Tennessee your home, make a quick run to Memphis to visit with Tisha Wright. Born and bred in the South, she specializes in the Western Tennessee region for Benchmark Realtors. Benchmark is known for offering some of the best realty training available. The company prides itself on the continuing education of its realtors and the advanced designations they consistently achieve. Tisha came to realty later in life and takes special pleasure in being able to help others achieve the dream of home ownership. She started out in corporate accounting in the Northeastern United States but found the career unfulfilling. "I didn't feel that what I did really mattered," she explains. Nostalgia for the South, its mild climate and culture of hospitality brought her back home and eventually, her sense of place inspired her to pursue an MBA with a concentration in real estate. After earning her realtor's license, she is happier than ever in her work. "This job has been extremely rewarding," she notes. "I've helped many families buy and sell homes and actually see the difference I help make in their lives." Let Tisha make a difference in your life when you're ready to come home to the South.

7900 Winchester Road, Suite 102, Memphis TN
(901) 692-9253

The Dance Academy of Bartlett

For more than ten years, The Dance Academy of Bartlett, under owner and director Tracy Hannon, has offered a balanced dance program that expertly mixes education and enjoyment. Students of varying ages and abilities at the school receive individual and group attention as

they learn steps and combinations, study French terminology and practice performing on stage. Since opening in 1997, the school has quadrupled in size. Students have performed on Carnival Cruise Lines, with the Moscow Ballet and with Neil Goldberg's Cirque. They consistently win high marks at dance competitions. The academy offers summer camps for children ages three and up with programming that soars beyond tap, jazz and ballet to modern dance, improvisation and dance history. Tracy has been teaching for 15 years. She's rehearsal director for the Moscow Ballet's traditional *Nutcracker* and has judged the international I Love Dance competitions. Introduce your child to a world of grace and dedication with lessons from The Dance Academy of Bartlett.

6238 Stage Road, Bartlett TN
(901) 385-2228
www.thedanceacademyofbartlett.com

Titan Home Mortgage

When you decide to buy a home or refinance a mortgage, you're taking a big step. You can trust Titan Home Mortgage to find the loan program that's best for you. With an accounting degree from Mississippi State University and eight years in the mortgage industry, owner and president Craig Cline has an eye for numbers and a nose for news. Helping customers with customized pricing is his specialty—he closely watches rates rise and fall to find you the best deal around. Titan works with 63 top lenders across the country, so it's well-placed to find the very best rates. Craig and his business partner, Mike Thomas, owe the success of their business to tireless employees who have the talent and knowledge to satisfy customers. Sixteen loan

officers give clients the personal attention they deserve. Whether scouting out your dream home or refinancing your current mortgage, Craig, Mike and their staff are dedicated to you. Don't overlook tapping into your home equity. You've been paying off your balance while property values have skyrocketed. Titan is here to help you find the best program for your goals. Titan Home Mortgage is licensed in Tennessee, Mississippi and Virginia. Call in the experts at Titan Home Mortgage for professional, fast and friendly service.

51 Germantown Court, Suite 210, Cordova TN
(901) 531-7070
www.titanhomemortgage.net

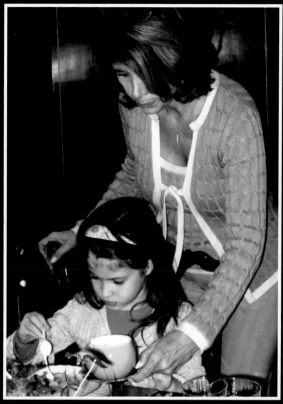

The School of Protocol and Etiquette

In the ever-quickening pace of modern life, it seems that much pleasantry and common politeness has fallen by the wayside. Thankfully, those among us who can't identify a crab fork or who have no idea how to properly shake hands can learn these age-old civilized practices at the School of Protocol and Etiquette. Founder Debbie Patterson Neal grew up in a traditional and formal German household where her father strictly enforced good manners both at home and in public. She went on to instill these values in her own daughters, as well as those she hired for her various enterprises. Debbie earned a certificate in etiquette training at the American School of Protocol before venturing forth to establish her own protocol academy in Tennessee. The School of Protocol and Etiquette offers training in a range of subjects, from table manners and proper introductions to preparing for interviews and making contacts at networking events. The school specializes in training hotel and restaurant staff in proper ways to serve guests. Whether you're looking to polish up your own manners, incorporate proper protocols into your business or have your children tutored in the concepts of etiquette, Debbie can meet your needs with grace and style at the School of Protocol and Etiquette.

7592 W Farmington Boulevard, Suite 115, Germantown TN
(901) 756-2688

R.B.'s Cyclery

If visions of state-of-the-art bicycles dance in your head, a visit to R.B.'s Cyclery is in order. Owner Rod Bickel, triathlete extraordinaire, started his venture in a garage in 1996. Since then, his thriving business has become a top destination for those who seek triathlon, road and mountain bikes. Rod is always on-hand to show you the latest. Looking for a 650c wheel? You'll find it here. How about a titanium frame? R.B.'s has it, plus steel, aluminum and carbon fiber. Accessories such as helmets, carriers, clothing, pumps and much more are available. R.B.'s specializes in custom-fitting you to your bicycle. A body-geometry-based fit system analyzes your measurements to maximize comfort and aerodynamics. While R.B.'s features top-notch equipment aimed at the biking connoisseur, beginning and intermediate cyclists are more than welcome. The friendly, expert staff is happy to introduce all riders to the next level of equipment, fit and accessories. Make a point of asking staff members about races, rides, and events for cycling enthusiasts. If you have questions, they have answers. Drop by R.B.'s Cyclery anytime for updates, schedules or just some chit-chat with biking buddies. Rod invites you to come when you can and stay as long as you like.

8500 Wolf Lake Drive, Suite #105, Bartlett TN (901) 937-4669 *www.rbscyclery.com*

Results Personal Enhancement Studio

The Mr. Tennessee trophy at the front desk of Results Personal Enhancement Studio indicates that this is the place where excuses come to die. Are you serious about bodybuilding? Do you have the discipline to subject yourself to the grind of grueling daily workouts? Are you willing to make the sacrifices in diet and lifestyle that are necessary to get yourself to the competitive level? If so, you couldn't find a more qualified person to be your trainer than Results owner Chris Caudy, who was crowned heavyweight champion on his way to winning the overall title in the 2004 Mr. Tennessee competition. Chris' fitness specialty is contest preparation. His wife, Chelle, is also a personal trainer devoted to helping each client develop the body and attitude of a champion. Chris has trained Mr. Mississippi and Mr. Alabama winners, guiding them not just with their workouts, but with their diet and posing. Not everyone who comes to Results is a professional. Since opening the studio in 2005, Chris and Chelle have catered to all levels of bodybuilders—old and young as well as beginners and experts. A willingness to accept the challenge of bodybuilding is the only requirement. Drop the excuses, go to Results Personal Enhancement Studio and get down to business.

**8095 Macon Road, Suite 105, Cordova TN
(901) 752-8499**

Quail Ridge Golf Course

In 1994, top golf course designer David Pfaff put the 18-hole Quail Ridge Golf Course on the map. Unlike the flat terrain that characterizes much of the Memphis area, Quail Ridge features rolling hills. Its tree-lined fairways, seven lakes and a winding creek give it a country feel, enhanced further by glimpses of such wildlife as deer, fox, ducks and (naturally) quail. The course features Champions Bermuda greens and Bermuda fairways. A fully stocked golf shop, snack bar and grill as well as beverage cart service add to the appeal of the establishment. Golfers can also improve their skills on the practice putting green or on the driving and chipping range. Quail Ridge offers special rates on Monday and Tuesday for clergy, police, fire and military personnel. Youngsters or parents playing with children also receive special rates on these days. Several professional and national qualifiers have taken place here, including the AJGA, the FedEx St. Jude Classic and the USGA PubLinks. In 2006, readers of the *Commercial Appeal* named Quail Ridge the Best Public Golf Club. Golf course Manager Brian Alexander can assist you with your next corporate meeting or party. Quail Ridge's flexible banquet facility features a view of the 18th hole and has hosted small weddings, poker parties and children's birthday events. For challenging golf in scenic surroundings, book your tee time at Quail Ridge Golf Course.

4055 Altruria Road, Bartlett TN (901) 386-6951 *www.thequailgolf.com*

All About Honeymoons

What is your honeymoon fantasy? Relaxing on a palm-lined pristine beach? Dancing to the sounds of the islands? Watching for wildlife in exotic locations? Going from port to port on a luxurious cruise ship? At All About Honeymoons, Eileen Civera is dedicated to making your

dreams a reality. Eileen is a home-based travel consultant with connections all over the world. Eileen specializes in customized honeymoons, destination weddings, romantic getaways and group travel. From all-inclusive resorts and cruises in the Bahamas, Mexico and the Caribbean to villas in Europe, she can put together a vacation to remember. Having planned her own vacations to places like Hawaii, Costa Rica, Quebec, British Columbia and Alaska, Eileen shares her excitement and expertise with family, friends and now newlyweds. Operating independently allows Eileen to work her schedule around the needs of her clients. Put her talent and enthusiasm to work for you, call Eileen to schedule a consultation or check out her web sites to learn more about what All About Honeymoons has to offer for a vacation of a lifetime.

(901) 626-6258
www.a-vacation-to-remember.com
www.eileenc.allabouthoneymoons.com

Windyke Country Club

Earl Dykema's vision for Windyke Country Club was that of an affordable, inclusive club for families to enjoy golf, swimming, tennis and socializing. The Memphis club, now owned by the Garner family, lives up to the founder's expectations every day. Windyke's 375-acre golf course was the largest course ever developed by an individual when Mr. Dykema had it built in the 1960s. Since then, Windyke has been host to every major junior, ladies, amateur and professional tournament in the state. That's in addition to the hobbyists and dedicated players you'll find there every day. The club's pro shop carries a full range of golf equipment. Families enjoy the club's eight tennis courts—five outdoor courts and three indoor ones. A tennis shop provides necessary supplies. Swimmers will want to dive right into the Olympic-size pool with its 10-foot-deep diving area. The Windyke Country Club's swim team has won 14 city championships. After all this exercise, you're bound to work up an appetite. The club's bar and grill offers a casual lunchtime environment, or you can grab a quick bite at the snack bar. A dining room,

tent and patio areas make ideal locations for parties and receptions of all kinds. Please the sports lovers in your family with a membership at Windyke Country Club, where you'll be welcomed with open arms.

8535 Winchester Road, Memphis TN
(901) 754-1888
www.windyke.com

Custom Travel

Mt..McKinley, Alaska
Photo by Uttam Shaw/Custom Travel

Did booking your last vacation online turn out to be a headache? If it did, then you are ready to join the many folks around Memphis who have re-discovered the convenience of working with an agent at Custom Travel. Why spend your precious time navigating site after site, looking for the best airfare and hotel deal? The staff at Custom Travel will do it for you. What's more, when you work with a travel specialist, you will never embark on your trip with a pile of unanswered questions. Are you really getting the best possible rate on your hotel room? Is the hotel really the modern five-star establishment that the online service says it is? Is it really right on the beach? At Custom Travel, you can pose your questions to a real person, someone who has the inside scoop on the rates and the range of services at the hotels at your destination. He or she can inform you about seasonal specials, arrange a car rental and reserve a space for you on that wildlife excursion. Do you really want to trust something as important as your destination wedding or honeymoon to an online service? Sit in on a honeymoon seminar at Custom Travel and see why this business is a well-known honeymoon specialist. Wherever you are heading, travel with confidence by letting Custom Travel make all your arrangements for you.

754 E Brookhaven Circle, Memphis TN
(901) 682-5550
910 W Poplar Avenue, #4, Collierville TN
(901) 854-2024
www.customtraveltn.com

Gus's World Famous Hot & Spicy Fried Chicken

With its nine tables and reach-in beer cooler, the original Gus's World Famous Hot & Spicy Fried Chicken might not look like a world-famous eatery, but world-famous is exactly what it is. Gus's has been featured on the Food Network and in several national publications. *USA Today* named Gus's fried chicken one of the Top 20 Dishes in the United States, and *GQ* even called it one of 10 Meals to Fly For in the world. Folks have been trying for decades to ferret out the secret recipe for Gus's spicy chicken batter, but you'll just have to eat at Gus's to experience it. Gus's will freshly fry your chicken in 100 percent peanut oil after you order, so it comes to your plate direct from the fryer. It takes a little while to make each order fresh, but it's worth it. You'll also find fabulous catfish and fresh, homemade sides and pies at Gus's, now in six locations. The legacy of Gus's World Famous Fried Chicken began with Napoleon Vanderbilt in 1953. Napoleon opened a small restaurant called Maggie's on the town square in Mason, a few miles east of Memphis. More than 50 years have passed since then, and the place has changed a lot. In 1973, the restaurant moved to its current location in Mason, and 10 years later, Napoleon's son Gus took over. Before long, people were coming from all over the country to taste the best fried chicken in the South. That's when Gus and his wife, Gertrude, decided to change the name, and Gus's World Famous Fried Chicken was born. Wherever you are in the greater Memphis area, stop in and taste for yourself how Gus's got to be world-famous.

**original location: 520 Hwy 70, Mason TN
(901) 294-2028
2965 Germantown Road, Bartlett TN
(901) 373-9111**

Gridley's Fine Bar-B-Q

Quality and quantity go hand in hand at Gridley's Fine Bar-B-Q. It was about 65 years ago that Clyde Gridley began slowly cooking the best beef and pork available over hickory wood and charcoal. He felt that customers would appreciate the soft and juicy meat of his barbecue once they tasted it. He also had a hunch that they would go for his sweeter sauce. Even Gridley's mayonnaise-based slaw was a break from convention, an alternative to the mustard-based slaw that was popular at the time. Gridley went out of his way to set his establishment apart from the typical barbecue shack by adding beautiful décor and employing the sharpest waiters he could find. The crucial final element in his formula for success was to serve very generous portions, sending customers home well-fed and feeling they had gotten good value for their money. Family favorites were gradually introduced to the menu, such as Gridley's Bar-B-Q shrimp, which caught on immediately. Gridley's has expanded several times to keep up with its popularity and now boasts five other Memphis-area locations in addition to the original Bartlett restaurant. Although ownership has changed over the years, the Gridley vision has always guided the business. Pork butts, prime beef brisket and barbecue ribs are still prepared with utmost care and attention. Pulled barbecue sandwiches are piled high. Try any of these favorites with a loaf of Gridley Bread and become a Gridley's Fine Bar-B-Q fan for life.

6842 Stage Road, Bartlett TN
(901) 377-8055

Abe's Ribeye Barn

At Abe's Ribeye Barn, a memorable fine dining experience may mean seafood, chicken dishes or steak freshly prepared over a charcoal grill. The certified Angus beef makes ribeye, filet mignon and a memorable New York strip steak. Sourdough bread with honey butter is a tasty way to start the meal, and the candied sweet potatoes make a delightful side. *Crème brûlée,* Chocolate Lover's Spoon Cake or bread pudding make a perfect ending to a perfect meal. Abe's is a place where you can feel equally comfortable in casual dress or a tuxedo or evening gown. The full-service lounge offers privacy to smaller groups and romantic couples. Naturally, Abe's offers a complete selection of spirits. Banquet facilities are available for special occasions. Owner Abe Hawatt opened the restaurant in 1995. Abe is originally from Lebanon and was headed for a degree in electrical engineering, but a stint in the restaurant business unleashed his culinary passions. After 15 years, Abe was able to follow his dream and open his own establishment. Whether you're out for a night on the town or a casual meal, come to Abe's Ribeye Barn. You're sure enjoy an evening to remember.

1130 Henry Street, Dyersburg TN
(731) 285-4648
www.abesribeyebarn.com

Big Foot Lodge

Big Foot Lodge in Memphis is named after the Sasquatch, the legendary super-sized biped that some say roams the North American wild. An eight-foot-tall statue of the Sasquatch stands by the front door, greeting families, business people, travelers and locals alike. As its name suggests, Big Foot Lodge is a serious contestant in the race for the largest meal portions anywhere. Take the signature Sasquatch, a four-pound hamburger complete with all the fixings and a pound of fries. If you can finish it by yourself in an hour, it's free. If you're still hungry, you can order a deep-fried Cornish hen or some of the other Big Foot treats, including BBQ egg rolls, fried pickles, live Maine lobster and s'mores you can make at your table. For dessert, there's the Yeti, 18 scoops of ice cream with tons of toppings. Owner Shawn Danko is originally from Montreal, and his menu contains some Canadian specialties, such as *poutine*, handcut fries loaded with cheese curds and smothered with Big Foot's own special gravy. And don't forget the Nanaimo Bar, a truly Canadian desert. Big Foot Lodge also has its own rendition of the corn dog, the Corn Brat, which uses delicious bratwurst instead of the traditional hot dog. Chicken wings come 12, 24, or even 50 at a time, the handcut rib eye steak weighs in at 20 ounces, and beer fills 34-ounce steins. The restaurant looks more like something out of the Northern woods than downtown Memphis, with trophies of wild game and fish lining the log cabin walls. For big food, big taste and big fun that would bring any Sasquatch out of the woods, visit Big Foot Lodge.

97 S 2ⁿᵈ Street, Memphis TN
(901) 578-9800
www.bigfootlodge.net

The Inn at Hunt Phelan

In 1990, when Bill Day moved into a home that has been in his family for more than 175 years, it was, as he says, in "wrecking ball condition." After 14 years of painstaking restoration based on the plans of original architect, Robert Mills, the Inn at Hunt Phelan once again reflects its antebellum elegance. Amazing attention to detail, down to replicating the original drapery fabric, has earned Hunt Phelan a national design award from the American Society of Interior Designers as well as more than 20 local and national restoration awards. This bed-and-breakfast features 12 sumptuous guest rooms that showcase antique furnishings and authentic fabrics. The spacious bathrooms create the spa-like ambience of an upscale hotel. The inn's restaurant, called Dinner in the Mansion, is one of Memphis' few four-star establishments. It serves up exquisite French Creole cuisine by Chef Stephen Hassinger in elegantly ornate dining rooms. The Veranda Grill offers cocktails, conversation and bistro fare either inside or on the patio. The beautifully landscaped grounds, New Orleans-style patio and large fountain with a stage gazebo create the ideal setting for a wedding or other special occasion. The mansion also features banquet rooms. Placed on the National Register of Historic Places in 1970, the inn has hosted three past American presidents and even (long ago) the president of the Confederacy. Come experience rich history and old-fashioned Southern hospitality at the Inn at Hunt Phelan.

533 Beale Street, Memphis TN
(901) 525-8225
www.huntphelan.com

Blue Plate Café

The vanishing tradition of the blue-plate special is alive and well at Blue Plate Café, where you can order a hearty breakfast all day long or pick a meat and three sides for lunch or dinner. The Poplar Avenue café opened in 1994 in a charming yellow building. The original location started as a family home, built in 1952 by Holiday Inn founder Kemmons Wilson. With breakfasts this satisfying, it makes sense that Blue Plate serves them all day long. Try the biscuits with creamy sausage gravy and the salty country ham. The waffles are round, thin and crisp and fill your whole plate. You can put grits or chunky hash brown with your omelette or pour warm maple syrup over a stack of pancakes. The café is a popular weekday lunch spot, where food arrives quickly but doesn't taste like fast food. Choose from salads, soups and an assortment of sandwiches, including fried peanut butter and banana. The meat-and-three lunches earned the Blue Plate its name. Meat choices include pot roast, chicken fried steak and meat loaf. There are baked pork chops, chicken and dumplings, plus fried shrimp on Fridays. Fried okra and real mashed potatoes are a couple of the favorite sides. Add the daily fruit cobblers and a courteous staff to the mix, and you'll see why the International Restaurant Association voted the café one of the Top 10 Cafés in America in 2004. It was also voted the number one restaurant in Memphis for breakfast and home cooking. For Southern soul food in a down-home atmosphere, visit any of the Blue Plate Café's three popular locations. The Blue Plate Café—A Memphis Tradition.

113 S Court Avenue, Memphis TN
(901) 523-2050
5469 Poplar Avenue, Memphis TN
(901) 761-9696
2921 Kirby Whitten Road, Bartlett, TN
(901) 213-1066

Central BBQ

In a town with its own barbecue style, standing out for your barbecue takes know-how and a dedication to getting the details right. Owners Roger Sapp and Craig Blondis prove fit for the task at Central BBQ, where the Memphis style reigns supreme. In the Memphis style, the quality of the meat stands out, with a dry rub of spices infused into the meat during smoking. Sauces come on the side to add after the meat is cooked. "The meat has such good flavor that it really stood on its own with no additional enhancement," said a Roadfood.com reviewer. Commercial Appeal raved about the ribs, the chicken, and the pork and brisket sandwiches as well as the "uniformly excellent" side dishes. Central BBQ makes a roasted potato salad with true roasted flavor and a chunky coleslaw lightly dressed with vinegar. Its fresh-made potato chips are thick and crisp; its beans with pork meat, sweet and savory. The restaurant offers such dreamy desserts as cheesecake and Ben & Jerry's ice cream. Central BBQ has been going strong since opening five years ago. Roger and Craig know their way around restaurants and are longtime participants in the Memphis in May International World Championship Barbecue Cooking Contest, an event that attracts national press and the foremost food magazines. Find out why Memphis brags about its barbecue at Central BBQ.

4375 Summer Avenue, Memphis TN (901) 767-4672 *cbqmemphis.com*

Rendezvous Restaurant

If you're searching for a real taste of Memphis, then gather the gang and head for the Rendezvous Restaurant, where thousands come each week to enjoy a true Tennessee sensation. This local favorite's walls are covered with memorabilia and nostalgic reminders of the colorful past of the city and the restaurant. Over the years, the Rendezvous has served U.S. presidents, the Rolling Stones and many a working man with the same tender and delicious food featured in the *Memphis Flyer* Best of Memphis, *Southern Living* and an array of other magazines. Best known for its amazing ribs, the Rendezvous Restaurant serves up a variety of other comfort foods as well, including sandwiches, chicken and meatless red beans and rice. If you can't make it down to the restaurant, the friendly staff will be happy to wrap up an order to ship out by Federal Express. In 1948, Charlie Vergos was cleaning out a basement below his diner when he discovered a coal chute. This chute was an essential part of a culinary legend. It acted as a vent for the Rendezvous grill, enabling Charlie's incredible talent with barbecue. Go ahead and give in to your barbecue cravings with a trip to the Rendezvous Restaurant, where barbecue has reigned supreme for nearly 60 years.

52 S 2ⁿᵈ Street, Memphis TN
(901) 523-2746
www.hogsfly.com

Mister B's Restaurant

The spicy Cajun fare, scrumptious seafood and colossal steaks at Mister B's Restaurant in Germantown are legendary, all thanks to founder Dick Baker, Mister B. Today, his heirs, Theresa, Brett and Debbie Baker, carry on his legacy. The popular establishment has only moved twice in its history. Today at Poplar Avenue, two beloved cooks, Miss Ernestine and Miss Essie, continue to work for the family. Both women began their culinary careers when Mister B's first opened its doors in 1975. Shrimp, crab, oysters and other seasonal seafood are delivered fresh several times a week. Try the crab imperial, prepared from the original recipe handed down from Mister B himself. Steaks and pork chops are cooked just the way you like them. Don't be surprised when a two-pound T-bone arrives at your table. If you feel a little adventurous, order oysters on the half shell, frog legs or crab claws. For a taste of New Orleans, bring on the Cajun. Daily delights include red beans and rice, gumbo, creole and étouffée. Vegetable plates and varying specials are served at lunch. Choose a glass of Chardonnay or Merlot from the full-service bar to compliment your lunch or dinner. Call on the Baker clan at Mister B's Restaurant to prepare a meal that satisfies long after you've left the building.

6655 Poplar Avenue #107, Germantown TN
(901) 751-5262

Fire-n-Stone Pizza

Fire-n-Stone Pizza reminds customers that Not All Pizzas are Created Equal. The Germantown pizza parlor proves its superiority every day with a huge variety of fresh ingredients and a special hot stone baking method. The restaurant's name comes from the way in which the pizzas are cooked. Fire-n-Stone places its pizzas directly on an open stone in a gas-fired oven for a difference you can taste. Owner Corey Dunavant brought this pizza-cooking style to the Memphis area after seeing it done in other parts of the country. Corey added the emphasis on fresh ingredients. Not only are the restaurant's dough and sauces made on the premises without prepackaged ingredients, but all meats and garlic are roasted and seasoned in Fire-n-Stone's own oven. A produce truck delivers fresh vegetables and fruits to the door. The pizza menu includes 52 ingredients, creatively combined for sensational bursts of flavor. You'll find several kinds of cheese, savory meats and seafoods and such exotic toppings as kalamata olives, portobello mushrooms, pineapple and cucumbers. If you're not in the mood for pizza, try one of Fire-n-Stone's salads, sandwiches or wraps. Those looking after their health will be pleased to note that *PMQ Magazine* declared Fire-n-Stone's Healthy Man Pizza the second healthiest pizza in the United States. For pizza that makes an individual statement, come to Fire-n-Stone Pizza.

9947 Wolf River Boulevard, Germantown TN
(901) 861-5140
www.firenstone.com

Folk's Folly
Prime Steakhouse

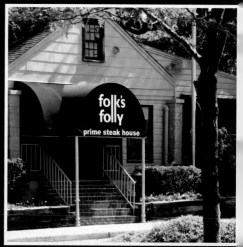

Local entrepreneur Humphrey Folk, Jr. was a fun-loving yet shrewd businessman who had a knack for recognizing opportunity, no matter how softly it knocked. A contractor by trade, Folk enhanced extensive travel with a passionate appetite for dining out, collecting recipes along the way. In 1977, he compiled his favorite dishes and began renovating a comfortable home in East Memphis for the area's first prime steak house. Against advice from his colleagues who referred to his lack of restaurant experience, he forged ahead with his plans and affectionately gave the business a tongue-in-cheek moniker, Folk's Folly. Thirty years and seven additions later, Folk's Folly is a well-established, a one-of-a-kind Memphis tradition, still serving the highest-quality hand-cut prime beef and still actively owned by Humphrey's four sons, along with managing partner and renowned restaurateur Thomas Boggs. An extensive wine list, distinctive appetizers, the freshest accompaniments and down-home desserts complement the mouth-watering steaks and other specialties, including live Maine lobster and Australian rack of lamb. Don't miss your opportunity to experience the excellent cuisine and service at Memphis' original prime steak house, Folk's Folly.

551 S Mendenhall Road, Memphis TN
(901) 762-8200
www.folksfolly.com

Automatic Slim's Tonga Club

"A restaurant is a piece of art to me," says Karen Blockman Carrier, a former artist and now one of Memphis' foremost restaurateurs. Her flair for the visual makes dining at Automatic Slim's Tonga Club a romp. Where else can you find barstools covered with pom-poms and fringe that are the creation of a New York hat designer? The food is an eclectic blend of Southwestern, Caribbean and Southeast Asian fare that is willing to take chances. Try the platter of grilled chicken wings stuffed with scallion-goat cheese and ground Thai pork. "You'll never look at Buffalo wings in a bar the same way again," said one food critic, who also praised the roasted chicken crusted with coconut and guava: "The combination of flavors and sensations was terrific." The jerk of the day, featuring secret spices wrangled from the women on the beach in Jamaica, cranks up the heat on any entrée at Automatic Slim's, a restaurant often credited with sparking a resurgence in the downtown area of Memphis. Opened in 1991, it has become a city institution, beloved as much for Karen's creative menu as for its hip, funky décor and potent atmosphere. The mezzanine dining area is one of the best spots in the city for people watching. For a dining experience that's a work of art, head to Automatic Slim's Tonga Club.

83 S Second Street, Memphis TN
(901) 525-7948

Cielo

Cielo, the Spanish word for *heaven,* is also a word that you'll hear around Memphis in association with stylish and trendy dining. Cielo is one of five Memphis restaurants owned by Karen Blockman Carrier, whose belief that dining should be an engaging experience for all the senses reaches its most romantic height at this location. Housed in the Mollie Fontaine Taylor home in the heart of Memphis' Victorian Village, Cielo serves Spanish and French dishes amid a backdrop of contemporary artwork, custom wood finishing and 18-foot ceilings with gold leaf. For appetizers, try the escargot or the pork dumplings Thai style. New Zealand rack of lamb and a crispy half duck atop a celery root slaw are featured entrées. Each dish showcases the creative style that is the owner's trademark. Diners entertained by Karen's sense of the offbeat at her Beauty Shop Restaurant & Lounge might be surprised that she can do elegant equally as well. She was involved in every detail when opening the restaurant in 1996, even down to choosing the sparkling glass chargers, which were handcrafted by a nationally renowned glass blower. Dine at Cielo, where one word captures an entire dining experience.

679 Adams Street, Memphis TN
(901) 524-1886

Do Sushi and Lounge

At Do Sushi and Lounge, you can enjoy your meal within the privacy of your own little tent. Floor-length muslin curtains can be drawn around tables to enclose you and your friends in your own world of good conversation and exotic tastes. You can also eat at the bar or get comfy in the front corner, sitting on cushions on the floor. In short, the experience at Do Sushi is anything but ordinary, which can be said for all of the Memphis restaurants that Karen Blockman Carrier owns. Do Sushi is located next door to the beauty salon that Karen transformed into a popular eatery called the Beauty Shop. All of the fish at Do Sushi is prepared fresh. *Memphis* magazine gave the food a four-star rating overall, noting that even some of the old standards have been revitalized with unusual twists. For example, the tempura approach to the shrimp roll is a "brilliant improvement" over the typical seaweed wrap. Other crowd pleasers include the dragon rolls, featuring spicy crawfish and plum puree, and the Tokyo Surf and Turf, which consists of a thin strip of seared beef draped over a tuna roll with leeks and arugula. To encourage sharing, just about all of the food is served on small plates, which calls for you to bring the whole gang and try lots of different sushi and nigiri at Do Sushi and Lounge.

954 S Cooper Street, Memphis TN
(901) 272-0830

Beauty Shop Restaurant & Lounge

Folks with a sense of humor and an appetite for an exotic sandwich or salad can bring both to the Beauty Shop Restaurant & Lounge, and they will walk away happy. This restaurant takes concept dining to a new level with décor from the famous Atkins Beauty Salon, where Priscilla Presley used to have her hair done. How did it all come about? Karen Blockman Carrier, already the successful owner of three Memphis restaurants, was thinking of opening a smaller neighborhood eatery when she stumbled upon a place for rent in the Cooper Young area of midtown Memphis. "I walked in and there was this beauty salon straight from 1941," she recalls. "Everything was intact, and I just started visualizing the booths where they used to get their hair done being food booths where you could sit down and eat." The idea of enjoying your ahi tuna while sitting in a hair dryer chair has gone over big since the Beauty Shop opened in 2002, mainly because the quality of the food equals the cleverness of the concept. This is the place for the adventurous palate seeking Italian, Asian and Latin flavors. Try the Bangkok Salad or the filling Ancho Pork Torta and finish with the pistachio bread pudding for dessert. With Barbicide canisters for straw dispensers and hair rinse sinks behind the bar, you might want to wear curlers to get into the proper spirit of the place. In the mood for something a little wacky? Then let your hair down at the Beauty Shop Restaurant & Lounge.

966 S Cooper, Memphis TN
(901) 272-7111

Molly's La Casita

The story of Molly's La Casita begins with one very special lady whose memory lives on in the homey Mexican restaurant that bears her name. Molly Gonzales opened the original La Casita in 1974. One of her first customers was Robert Chapman, who enjoyed the meal so much that he returned each week for several years. In 1982, Molly, then 80 years old, confided in Robert that she would have to close the restaurant due to problems with the building. As luck would have it, Robert had just seen the perfect building for the restaurant, complete with tiled floors and exposed brick and stucco walls. The two friends worked out a deal in which Molly would run the kitchen while Robert tended to the business end. Though Molly passed away several years ago, Robert and his wife, Jamie, continue her tradition of authentic Mexican meals. Because Molly cooked completely by instinct, Robert spent many hours in the kitchen measuring and recording Molly's pinches and dashes to ensure the flavors were just right. Choose a steak fajita that comes to your table sizzling hot or try one of the delicious red snapper or shrimp dishes. The chunky guacamole is a must-have, while the Margaritas are loved by locals and visitors alike. Visit Molly's La Casita and remember a remarkable woman who added spice both to her dishes and to the lives of her customers.

2006 Madison Avenue, Memphis TN
(901) 726-1873
www.mollyslacasita.com

Tops Bar-B-Q

While you're on your musical tour of Memphis, drop in at Tops Bar-B-Q, one of Elvis Presley's favorite pit stops. Celebrating its 54th year, Tops is famous for its awe-inspiring barbecued pork shoulder, slow-cooked in a pit over hardwood, charcoal and green hickory wood, and available as a sandwich or dinner plate. Tops also barbecues beef, chicken and ribs—just let the staff know what you prefer. The restaurant makes specialty hamburgers from freshly ground beef and cooks them to order. For a side dish you have a choice of beans, coleslaw, French fries or chips. Tops Bar B-Q is a favorite among Memphis locals, and recently won the Readers Choice Award from

the *Commercial Appeal*. Now owned by George Messick, Tops has a long history. The first restaurant opened in 1952, and its popularity has grown ever since. Tops currently has 14 locations in the Memphis area. If you're planning a company picnic or family reunion, Tops offers party packages and catering, a great way to wow your friends and family. On your next tour, break-step into a Tops, and find out for yourself why Tops Bar-B-Q is fit for the King.

5720 Mt. Moriah Road, Memphis TN
(901) 363-4007
www.topsbarbq.com

Photo by Jim Kiihnl

The Side Porch Steak House

The Side Porch Steak House opened a century or so too late to cater to the stagecoach and train travelers passing through what was then the depot town of Bartlett. Nevertheless, it's still the oldest steak house in town. According to the readers of the *Bartlett Express,* it's also the best. For six years they have voted it their favorite place to bite into thick, juicy T-bone and filet mignon as well as New York strip and rib eye. This family-owned and operated restaurant serves onion petals, hot wings and many other delicious appetizers to complement the entrées, which include

seafood and chicken in addition to the steaks. Would you like to know the recipe for the marvelous steak marinade? Sorry, it's a secret. Established in 1976, the restaurant is located in a converted house where the local telegraph operator once lived. A former mayor and his family made the house their home from 1946 to 1971. Come to the Side Porch Steak House, and leave raving about your meal, just as the locals do every night.

5689 Stage Road, Bartlett TN
(901) 377-2484

Buns on the Run

The bakery background shared by Buns on the Run owners Sharron Johnson and Pam Hardin, combined with a homey and inviting atmosphere like grandma's kitchen, sets this Memphis restaurant apart. Housed in a duplex bungalow in the Midtown residential area, the restaurant serves the kind of breakfasts you want to savor. Choose from fluffy omelettes, creamy quiche Lorraine or eggs made just the way you like them with your bacon on the side. The French toast uses freshly made bread, and the crêpes come with lingonberry butter. Lunch is equally extraordinary, with sandwiches on bread that's baked daily on the premises and specials featuring a choice of meat with three side dishes. Service is fast and friendly, and desserts are sublime. Sharron and Pam started out with a to-go bakery in 1997 that offered pastries, pies and cakes. When customers requested lunch and breakfast items, Sharron and Pam created a menu to accommodate them. A local television feature on the sandwiches had customers lined up around the block to sample the breakfast menu. The restaurant actually ran out of food that Saturday, and Buns on the Run has been popular ever since. Bakery goods are still available, including pecan pie squares, cinnamon rolls and muffins, with special baked goods during the holiday. Gain a new appreciation for breakfast and lunch fare with a visit to Buns on the Run.

2150 Elzey Avenue, Memphis TN
(901) 278-BUNS (2867)

Bhan Thai Restaurant

Since 2002, Bhan Thai Restaurant has been the place to go in Memphis for award-winning Thai food. The restaurant, owned by Molly Smith, has been voted Best Thai for five years in a row by both *Memphis Magazine* and the *Memphis Flyer*, and was recently awarded Most Thai by *The Commercial Appeal*. Bhan Thai is renowned for its homey feel and possesses a beautiful patio dining area and bar, plus a banquet facility. Molly calls the menu at Bhan Thai "slightly Americanized." Chef Alex Kasmrijan, a native of Thailand, takes his inspiration from the family-style fare he grew up on in his homeland, such as the popular Yum Tuna, served with a sauce from northeastern Thailand that dates back 2,000 years. *Memphis Magazine's* reviewer praised the cuisine for its variety and intense flavors that don't rely over-much on fiery spices. The restaurant is housed in a former private home and retains a domestic charm. As at many homes, one of the most fun places to be is out on the patio with a drink in hand. *Memphis Downtowner* magazine called Bhan Thai's patio "one of the best outdoor dining and drinking spots in town." With its umbrellas, flowering plants and the sounds of live acoustic music on the weekends, the three-tiered deck and patio is the ideal spot for relaxing with friends while enjoying Thai tea, an order of spring rolls or the spicy tang of Tiger Cry. For balanced flavors in authentic Thai cuisine, visit Bhan Thai Restaurant.

1324 Peabody Avenue, Memphis TN
(901) 272-1538
www.bhanthairestaurant.com

BooYa's Burritos

Jay Kupiszewski and his wife, Kim, describe their fun restaurant as fast-casual, with the speed and low prices of a fast-food restaurant but with the great atmosphere and high-quality food of a fine dining establishment. At BooYa's you get to tell the friendly staff members just how you want your food prepared and to watch as they make it. Select a main dish, then choose your add-ons. The Buffalo chicken burrito adds a classic American zing to a Mexican favorite. For seafood lovers, the Beach Burrito is full of shrimp, scallops and fish sautéed with garlic, veggies and white wine. The Fish Tacos are sure to please; try the freshly grilled tilapia or the hand-dipped, beer-battered catfish, each with its own special sauce. Add the final touch to your meal with your choice of seven homemade salsas and several hot sauces. Make any gathering a beach party with party packs from BooYa's catering department. Grilled fajitas, tacos and enchiladas are all sure to be crowd pleasers. Jay began dreaming about opening his own restaurant in 1988, when he helped a friend with a start-up. After nine years in the Air Force and several years as a commercial airline pilot, he made his dreams a reality by opening BooYa's in 2006. Come on in to BooYa's Burritos at the Shops of Wolflake for good food in a laid-back atmosphere.

2695 N Germantown Parkway, Suite 115, Bartlett TN
(901) 386-7919
www.booyasburritobeach.com

Fino Villa Cucina Italiano

At Fino Villa Cucina Italiano, Italian food is prepared with a particular pride. Traditional Italian dishes such as lobster ravioli are created from scratch when you order, using only the highest

quality ingredients. Some dishes, such as Steak Diane and halibut, are prepared tableside. The world-class chefs can also fulfill special requests for Italian favorites you may not see on the menu. Fino Villa offers chef's features and new desserts every day as different seasonal ingredients become available. The dining room is spacious and elegant, its walls adorned with murals. The staff members have all chosen restaurant service as their career. Tony Sarwar owns the restaurant, which is the manifestation of a dream based on a long tradition of family cooking. Tony, trained by top chefs in Chicago, opened Fino Villa in 2005, which he now runs along with his mother, Maria, his brother, Dino, and his sister, Lyla. Come to Fino Villa Cucina Italiano to experience three generations of cooking excellence.

875 W Poplar Avenue, Collierville TN
(901) 861-2626
www.finovilla.com

Sauces

Our Plate Your Canvas is the tag line at Sauces, a hip restaurant tucked along historic Main Street in downtown Memphis. Rosemary basil halibut, pork Dijonaise and Thai grouper are just a few of Our Plate entrées, and guests are invited to complete a masterpiece from the Your

Canvas section. The mango bruschetta pairs nicely with any of the seafood choices. The lobster cream sauce is heavenly enough to drink on its own, though you should try it on the halibut. The fried mozzarella Caprese is the top appetizer at this hot spot, which also scores big with its she-crab soup and seared tuna salad. The bar at Sauces was one of the first in Memphis to serve mojitos, now everybody's favorite South Beach drink. Work a little culinary magic with the chef at Sauces.

95 S Main Street, Memphis TN
(901) 473-9573
www.saucesmemphis.com

Miss Cordelia's

The big city of Memphis somehow seems a little smaller inside Miss Cordelia's. Housed in a quaint storefront, this restaurant, grocery and after-work wine bar is a social hub in the vibrant Harbor Town neighborhood. Folks stop in the aisles to chat with each other just as they would in a small-town market, and the person at the deli knows what the regulars will probably order before they ask. If you are putting a Mud Island picnic together, Miss Cordelia's promises a fabulous selection of fresh salads, cheeses and sweet treats. The deli sandwiches are delicious and the shelves are stocked with paper plates and other necessities. The restaurant always offers healthy options and pleasant surprises, such as the mango coconut rice that accompanies the jerk pork tenderloin. Executive Chef Nancy Kistler, considered by many to be the friendliest chef in Memphis, ran her own fine catering business for 18 years before bringing her talents to Miss Cordelia's. Her nightly meal specials, which come at a very affordable price, typically feature a classic crowd pleaser such as fried catfish or spaghetti and meatballs. Experience old-fashioned charm while you shop and eat at Miss Cordelia's.

737 Harbor Bend Road, Memphis TN (901) 526-4772
www.misscordelias.com

Café Olé

Café Olé has always been ahead of the trends. It was the first restaurant to open in the now-popular Cooper-Young Historic District. It was the first restaurant in Memphis to offer fish tacos. Don't be surprised if the bacon-wrapped stuffed shrimp, a favorite of Café Olé's customers, catches on and becomes a staple on menus throughout the country. The margaritas at Café Olé are something special, too. They are made from an original recipe that you'll have to pry out of the bartenders. Food recipes use only fresh ingredients, and all sauces are made in the kitchen. As a result, Memphis readers' polls consistently heap honors upon Café Olé, including Best Mexican Restaurant. Take a seat on the patio and see why Café Olé is considered one of the best places in Memphis to eat outside. Steve Wineberg loved the food at the restaurant so much that he was a frequent customer before he bought it in 2003. He has been in the restaurant business since he was 14, and the purchase fulfilled his dream of having his own establishment. In addition to serving dinner, Café Olé is open for lunch, with Mexican-flavored sandwiches as a popular staple. Enjoy a meal at Café Olé, a real Memphis trendsetter.

959 S Cooper Street, Memphis TN
(901) 274-1504
www.cafeolememphis.com

Café Toscana

A great Italian meal at Café Toscana might begin with shrimp sautéed in a spicy Calabrese sauce and served over four-cheese soft polenta. If you are thinking that this sounds like an appetizer from the menu of a trendy restaurant in, say, Florence, you are on the right track. Chef and owner Giacomo Ciabattini grew up and attended culinary school in that city. He credits his first job in a restaurant near the Piazza Duomo for teaching him the value of using fresh ingredients of the highest quality. Before settling permanently in America, Giacomo taught classes three months a year in Tuscany, passing his knowledge of authentic Italian cooking to some 500

chefs-in-training for the Olive Garden restaurants. He makes everything fresh at Café Toscana, including the sauces, which range from the classic Bolognese sauce of beef and pork he serves with the tortellini to a Gorgonzola cream sauce that comes with the beef tenderloin. Parmesan tilapia and *ravioli di astice*, lobster ravioli, are among the most popular dishes. For a contemporary Italian dinner complemented by a glass of fine wine, come to Café Toscana.

5007 Black Road #150, Memphis TN
(901) 761-9522
www.cafetoscanausa.com

Buckley's Fine Filet Grill

Buckley's Fine Filet Grill is a dream come true for its owners and for lovers of steak, seafood and pasta. Owners Jeff Fioranelli and Ken Dick, friends since high school, worked together in the restaurant business and created a plan to open a restaurant shortly before graduation from college. The restaurant's first location, with evening hours, opened in East Memphis in 1994. A Cordova location opened in 2004 with day and evening hours. Whichever location you choose, the food will be worthwhile. Buckley's uses corn-fed beef trucked in fresh from its Nebraska supplier. You'll taste the difference in the Buckley's Filet, an eight-ounce cut of tenderloin brushed with garlic butter and served with the famous Buckley Buds, garlic mashed potatoes with generous toppings. You'll also find specialty Italian dishes here, made according to the authentic recipes provided by Jeff's Italian grandmother, such as the mouth-watering Ravioli Noni, with marinara, meat or garlic cream sauce. If you're hungry for something besides beef,

check out such seafood dishes as encrusted grouper or blackened wild salmon. The restaurant features a romantic, casual atmosphere, with original artwork from Ken's wife, Lisa, hanging on the walls. For hearty meals, come to Buckley's Fine Filet Grill seven days a week.

5355 Poplar Avenue, Memphis TN
(901) 683-4538
714 N Germantown Parkway, Cordova TN
(901) 756-1639
www.buckleysgrill.com

Belmont Grill

Friendly faces, over-the-top service and award-winning food and drink combine for a delicious dining experience at Belmont Grill in Germantown. The neighborhood grill celebrates its 10th anniversary in 2007. Its history as a social center goes back still further to life as a general store in the whistle stop town of Forest Hill in the early 1900s. Belmont Grill is the kind of place where people from all walks of life gather for lunch, dinner or drinks. In 2006, the Belmont won *Memphis Magazine*'s Gold Award for Best Burger, a crowning achievement that followed a decade of second place finishes. The food critic for *Memphis Commercial Appeal* called the Belmont's hot wings the best in town. Seafood is a favorite here, and you will find a fried shrimp dish with a handmade sauce that is the talk of the town. The restaurant sells up to 100 pounds of fried catfish every week, which speaks for its popularity. The Belmont takes the extra steps to assure this kind of consistent praise. Steaks are hand-cut in-house, onion rings are hand breaded daily and every soup gets its start right on the premises. Whether it's beer, wine or the latest coffee drink, you'll find an excellent beverage choice here that's bound to result in a favorite or two. Everything about the Belmont is friendly and casual, so no one will think twice if you engage in a lively discussion with your friends over dinner or drinks. For a place that puts you and your appetite at ease, visit Belmont Grill.

9102 Poplar Pike, Germantown TN
(901) 624-6001

Blues City Café

Since 1991, the Blues City Café has been a top local hangout and tourist destination in Memphis. Celebrities stop here frequently. Bill Clinton, Robert DeNiro, James Earl Jones and Jerry Seinfeld, among others, have all enjoyed a meal or two. Southern favorites such as barbecued ribs, fried catfish, broiled steaks and homemade tamales are always available. Other popular items on the world-famous menu include the homemade chili with Texas toast, Memphis soul stew and seafood gumbo. The Food Network's *Bobby Flay Show* and the Travel Channel's *Taste of America* have both featured the restaurant. Music is in the air, with live entertainment nightly in the Band Box. You may hear the next big thing or catch a famous act such as blues legend B.B. King, Queen Latifah, Yanni or old-time rock and roller Jerry Lee Lewis. The dance floor is always open. The look at the Blues City Café is intentionally weathered, with corrugated iron and glass blocks. *The Firm,* a Tom Cruise movie, filmed the interior of the restaurant almost unchanged. The Blues City Café offers catering for up to 1,000, or you can rent the Cadillac Room for groups of up to 40. Great music and great food have always gone together. At the Blues City Café you have both. Stop by today to enjoy the best meal on Beale.

138 Beale Street, Memphis TN
(901) 526-3637
(901) 525-1724 (catering)
www.bluescitycafe.com

Alfred's

To paraphrase master bluesman W.C. Handy, if Beale Street could talk, it would be singing the praises of Alfred's. With delicious old-fashioned Southern food and drink and the joyous sounds of music and conversation, this Memphis club offers a fun-filled night on the town. Currently owned by Sandy Robertson, Alfred's was one of the first clubs to open on the storied Beale Street. Memphis is widely known as the birthplace of rock n' roll, and Alfred's was one of the first clubs where rock was played. Live music is still on the menu at Alfred's, with Kevin Paige & the Amazing Flea Circus performing often. Kevin is well-known for his American Top 20 pop hits, "Don't Shut Me Out" and "Anything I Want." You'll find many other acts here, including DJs and karaoke singers who just might be the next big star. There's a large floor to dance the night away on and a double-decker patio to relax with a drink on. The food includes such Southern classics as barbecued pork, fried green tomatoes and catfish. You'll find the steak and ribs cooked to perfection. The atmosphere is festive, with the neon letters from the famed Stax recording studio serving as a bright backdrop to the main stage. For a plate full of delicious Southern food and an earful of sweet Southern sounds, come to Alfred's, open for lunch and dinner.

197 Beale Street, Memphis TN
(901) 525-3711
www.alfredsonbeale.com

Dyer's Burgers

How's this for old-fashioned food? Dyer's Burgers has been making its legendary hamburgers since 1912—with the same grease. A Memphis landmark, Dyers was originally owned by Elmer "Doc" Dyer. Local legend has it that the secret to Doc's delicious burgers was the grease he deep-fried them in. That's why Dyer's uses that very same grease, carefully strained every day, to prepare its delicious burgers. Whenever the restaurant has moved, they've had the grease transported to the new location under police escort. Dyers serves a burger like your parents and grandparents told you about, dripping with mustard, onions and cheese. You'll also find chicken tenders and hot wings on the menu. If you're looking for a bowl of spicy chili with onions and cheese, you've come to the right place. Enjoy an authentic soda jerk float or a milkshake to drink and a slice of homemade peach cobbler for dessert. Come to Dyer's Burgers for the same greasy goodness customers have been enjoying since 1912.

205 Beale Street, Memphis TN
(901) 525-3711

Memphis

Murfreesboro

Jackson

Collierville

Bumpus Harley-Davidson

Live to ride, ride to live. Anyone with a Harley-Davidson automatically becomes a member of a worldwide family. If you purchase the great American motorcycle in Tennessee, you can also join the Bumpus family of riding enthusiasts. With four locations in Tennessee, Bumpus has become a household name in the state. The Bumpus family opened its first Harley dealership in 1986, beginning in Memphis and then adding a second and third store in Murfreesboro and Jackson in 1993 and 1995. The newest dealership in Collierville, which opened in 2005, holds a large part of the Bumpus antique collection of Harley-Davidson motorcycles. Bumpus Harley-Davidson carries a complete line of America's best-known motorcycles, from Sportsters to Touring models. For one-stop shopping, each Bumpus dealership includes departments for clothing, sales, financing, parts and services. You can also rent motorcycles or even learn to ride at Bumpus Harley-Davidson. Bumpus' customer-friendly employees will share their expertise with you, guiding you to the motorcycle that fits your lifestyle, your taste and budget. There is always something exciting happening at Bumpus Harley-Davidson. Check the website for a calendar of events, shows and sales. When you rev up, head out to Bumpus Harley-Davidson.

2160 Whitten Road, Memphis TN
(901) 372-1121
2250 NW Broad Street, Murfreesboro TN
(615) 849-8025
326 Carriage House Drive, Jackson TN
(731) 422-5508
325 S Byhalia Road, Collierville TN
(901)316-1121
www.BumpusHarleyDavidson.com

Bella Notte

Bella Notte is an interesting gift shop located in the artistic community of Cooper-Young, 10 minutes from downtown Memphis. The historic Cooper-Young area has evolved into one of the city's most popular destinations. Bella Notte is nestled among great restaurants, art galleries and clothing boutiques, and features beautiful gift items. Discover designer jewelry, home accessories, cards, paper products, baby clothing and toys and French and Italian toiletries. Local artisans whose creations add to the ambiance of the shop say their works of art shout *Bella Notte*. The store was established in 1999 by Nicco Anderson, who came into the business with an Art History degree and a passion for travel. After experiencing years of successful business, Nicco married and began the journey of motherhood. Nicco's mother, Patricia Anderson, manages the shop today, making it the third multi-generational family-owned business in their hometown. Bella Notte was described by *Commercial Appeal*, a local newspaper, as having "a great selection of journals and the most adorable baby clothes in town." *Northwest Travel and Leisure* also praised the "hip baby room," while *Memphis Magazine* called the shop as "unself-consciously wonderful as they come." Pamper yourself with a selection of fine gifts and home décor on the playful side at Bella Notte.

2172 Young Avenue, Memphis TN
(901) 726-4131

Photo by Hal Jaffe

Babcock Gifts

Babcock Gifts began as an antiques business more than 30 years ago, but Bernice "Buzzy" Hussey and her late husband Richard turned it into an impressive gift shop by adding china, silver, crystal and gifts. Whether you're searching for that perfect wedding gift, a special remembrance for a loved one or something exquisite for yourself, you're sure to find it at this Memphis shop. A computer bridal registry means convenient one-stop shopping and the assurance that whatever gift you pick will be treasured by the wedding couple. Babcock's china collection features Haviland, Royal Crown Derby, Herend and Anna Weatherly along with many other top brands. Fine names in crystal include Waterford, Baccarat, Kosta Boda, as well as Varga, St. Louis, William Yeoward and Tudor. The extensive selection, artfully displayed throughout the store, is matched by knowledgeable customer service. The shop also offers complimentary gift wrap and free local delivery. Babcock Gifts sells pottery produced by local artisans and often hires students from nearby high schools to work in the store. The business donates merchandise for fundraisers to such charity organizations as the Junior League of Memphis, Children's Museum, WKNO, Brooks Museum of Art and the Dixon Gallery and Gardens. Both the *Commercial Appeal* and the *Memphis Flyer* readers voted Babcock's the number one gift shop in 2006. For top-notch service and an outstanding selection of timeless treasures, visit Babcock Gifts.

4626 Poplar Avenue, Memphis TN (901) 763-0700 or (800) 489-0701 *www.babcockgifts.com*

Bella Vita

After six years in business, Stephanie Losorwith can say with certainty that her concept of *bella vita*, meaning *the beautiful life*, is a hit with gift shoppers. Bella Vita provides two locations, in Collierville and Cordova, for its fine selection of dinnerware, home décor and gifts. The shop supports local artists and craftspeople by selling their pottery and other handicrafts. Bella Vita also carries the largest inventory of Good Earth Pottery in Memphis, including lovely handmade dinnerware coveted by brides. In fact, the store is so enticing to brides that it offers a bridal registry to help fulfill some of those dreams. Hand-painted European tableware by Casafina is a perennial favorite. In 2006, the Vesta Home Show recognized the store for Best Interior Design. Gifts from Bella Vita celebrate those gatherings of family and friends that make life sweet. Items of spiritual and Christian interest also figure prominently among the store's gift selections. For gifts that grace homes and raise spirits, visit Bella Vita.

3670 Houston Levee Road, #101, Collierville TN
(901) 850-0892
7990 Trinity Road, Cordova TN
(901) 755-2279
www.shopbellavita.com

Hastings Entertainment–Dyersburg

Hastings Entertainment pioneered the media entertainment superstore concept, so it's no surprise the store in Dyersburg is everything you would want an entertainment store to be. People come to Hastings to buy, rent, sell or trade their movies, music, books and games, but they also come to relax and read, or to congregate with friends and family and say hello to the staff, who often know their names. Over the years, Hastings has expanded its merchandise to include a plethora of items that relate to media entertainment. From graphic t-shirts to iPod covers, this is a store that knows what you need in media entertainment and related items. Hastings provides a children's play area for visiting families and space for readers to settle in with their books. There are listening stations for exploring the music and musical instruments if what you really want to do is make your own. Check with the staff on upcoming in-store events. When you can't make it in, you can still browse the convenient e-commerce store on the website. For the full Hastings Entertainment experience, spend some time in the Dyersburg store. You will find that you're always welcome at Hastings.

650 U.S. Highway 51 Bypass W, Dyersburg TN
(731) 286-4881
www.hastings-ent.com

Toad Hall Antiques

Toad Hall Antiques offers the wares of 15 dealers in the quaint Antique & Design District of Midtown Memphis. After completely renovating a century-old building, which had been slated to be condemned, owner Dana Whitehead opened her store in March 2003. Named after a character's home in Kenneth Grahame's *The Wind in the Willows*, the sunny yellow building sports a whimsical painted mural of Mr. Toad on its two-story exterior. Known for both the variety and affordability of its offerings, the 5,000-square-foot store features not only antiques but lighting, mirrors, rugs, artwork, jewelry and gift items. The antiques come from all over the world—shipments arrive weekly and from England four times a year. The goods range from primitives to painted pieces and from European and French furnishings to accessories. Toad Hall showcases the work of local artists as well as imports. Dana truly enjoys helping folks find specific items that fit their homes and their tastes. Loyal local customers and families all over the country have decorated their homes with items found here, which explains why the readers of the *Memphis Flyer* named Toad Hall as Best Antique Store in 2004 and 2006. Come browse through the treasures at Toad Hall Antiques, where there's always something new to see.

2129 Central Avenue, Memphis TN
(901) 726-0755
www.toadhallmemphis.com

The Cup Lady

In the beginning, Debbie Neal was famous for her custom-printed cups. So many people asked her whether she was the cup lady that she decided to turn the constant query into the name of her small printing business. Today, Debbie does much more than cups. The Cup Lady specializes in creating small batches of personalized or monogrammed products that are ideal for weddings, trade shows, special parties or occasions such as bar mitzvahs, anniversaries or reunions. Debbie can add drawings, doodles, company logos and nearly anything else you can think of to glasses, napkins, cards, matchbooks, t-shirts or key chains. Do you love the look and convenience of personalized Koozies, those clever foam can holders? Do you have an unusual or unusually spelled name? Not a problem for the Cup Lady. She can add any name or phrase in a variety of colors and fonts to create completely original items. Debbie sells most of her creations though her website, but you can also find her delightful designs at several metro Memphis shops as well as niche shops in Nashville, Atlanta and Florida. You might not be able to customize everything in life, but you can surely try with a little help from the Cup Lady.

7592 W Farmington Boulevard, Suite 115, Germantown TN
(901) 756-2688
www.thecuplady.com

S. Y. Wilson & Co. Antique and Artisan Market

For more than a century, S. Y. Wilson's has stood at the center of Arlington's commercial and social life. Founded in 1893, it is the second-oldest continuously operating business in the county. Today, Susan Wilson Hoggard, a fourth-generation descendent of founder Samuel Young Wilson, and her husband, Mark, run the S. Y. Wilson & Company Antique and Artisan Market in Arlington's Historic Depot Square. The store offers antique booths, original local art, and gifts on two floors and from the store on the mezzanine. In 1912, when Samuel S. Y. Wilson raised the current building, it was a general store that stocked necessities that took customers from the cradle to the grave. In fact, the mezzanine displays one of the store's original baby carriages, now 80 years old. You'll find aged wooden caskets in the attic. Wilson's has

its original floors, walls and ceilings. In the 1960s, the store stopped selling clothing and food and became a true hardware store. Susan, who bought it in 1994, initially ran it as a garden center before settling on the current format. Wilson's retains its general-store charm. You can still buy country candy and soft drinks, galvanized washtubs and baskets. You can play checkers on the porch. Stop by S. Y. Wilson & Company Antique and Artisan Market, and see what its antique vendors and artisans have to offer you.

12020 Walker Street, Arlington TN
(901) 867-2226

Army Surplus Collierville

Whether it's medals, camping supplies or clothing, Army Surplus Collierville is the place to go for Army-style equipment with civilian uses. Al Klug III and his father started the business in 1984, when the Klug family was heavily involved in scouting. Al's dad wrote and published a book called *Camping Log*, which the Klugs marketed at flea markets and gun shows along with camping supplies. When the camping supply business took off, they opened their store in 1986, and moved to their current location in 1989. Al's dad has passed away, but Al continues the tradition of stocking Army surplus items at the store. He and his staff head to sales at military bases in the area, purchasing all sorts of useful outdoor gear dating from World War II to

the present day. Army Surplus Collierville is the only Army surplus store in the Mid-South and attracts customers from throughout the region. Veterans are often able to purchase medals like those they were awarded to pass along to children and grandchildren. For the best in authentic fatigues, decorations, memorabilia and other gear used by our fighting men and women, come to Army Surplus Collierville.

127 N Main Street, Collierville TN
(901) 853-7578

Kitchen Extras

Linda Gilkey has been entertaining guests for most of her adult life, so opening Kitchen Extras in 1998 was a logical move for her. This store is the place to find kitchen items that are both beautiful and practical. Kitchen Extras is the exclusive dealer for the unusual pieces from Earthborn Pottery of Alabama. Like many of the items in Kitchen Extras, these charming items are beautiful, yet usable as well. Linda also carries Tervis tumblers and is the only merchant in Jackson with Skyros dishes. Linda became adept at the art of hospitality while supporting her husband's career. She has lived all over the country, and the kitchen has always been the

heart of her home. Countless guests have complimented her recipes. Guest after guest has admired her table settings. Linda couldn't have fed as many people as she has without an array of kitchen gadgets, such as the ones you'll find at Kitchen Extras. From the shelves of cookbooks to the selection of gorgeous European glassware, everything in Kitchen Extras has been selected by someone who knows how to be a gracious host. Buy your kitchen wares from the hospitality experts at Kitchen Extras.

**100 Vann Drive, Suite D, Jackson TN
(731) 660-7936**

Forty Carrots

Forty Carrots is the only independently owned culinary store in the Memphis area. It is owned and operated by food loving Phyllis Cline. Phyllis always has something cooking at Forty Carrots, and the delicious smell of her homemade Parker House rolls and other delicacies are the first thing that greets customers as they walk through the door. You can even buy some of Phyllis' delicious entrées from the freezer to have for dinner when you don't feel like cooking.

The shop has everything you need to equip a gourmet kitchen. You'll find a vast variety of pots and pans, pot racks, cutlery and bakeware, along with many specialty items. The store stocks all sorts of gadgets for your kitchen, with items in many price ranges. If you're looking to sharpen your cooking skills, you can sign up for a cooking class, ranging from Basic Knife Skills to An Evening in Tuscany. Phyllis and her family staff are glad to share their knowledge and cooking enthusiasm with their many loyal and repeat customers. To cook up a storm, or to surprise your family with extraordinary freezer entrées, pay a visit to Forty Carrots.

**5101 Sanderlin Avenue, Memphis TN
(901) 683-5187**

Diane's Gift Emporium

Your dearest aunt turns 80 next week, your niece is having a baby and your daughter made the dean's list at college. Where can you find a gift for all of them? Diane's Gift Emporium, named the 2007 Best Accessory Store by readers of the *Germantown News*, is a sure bet. Its vast assortment of merchandise includes home décor, bath items and linens as well as jewelry, stationery and outdoor ornaments. Diane Arnold and her staff will help you pick out the perfect baby shower gift. You will also find cookbooks and kitchen gadgets for your husband the gourmet, along with fancy collars and other specialty items for your pooch. Are you going on a trip soon? If so, you will love traveling in style with a Vera Bradley bag and luggage from Diane's. Since 1998, Diane has used her background in home interiors to choose stylish and tasteful items for her store. She is proud that her business was named one of the top gift shops in all of metro Memphis. Try Diane's Gift Emporium for all your gift shopping needs.

**9056 Poplar Pike, Suite 101,
Germantown TN
(901) 751-0902**

Pyramid Racing Collectibles

Jim Kiefer dreamed of starting his own business centered on his passion for stock car racing and founded on the principle of outstanding customer service. He and his wife, Patti, started Pyramid Racing Collectibles as an Internet-based company in 2000 and opened their retail store in Memphis in 2002. Both online and in the store, Pyramid Racing carries one of the largest selections of authentic die-cast motorsports items around, including authentic NASCAR and NHRA merchandise. Pyramid offers the most collectible brands of realistic die-cast race car replicas, including Motorsports Authentics and Action Racing Collectables. Although Pyramid Racing Collectibles offers the same items that are sold by trackside vendors, Jim offers Internet pricing on merchandise in the retail store. In addition to quality products and reasonable pricing, Pyramid Racing is a place where customer service matters, which makes web shopping a breeze. All in-stock items are shipped within 24 hours from the time your order is placed, and Jim's e-mail responses to your questions usually come within 30 minutes to an hour. Customers can also receive answers to their questions via a toll-free telephone number. Items not found on the website, including shirts, jackets and caps, can be special-ordered. For all your racing memorabilia and collectibles, come to Pyramid Racing Collectibles.

2235 Whitten Road #105, Memphis TN
(901) 385-0525 or (800) 792-3142
www.pyramidracing.com

Gild the Lily

Geneva Chandler, owner of Gild the Lily, has treated her Memphis patrons and tourists alike to a delightful selection of unusual gifts for more than 15 years. Affectionately known to her local customers as Gee Gee, Geneva's hand-picked selections include fun and thoughtful gifts, some with a humorous twist and others just plain sweet. Among the sweet choices, you'll find baby items from Bellatunno that range from burpie bibs to diaper ditties. On a more practical but elegant note, look for the all-cotton Simple Pleasures sleepwear and Lady Primrose bath products. The product line from Pylones includes whimsically designed kitchen utensils, handbags, dog leashes and desk accessories. You won't want to miss the pottery section; most

of the pieces are handcrafted by local and regional artisans. Gee Gee's family was one of the first to move into the post-World War II neighborhood of High Point Terrace. Originally a rural area on the outskirts of Memphis, the neighborhood is now an upscale part of the city. A favorite of the carriage trade, Gild the Lily is staffed by a cadre of friends and is a vibrant shop full of color and fun. Come see Gild the Lily and find extraordinary wares. As Gee Gee says, "It's all about friends, old and new."

485 High Point Terrace, Memphis, TN
(901) 458-5471

A Little Something Special

A Little Something Special is a resource for gift-giving that you won't want to miss. Handcrafted jewelry, Maggie B quilted handbags and Alexandria Fragrance lamps line the shelves of this friendly business. Collectors are always welcome. Collegiate Tervis Tumblers display logos from Auburn to Ole´ Miss. In addition to one-of-a-kind hand crafts, the shop is an authorized dealer for Arthur Court, Mudpie and Village Candles. You'll find Willow Tree Thank You angels and goods from Ganz and Camille Beckman. Check out the Webkinz Pet Shoppe, which sells lovable plush pets and accessories. You can also design your own customized gift

bag, both beautiful and affordable. Have your gift monogrammed to add extra splash and dash. Staff members offer first-class services. Online shopping is available to those who are long on giving, but short on time. A Little Something Special is the work of Bill Liverseidge and his wife Marcia. Both have artistic backgrounds—he's a woodworker and she participates in the folk art tradition of tole painting. For the past six years, this dynamic duo has been building a fascinating inventory. Next time you're in Oakland, take a few minutes to shop at A Little Something Special. Without a doubt, you'll walk out with a little something wonderful.

7060 Highway 64, Oakland TN
(901) 466-0102
www.shopsomethingspecial.com

RAM Entertainment

Whether you dream of an intimate wedding with only your closest friends and family, a gala dinner for hundreds or a private concert with national headline entertainment, let Russ Madry and his team at RAM Entertainment turn your ideas into reality. For more than 19 years, Russ and the company that bears his initials have provided one-stop shopping for all your event-planning needs. Your wedding day is one of the most memorable events of your life. Make sure you have the time to enjoy it without worrying about pesky little details. Corporate functions deserve the same attention to detail, and RAM makes your award ceremonies, conventions and company meetings flow seamlessly. It all started when Russ was growing up. He enjoyed helping his mother with fundraising events for local charities. While at the University of Memphis and then later while working in medical sales in Dallas, Russ booked bands as a sideline. In 1994, he returned to Memphis to stay with his parents, whose health was failing. He made the most of a difficult situation and decided to remain here, pursuing event planning on a larger scale and organizing a team to do it. Call RAM Entertainment today to plan those special events your guests will remember for years to come.

5050 Poplar Avenue, Suite 1702, Memphis TN
(901) 757-4900 or (800) 935-3555
www.ramentertainment.com

Steven Russell
photographic art + design

Steven Russell Wedding Traditions Photography

After 27 years and nearly 2,600 weddings, Steven Russell still finds his job as a professional photographer fascinating. "Every face tells a story," he says. "I love to capture that story by photographing people in their natural element." Through his photographs, he continues to find ways of showing people how interesting they are and allows them to relive moments and rediscover loved ones from new angles. Steven specializes in candid shots and especially enjoys capturing spontaneous, natural moments at weddings. He typically shoots 400 to 600 images per wedding, giving the family a plethora of options to choose from that go far beyond the standard array of posed ensembles. To take full advantage of Steven's artistry, consider ordering one of his custom design albums and let him do the selecting for you. He will assemble the photos in beautiful vignettes and collages using Photoshop. The pages typically use a large photo turned black and white or faded for a background, with other photos artfully arranged on top. These pages seem to create a three-dimensional experience of the moment, with multiple takes, close-ups and variations. The effect is highly individualized yet always classy. Steven notes that 65 percent of his business comes from referrals, a testament to his customers' satisfaction. If you'd like an artistic document of your special event or special someone, contact Steven at Wedding Traditions Photography.

6779 Poplar Pike, Memphis TN
(901) 759-1881
www.weddingtraditions.com

Food Architects

Build an exquisite affair and they will come. Owner Bill Donofrio and his creative catering staff at Food Architects promise mouth-watering treats that will linger in the memories of your guests for a long time. Their bountiful buffets, sumptuous food trays and delicious plated meals whet the most discerning appetites. Whether you're planning an event for 500 or an intimate gathering for six, Food Architects offers choices galore. Down-home favorites include barbecue meatballs, crunchy chicken tenders and seasonal fruit displays. Prefer a more exotic array? Try the crab-stuffed pork chops crowned with a white wine demi-glaze, or a swan-shaped puff pastry swimming in a vanilla cognac sauce. The customer always comes first at Food Architects—you can choose from its menu or design one of your own. This catering company is a member of the Wedding and Event Association of Memphis, and its highly trained consultants offer comprehensive wedding services that can help make your dreams come true. Whether it's a wedding reception, a corporate event, an intimate gathering or a rehearsal dinner, invite the folks from Food Architects to help create memories that last forever.

3222 Airways Boulevard, Memphis TN
(901) 461-2232
www.caterersmemphis.com

J. Herndon Photography

As you look at the tiny hands of a baby, or the reflection of a beautiful young bride in the mirror, it may be hard to imagine that someday the baby will go off to college, or the bride will be someone's grandmother. Capture those fleeting moments with the skills of J. Herndon Photography. Owner and photographer Jody Herndon's interest in photography began on the streets of Europe, where faces of strangers called to him. In 2002, after six trips to Europe, Jody started J. Herndon Photography with the help of his wife, Kimberly. Jody says that a photograph is a celebration of the moment, and that capturing that moment is almost like cheating time. For wedding memories that last a lifetime, invite Jody to your special day. He can chronicle the ceremony as well as the little moments that might otherwise go unnoticed. In portraits from J. Herndon Photography, a person's spirit is highlighted, and Jody encourages sittings in places the subjects are most comfortable. Jody's commercial talents allow him to create dramatic shots of your business and professional group photos. Whether it is a special occasion or just an everyday moment, it only happens once. Make sure you capture it with photographs from J. Herndon Photography.

4486 Fair Meadow Road, Memphis TN
(901) 848-9790
www.jherndonphotography.com

Harpist Bill Butner

The harp wasn't Bill Butner's first instrument, but it's the one that has obsessed him since the 1960s. It is also the one that gained him an audience at the White House in 1994 and appearances on the *Oprah* and *Today* shows. Bill has performed with the Germantown Symphony for more than 30 years and is a member of the Memphis Symphony ensemble that plays at Central Church. When he provides music for weddings and parties, most people request old movie love songs and classical melodies. What tune wouldn't sound good on the harp? Even the melodies to those rock and roll songs that Bill played on his guitar in high school would chime sweetly on its strings. Its sound is often described as heavenly, though learning to play this demanding instrument could cause one to mutter words in frustration that no angel would ever speak. Once Bill got hooked on the harp in college, he devoted seven hours a day to practicing. Today, after a career as the assistant director of a credit union, he is one of only a few professional harpists in Tennessee. Ask Bill Butner to bring the heavenly strains of harp music to your special event.

**3300 Patches Drive, Bartlett TN
(901) 383-9356**

Michael Allen Photography

For 15 years, Michael Allen Photography has created contemporary storybook wedding journals. Owner Michael Allen is famed for the passion, artistry and expertise he brings to the photographs of your most romantic day. Michael and his wife, Janice, have extensive experience in the bridal fashion industry. Michael's work has been featured in publications such as *Southern Bride* and *I Do*. He has studied with world-renowned photographers such as Denis Reggie and Mike Colon in the Masters Series of wedding and portrait photography. Michael's wedding photojournalism is executed with an artful modern edge. He works closely with you to create a customized portfolio that you'll treasure. He uses the latest high-definition digital cameras, among them the state-of-the-art Canon 5D 13-megapixel. Michael and Janice also own one of the top 200 salon spas in America, which gives them a decided advantage in making certain your appearance is perfect on your big day. Janice has been hailed as one of the South's most accomplished hairdressers, and the rest of the salon's staff is equally gifted in makeup and beauty treatments. Michael is typically booked months in advance, so you'll want to contact the studio early to reserve your date. Let Michael Allen Photography share its secrets of romantic photography with you.

8100 Macon Station, Suite 105, Cordova TN
(901) 489-5237

Extreme Events Catering

In downtown Memphis's picturesque Mud Island River Park, Extreme Events Catering offers a variety of lovely riverside venues that can accommodate events for up to 10,000 people. Wedding receptions, banquets, corporate meetings and holiday parties are taken in stride at Extreme Events Catering. The third-level observation deck features spectacular views of the Memphis Skyline and the Mississippi River. The River Terrace and Harbor Landing banquet rooms are perfect for wedding ceremonies and receptions. The Southfield and North Courtyard locations are favorite choices for picnics, festivals or family gatherings. Extreme Events also offers off-site services for parties of 40 people or more. From business lunches at your office to wedding receptions at the Botanical Gardens, Extreme Events Catering can be there. Chef Christopher Miller trained at the prestigious Culinary Institute of America, and Chef Seth Feibelman trained at Johnson & Wales University. Together they are masters of menus, whether they include fried chicken or foie gras. They use only the freshest ingredients in their lineup of traditional and creative dishes, which are beautifully presented and designed to serve your function and budget. The able staff of event planners works with you one-on-one to organize your event and menu. Staff members will make your party an extreme delight that lives in the memory of your guests long after the party is over. Whatever your party needs, Extreme Events Catering can make your dreams come true.

280 N Mud Island Drive, Memphis TN
(901) 528-0001 or (901) 827-1402
www.extremeeventscatering.com

Draper's Catering of Memphis

Isn't it about time that you had that big party you've been denying yourself for so long? You will love being a guest at your own bash when the folks at Draper's Catering are handling the details. They will set everything up and bring in the tables and linens in addition to preparing all the food. Package options allow you to throw anything from an Italian feast to a Southern barbecue. It's fried chicken, potatoes and gravy for the whole family and all your friends when you choose the Southern Comfort Buffet. Let someone at Draper's help you plan a glorious, hassle-free wedding reception. Draper's Catering will work with any budget to put together a menu that suits your needs, the wedding cake included. Corporate luncheons are another specialty, with menus ranging from delicious sandwich combinations to elegant hot entrées. Draper's has been bringing the cheer to Memphis celebrations since 1990. The company even delivers box lunches city-wide to meetings and large groups. Think big for your next party, and think Draper's Catering to make it a success.

6116 Macon Road, Memphis TN (901) 385-7788
www.draperscatering.com

Conroy Studio

As you skim through Steven Conroy's portfolio of wedding photos, bear in mind that many of these gorgeous and handsome people considered themselves camera shy before Steve made them glow. In fact, the compliment he received recently from a mother-of-the-bride is typical: "My daughter, my mother and I usually do not photograph very well," she wrote in a thank-you note, "but you somehow made everyone look great over and over again." Steve started working in the dark room when he was just 13 years old. His boss was his father, Jack, who started Conroy Studio in 1956. The studio, one of the first to use color and digital photography, has always had a knack for seeing the future. Family portraits and senior pictures are specialties in addition to wedding photography. With a positive attitude and a smile, Steve provides his trademark photography to doctors, attorneys and many other professionals. Sit for your portrait at Steve's full-service photography studio, where he keeps a variety of creative props and backgrounds, or let him come to your special event to create beautiful memories. Say goodbye to being camera shy, courtesy of Conroy Studio.

2832 Bartlett Road, Bartlett TN
(901) 624-6535
www.conroystudio.net

Just Write Stationery & Gifts

No matter what you require in paper goods and stationery, Just Write Stationery & Gifts can provide it. Just Write, in the heart of Germantown, is a name associated with printing and stationery for more than 20 years. This shop puts your personality on paper with a full line of stationery products. From bright and bold designs to monogrammed elegance, you'll find a style that makes the statement you desire. Hundreds of choices are available to cover any type of celebration, greeting or announcement, with a special emphasis on wedding invitations and birth announcements, celebrating two of life's major passages. To go with your card, you'll find a selection of gifts for the person in the spotlight or for a hardworking hostess. Along with notes and stationery, Just Write Stationery & Gifts offers monograms, cute holiday themes, corporate logos and custom stamps. You'll find trusted brands such as Crane & Co., William Arthur and Sweet Pea, just to name a few. Gift packages include ensembles of matching cards, name cards, bag tags and gift enclosures in an assortment of themes, from botanicals to polka dots. Just Write Stationery & Gifts has everything you need to help you celebrate the special friends and family in your life.

2135 Merchants Row, Suite 5, Germantown TN
(901) 755-GIFT (4438)
http://justwrite.egbreeze.com

Sweet & Sassy

In Memphis, Sweet & Sassy is the place to take girls for an unforgettable party experience. The children's salon, spa and celebration center features theme packages for just one girl or up to 30 girls. For a special outing for just one young star, the shop offers a choice of four fun packages. From the Diva for a Day to the Glittery Glam Girl, you're sure to find a spa-inspired package your special girl will love. For a birthday party, this salon has six packages geared to different age groups and interests. The Rockin' Rock Star, popular with the nine to 12 age group, starts with a sassy hairdo and hair extensions, followed by glam makeup and glitzy nail polish. The girls then choose a chic rock star outfit to complete the mood. The birthday girl picks her favorite pop song, and Sweet & Sassy's talented choreographer teaches dance moves and lyrics. Then the show begins. Party take-homes include pop-star makeover items, hair extensions, powder tubes, T-shirts, DVDs and a magazine cover group photo. Another of the salon's popular themes is the Sleepover at the Spa. The store is closed just for your group. PJs and sleeping bags come out and two-and-a-half hours of fun and giggles ensues. Girls learn to braid and style each other's hair and craft take-home flip-flops. Each enjoys a mini-facial. Singing, games and activities add to the fun. The party ends with a cake. You can purchase add-on activities for any of the parties, such as bracelet-making. In Memphis, extraordinary adventures for girls start at Sweet & Sassy.

2886 Wolf Creek Parkway, Suite 1300, Memphis TN
(901) 379-9993 *www.sweetandsassy.com*

Red Flair Affairs

Kelly Smith came through for the client who liked bold blues and feathery things, and she will come through for you when you need a distinctive look for your special event. Owner of Red Flair Affairs since 2001, Kelly provides flowers and arrangements that set the tone for everything from small intimate gatherings to galas with several hundred people. She particularly enjoys the challenge of designing weddings and other large celebrations such as Bar Mitzvahs, anniversaries and corporate events. "You really do have a gift and an eye for beauty that complemented the emotions of our beautiful day," wrote one couple, thanking Kelly for her fabulous work. Although praise for what she does is common, Kelly takes none of it for granted. She and her staff at Red Flair Affairs start from scratch with each client, not relying on templates to come up with a design plan. They listen closely to their clients' style preferences and think outside the box to create an original look for each event. For flowers and arrangements that express your individual style, consider Red Flair Affairs.

(901) 603-6624
www.redflairaffairs.com

Jake's Outpost

There is nothing quite like the wind in your face and a long road beckoning ahead. Whether it's a night out on the town or a road trip, it's important to wear clothes that fit the part, not only because it's cool but more importantly, for comfort and safety. Since 1991, Jake's Outpost has been upholding the image of those who were born to be wild. The shop sells motorcycle apparel that captures the spirit of endless highways, adventure seeking and rugged individualism. Owner Kelly Carter Smith says that her goal is to provide customers with the largest selection of motorcycle fashions in the area, especially leather goods such as jackets, boots and chaps. Riders shopping Jake's Outpost for gloves and T-shirts will also find helmets that score points for style while offering maximum protection. Kelly is the latest in a line of businesspeople in her family. Her grandfather, Cecil, opened a seed store on Front Street in Memphis in 1928. In addition to running Jake's Outpost, which her father founded, Kelly owns Red Flair Affairs, a design company specializing in weddings and other special events. Find everything you need to dress like you own the open road at Jake's Outpost.

16228 Highway 51 N, Millington TN
(901) 603-6624
www.jakesoutpost.com

IF IT'S NOT FUN,
We Don't Recommend It!

When people think of their favorite sports team, the first thing that pops into their heads is the zany mascot. In 2001, Chris Pegg founded **Mascot Central** to continue his dream and love of entertaining people. With many performers, Mascot Central brings a wealth of experience that has entertained crowds at NFL, MLB, NBA, NHL and MLS teams.

Regional businesses and universities have also benefited from their ability to **design costumes, staff characters**, and even coordinate performer tryouts. Their team of creative minds can design and market a mascot to promote your team, product, or service.

Whether **starting from scratch or updating an existing character** to better fit your company's marketing plan, they can get you noticed at your next big event. Existing characters showing some age and may need to have touch-ups. Mascot Central can update, clean, and store the costume to increase the life of your investment.

If no one is clamoring to climb in and perform, you can always consider one of Mascot Central's **talented and professional performers** to don your costume. The level of Sweat Equity in the performance will make your character's Fur Fly and get it noticed.

In their support of Special Kids and Families, Inc., the team enjoys clowning around, but is still serious enough to give back to the community. The company motto is lived every day: "If It's Not Fun, We Don't Recommend It!"

Let Mascot Central design a Fun Character that will add some energy to your organization for years to come.

MASCOT CENTRAL

www.mascotcentral.com
(901) 377-7101

Barley's Brew House & Eatery

Jerry Gay remembers 1996 as a great year for a road trip. That's when he and his partners traveled to various states, sampling the beer and ale in microbreweries as they rambled from here to there. It was a time of resurgence in the microbrewing industry, and when Jerry got back to Jackson, he decided to open Barley's Brew House & Eatery. At the time, there were only seven microbreweries in all of Tennessee. Those in and around Jackson who love a pint of craft beer have been grateful for Barley's ever since. Barley's Brew House serves beer that its brewmaster produces on the premises, as well as other brands. Barley's bakes the New York-style pizzas that are the stars of its menu in stone ovens with only the freshest ingredients, including the crust. The atmosphere is very relaxed. Live musicians perform several nights a week. "There is a great amount of talent in the region," Jerry points out, "and this is a showcase for it." He invites you to come by Barley's if you are looking for a pleasant place to enjoy micro-brewed beer, delicious pizza and fine musicians. You might even be inspired to open your own brew house while you're there.

2254 N Highland Drive, Jackson TN
(731) 668-2038

Boscos

If you take your beer seriously, you may have heard of Boscos, the restaurant for beer lovers, even before coming to Memphis. Michael Jackson, one the world's foremost beer authorities, has written about Boscos in his beer guides as well as naming Boscos' Famous Flaming Stone Beer one of the world's most interesting beers in his *Ultimate Beer*. No doubt he was intrigued by the brewing process, which calls for red rocks to be added while this beer is fermenting. This light-bodied golden favorite is one of the 50 varieties of beer that Boscos produces each year. Head brewer and founder Chuck Skypeck has been awarded the Brewers Association Recognition Award, which is the craft brewing industry's highest individual honor. Beloved for its beer, Boscos is also renowned for its food. In fact, its very name calls attention to its wood-fired ovens. The word *boscos* is Italian for *woods* or *forest*, and the gourmet pizzas here, as well as the Wood Oven Roasted Shrimp, are all prepared over oak and hickory in those ovens. The signature item is the fresh salmon, baked on a cedar plank. Celebrate good beer and food at the Memphis location, and then check out the Nashville or Little Rock, Arkansas locations during future travels. Hoist a pint at Boscos soon.

2120 Madison Avenue, Memphis TN (Boscos Squared)
(901) 432-2222
www.boscosbeer.com

Huey's

Blues, brews, and burgers are what Huey's is all about. Since 1970, the legendary Memphis eatery has been serving up mouth-watering food and weekly live music. With the longest-running continuous jazz ensemble in Memphis, Huey's is much more than just a burger joint. Some of the most accomplished musicians played at Huey's long before they found fame—Koko Taylor and Robert Cray, to name a few. Home of the world-famous burger, the casual, tavern-like setting makes Huey's a welcoming spot to share a few pints with your buddies or to test your skills at Frill Pick (toothpick-shooting through your straw). Scrumptious, big, tasty steak fries, salads and sandwiches have earned Huey's a reputation for dishing up the best pub grub in town. *Memphis Magazine* has given Huey's the Best Burger award for more than 21 consecutive years. Over the years, Huey's has expanded to downtown, midtown, Cordova, Southaven, Winchester, Collierville and east Memphis. Thomas Boggs, one of the owners, truly values community involvement. Boggs has served on numerous boards and has been past presidents of Memphis in May, the Zoological Society, the Memphis Restaurant Association and many others. He also has established Huey's as one of the city's most philanthropic businesses. Besides monetary donations, Huey's employees have donated hundreds of volunteer hours to nonprofit organizations. If you are traveling to Memphis, make sure at least one of your stops is at Huey's. For the menu and live music schedule, please visit the website.

Midtown: 1927 Madison Avenue, Memphis TN
(901) 726-4372
Downtown: 77 S Second Street, Memphis TN
(901) 527-2700
Poplar: 4872 Poplar Avenue, Memphis TN
(901) 682-7729
Southwind: 7825 Winchester Road, Memphis TN
(901) 624-8911
Cordova: 1771 N Germantown Parkway, Cordova TN
(901) 754-3885
Collierville: 2130 W Poplar Avenue, Collierville TN
(901) 854-4455
Southaven: 7090 Malco Boulevard, Southaven MS
(662) 349-7097
www.hueyburger.com

Rum Boogie Café

Rum Boogie Café has been the cornerstone of historic Beale Street and Highway 61 since 1985. It's appropriate that this renowned Memphis restaurant, with some of the best down-home cooking around, is also home to a large collection of Memphis music memorabilia. If it's real Southern cooking you're looking for, sit yourself down and order up a plate of red beans and rice, fried catfish or hickory-smoked ribs. While your taste buds are enjoying the lip-smacking good meal, let your ears take in the sweet blues sounds of James Govan and the Boogie Blues Band, playing five nights a week. You never know who might show up to join James and the boys. Michael Bolton, Bo Diddley and Greg Allman have all played here. Some of the greats of the Memphis music scene have left a piece of themselves behind at Rum Boogie. Whether it's a guitar autographed by rockabilly legend Carl Perkins—one of 200 autographed instruments here—or the cape that soul singer Isaac Hayes wore to the Oscars to claim his award for the *Shaft* album, you'll find something of note in this huge collection of memorabilia. You'll also find some of the STAX Records signs that adorned the famous studio as well as concert posters from the 1920s through the 1980s. Discover the soul of Memphis with a visit to Rum Boogie Café.

182 Beale Street, Memphis TN
(901) 528-0150
www.rumboogie.com

King's Palace Café

With blues clubs everywhere on Beale Street, the King's Palace Café stands apart as a cozy little jazz joint with some of the best Southern food anywhere. The Memphis restaurant features the old-time Beale Street atmosphere, with dim lights and great music blending with the aroma of hickory-smoked ribs and shrimp and crawfish étouffée. Grilled steaks, blackened catfish and such perennial Southern favorites as fried green tomatoes and gumbo just scratch the surface of the restaurant's extensive menu. The King's Palace Creole Gumbo took the top prize for two years in a row at the Rajun Cajun Crawfish Festival and Gumbo Cookoff, and the restaurant's Shrimp Velvet has been featured on television's Nashville Network. King's Palace offers lunch specials every day, including lighter fare, such as the Cajun chicken salad. Diners can enjoy their meal in the spacious dining room or on the lazy outdoor patio. Step into the Jazz Room for live blues, jazz and other kinds of music that make up the Memphis scene's rich tapestry of sounds. House band Memphis Groovetet packs 'em in every weekend. "Beale Street atmosphere is what attracts people to King's Palace Café; the good food and great music are what keep them coming back," writes critic Dana Avent of the *Downtowner*. Come to King's Palace Café for some of the best sounds and flavors Memphis has to offer.

162 Beale Street, Memphis TN
(901) 521-1851
www.kingspalacecafe.com

The Dan McGuinness and T.J. Mulligan's Family of Restaurants

The Dan McGuinness pubs are the most authentic Irish pubs in Memphis. They were built in Ireland, after all, before being shipped to the states and assembled by five Irish gents from Sonas Design. The floors, ceilings, tables and chairs are just as you'd find them in Cork or Dublin. Quench your thirst for all things Irish with a pint of Guinness and some of the authentic Irish cuisine you'll find here, including Irish lamb stew, shepherd's pie and Irish breakfasts on Saturday mornings. On the weekends, you can watch English Premiere League football (or soccer, as it's known to the Yanks) with the lads. On Thursday, Friday and Saturday, you can dance to the sounds of live Celtic music. Bring your wee ones in to enjoy items from the Kids Corner, including such favorites as corn dogs and grilled peanut butter and banana sandwiches. Dan McGuinness is a part of the Dan McGuinness and T.J. Mulligan's Family of Restaurants, which includes three T.J. Mulligan's locations in Memphis. At T.J. Mulligan's, you'll find some of the best pub grub and specialty sandwiches in Memphis. If you're looking for some fun and spirited competition, you'll appreciate the pool and poker tournaments as well as the trivia contests. T.J. Mulligan's is also available for private parties. For a lively time with family and friends, drop by Dan McGuinness or T.J. Mulligan's.

4698 Spottswood Avenue, Memphis TN
(901) 761-3711
150 Peabody Place, Suite 115, Memphis TN
(901) 527-8500
www.danmcguinnesspub.com
www.tjmulligans.com

The Parthenon in Centennial Park, Nashville

Middle Tennessee

End O' The Bend Lodge & Landing

A log cabin on the banks of the Cumberland River is just the place to get away from the crowds and enjoy some privacy. End O' The Bend makes a tranquil retreat for a busy executive or the perfect spot to stage a romantic getaway. The cabin is close to Opryland, downtown Nashville and the airport, but feels far away from everything. Jump off into an exploration of the sights and sounds of Nashville or kick back on the large, screened-in porch, where you can listen to the river and watch the General Jackson Showboat float by. The cabin, made of 150-year-old logs, boasts modern conveniences, lovely light and a splendid décor with antiques and fine art prints. Two large bedrooms feature easygoing style. End O' The Bend offers two full baths, a fully equipped kitchen and an outdoor grill. A great room with soaring ceilings and a fireplace promises relaxed entertaining. Ceiling fans, air conditioning and housekeeping services ensure your comfort. The big screen television with DVD/VCR keeps you entertained and wireless Internet keeps you connected. End O' The Bend has been named in Best Places to Stay in the South, Best Places to Stay in American Cities and A Guide to Unique Places to Stay. For a country setting close to the city and a home you will have all to yourself, make reservations with Rachelle Anthony and find out why so many vacationers return year after year to End O' The Bend Lodge & Landing.

2523 Miami Avenue, Nashville TN
(615) 884-8090
www.bbonline.com/tn/bend

Photo by rjones0856

The Hermitage Hotel

If buildings could tell stories, the Hermitage Hotel in Nashville would fill several volumes with chapters on its six presidential visits and its national suffragist convention. Bette Davis, Greta Garbo and Gene Autry lodged here. Pool legend Minnesota Fats called the hotel his home for eight years. Built in 1910 as the city's first million-dollar hotel, the Hermitage combines shine and splendor with superior service to earn recognition as a Mobil Four Star and AAA Five Diamond hotel. The lobby sets the tone with its stained glass ceiling, marble staircases and Russian walnut paneling. Guests stretch out in spacious guest rooms, which include custom-made beds, marble bathrooms and fully stocked refreshment centers. Beverages in the lobby come compliments of the house, as do the overnight shoeshine, newspapers and personalized concierge services. The hotel's restaurant, the Capitol Grille, was named one of the best restaurants in America by *Gourmet* magazine. Though musical styles may have changed, the Oak Bar serves as a hub of social activity, much as it did when the Francis Craig Orchestra entertained here in the 1930s and 1940s. For accommodations that defined luxury yesterday and still surpass the mark today, stay at the Hermitage Hotel.

231 6th Avenue N, Nashville TN (615) 244-3121 or (888) 888-9414 *www.thehermitagehotel.com*

Holiday Inn Brentwood

Revel in all that Nashville has to offer while basking in the comfort and luxury of a first-class hotel when you stay at the Holiday Inn Brentwood. Located in the Music City's prestigious southern suburb of Brentwood, this elegant hotel is a five-time recipient of the Holiday Inn Quality Excellence Award, thanks to its gracious hospitality, which is generously doled out in true Southern fashion. Guests of the hotel have a myriad of modern amenities at their disposal, including complimentary airport shuttles and transportation to locales within a five-mile radius, as well as Thrifty car rentals, guest laundry and express checkout. Holiday Inn Brentwood also offers an outdoor pool, whirlpool and dry sauna for your pleasure. Lafitte's New Orleans Food & All That Jazz restaurant provides an abundant menu of authentic dishes perfectly prepared in the Louisiana style. You'll find comfortable dining room and lounge seating in the restaurant as well as full room service and gourmet pizza delivery. Holiday Inn Brentwood is the ideal place to celebrate one of life's most momentous occasions—your wedding day. The hotel employs a professional wedding consultant along with an entire staff dedicated to ensuring that your special day is perfect in every way. Discover your new home away from home at Holiday Inn Brentwood.

760 Old Hickory Boulevard, Brentwood TN
(615) 373-2600
www.holidayinnbrentwood.com

East Hills Bed & Breakfast Inn

Located near Dickson in the rolling hills of middle Tennessee, East Hills Bed & Breakfast Inn welcomes weary travelers with true Southern hospitality. The inn's amiable hosts, John and Anita Luther, even leave the front door open and the light on for late arrivals. Built in the 1940s by John's father, the inn features five spacious bedrooms and five private baths tastefully decorated with period antiques and reproductions. Accommodations include cable television with VCRs and access to telephones and wireless Internet. Three secluded cottages behind the main house provide the ultimate in privacy and come equipped with kitchens, perfect for extended-stay guests. The main house's extensive front porch and enclosed back porch offer ample vantage points for viewing the gardens and wildlife. Inside, guests can snuggle down in front of the fireplaces in the common areas. The bountiful Southern breakfast, served family-style, might include homemade Belgian waffles, omelettes, blueberry pancakes or hash brown casserole. Bacon, sausage, country ham, homemade biscuits and cheese grits make up the sides. The inn is close to dining, shopping, golf, live theater, tennis, canoeing, horseback riding and Miss Mable's Tea Room. Whether you're seeking a restful retreat for the night, the weekend or the week, try the East Hills Bed & Breakfast Inn for the ultimate in Southern charm and hospitality.

100 E Hills Terrace, Dickson TN
(615) 441-9428 or (866) 613-3414
www.easthillsbb.com

Hearthstone Inn

No two guest rooms at the Hearthstone Inn are the same, which is appropriate since the English Tudor beauty was built in the 1930s for a true original, Clareen May King. Her father built it as a wedding gift when she married a poor Russian immigrant peddler, who rose to become one of the richest men in Coffee County. Clareen became a successful business woman. Between them, they owned many businesses including a furniture store, saw mill, real estate firm and others. Lavish features of the inn include a generous hall with marble fireplace and raised wood walls, a sunroom and a parlor. The oak stairway leads to a large marble bath and three guest rooms full of antique furnishings. Owner Victoria Taylor uses her creativity and years of design experience to give guests the utmost in luxury accommodations. The inn hosts private affairs such as weddings, receptions, corporate events, and church functions. The main dining room accommodates 50 people and the bricked courtyard 100 plus. Outside events are enhanced by the outdoor kitchen and the namesake stone fireplace. For events, the chef on staff prepares such favorites as the signature steak and grilled salmon. The homemade deserts are so popular that guests, though full from their meals, insist on taking them home. Treat yourself to royal splendor at the Hearthstone Inn, where a king once lived—David King.

212 W High Street, Manchester TN
(931) 728-3003
www.hearthstoneinntn.com

Magnolia House Bed & Breakfast

From May to June, the lovely old magnolia tree that shades the front porch of the Magnolia House Bed & Breakfast is in full bloom, filling the air with lemon-like fragrance. If you cannot visit then, don't worry. The Magnolia House casts a spell of comfort and charm any month of the year, and the Southern-style breakfast provides a delicious start to any day of your week. Each of its four rooms features a private bath, antiques and Egyptian cotton linens. Guests can make themselves at home in the communal sitting room, on either of the two shaded porches or on the large deck that overlooks flower gardens and a goldfish pond. Innkeepers Jimmy and Robbie Smithson love it when folks gather round the player piano in the living room for some old-time entertainment. This Craftsman-style home was built around 1905 on land that was the site of the Battle of Franklin. It sits two blocks away from the Carter House, which served as Federal headquarters during the battle, and just a mile and a half from the Carnton Plantation, which the Confederate army used as a field hospital. Both of these national landmarks are open to the public. Of course, going only as far as the front porch is also an option. When in Franklin, consider the Magnolia House Bed & Breakfast.

1317 Columbia Avenue, Franklin TN
(615) 794-8178 or (888) 794-8178
www.bbonline.com/tn/magnolia

Top O'Woodland
Historic Bed & Breakfast Inn

Owner Belinda Leslie purchased Top O'Woodland in 2000 from the estate of Mrs. Virginia Green. After extensive renovations to bring back the beauty of this Queen Anne-style home, Top O'Woodland opened for guests in 2002. Top O'Woodland has been designated historically significant by the Davidson County Historical Commission, and the history of each owner's family has been researched back to 1890. The Master Room has a tall king bed, velvet feather couch, fireplace and private outside door easily accessible to the parking area. Mr. Greens Cottage, a separate building through the courtyard, hosts a queen bed, full bed, twin bed, kitchenette and sitting area, making it a family favorite. More than just a bed-and-breakfast, this is an ideal location for wedding ceremonies, wedding receptions and all manner of celebrations. Belinda's talent and her credentials as a certified wedding director makes the inn's offerings attractive for the couple seeking a beautiful, stress-free wedding day. The wedding and reception area easily accommodates 75 guests, and the house offers many perfect backdrops for photos. With local pubs and restaurants within walking distance, Top O'Woodland is only blocks from downtown, making it a one-of-a-kind destination. For some of Nashville's authentic Southern hospitality, visit Belinda Leslie at Top O'Woodland Historic Bed & Breakfast Inn.

1603 Woodland Street, Nashville TN
(615) 228-3868 or (888) 228-3868
www.topofwoodland.com

Chigger Ridge Bed & Breakfast

Located just 30 minutes west of downtown Nashville, Chigger Ridge Bed & Breakfast encompasses 67 acres of serenity, seclusion and stunning mountain scenery. Innkeepers Jane Crisp and Doug O'Rear have created a relaxing haven for any special occasion, whether it's a reunion, party, meeting, conference, retreat, wedding or honeymoon. Perched on a ridgetop and located on the scenic Harpeth River, Chigger Ridge offers miles of beautiful hiking trails, abundant wildlife and a gorgeous 25-foot waterfall. The main house, a 5,800-square-foot log home, boasts natural stone fireplaces, vaulted ceilings, skylights and a multitude of porches equipped with rockers. Guests enjoy hearty country breakfasts in the massive dining room with large windows and French doors overlooking the wooded countryside. The private Guest House, which may be rented as a whole unit or as separate rooms, features vaulted ceilings, skylights and multi-level decks that are ideal for viewing the sunsets. A 26-foot screened gazebo, complete with refrigerator, sink, ceiling fans and festive lighting for evening entertainment, easily accommodates social gatherings. Chigger Ridge offers horseback riding with prior arrangements and horse camp for children in the summer. Beautiful in every season, Chigger Ridge Bed & Breakfast invites you to a peaceful mountain getaway.

1060 Highway 70 W, Pegram TN
(615) 952-4354
www.bbonline.com/tn/chigger

Old Marshall House Bed and Breakfast

A peaceful country retreat just 25 minutes from Nashville, the Old Marshall House Bed and Breakfast is a beautifully restored example of a two-story 1860s farmhouse. Joseph Kennedy Marshall built the house after returning from the Civil War. Today, its parlors, porches and gazebo are yours to enjoy. A lovely garden with lily ponds and a stream form the centerpiece of the immaculately kept grounds. Your hosts Glenn and Ursula Houghton offer three guestrooms and a log cabin dubbed the Cat's Meow. Mr. Marshall lived in the cabin while the main house was under construction. It's such a pity that he never enjoyed lemony ricotta pancakes or a bacon, mushroom and cheddar frittata for breakfast, as you will. Since you're staying in the home of a Confederate soldier, you might wish to visit one of Williamson County's Civil War sites, the Carter House or the Carnton Plantation with its Confederate cemetery. Other attractions in and around Franklin include antique malls and golf courses. The Pull-Tight Theatre and the Boiler Room Theatre both stage plays. For more than 10 years, the Houghtons have extended their hospitality to visitors from all over Tennessee and beyond. A couple from Minnesota left this note in the guestbook: "Our time in Tennessee was extra special because we found you and the Old Marshall House." Plan a country escape to the Old Marshall House Bed and Breakfast.

1030 John Williams Road, Franklin TN (618) 591-4121 or (800) 863-5808
www.oldmarshallhouse.com

Posh Puppy

Posh Puppy is certainly the most luxurious pet store in Franklin. At this shop, you can buy your dog a T-shirt for his birthday or a pearl necklace for being a good girl. Your dog will walk with a proud strut when sporting products from such designers as VIPoochy, Lady Churchwell's and Doggy Style Designs. From chic apparel and fancy leashes to strollers, car seats and dog beds, Posh Puppy has everything you need to make your pet feel like a superstar. The idea for Posh Puppy began when April Kaiser adopted a tiny Chihuahua named Junior in 2004. Tired of seeing Junior shiver whenever she took him out into the cold, April began searching for products to make the little guy comfortable. One thing led to another, and soon April launched her luxury dog boutique with great products that satisfy pets and owners. With Junior's help, April tests as many products as she can before deciding if they are right for Posh Puppy. Junior gets to try on raincoats and sample gourmet treats that simply cannot be found anywhere else in the area. Posh Puppy has the largest selection of luxury pet items in Tennessee, possibly in the entire Southeast, according to April, who hasn't let a taste for pet luxuries keep her from helping underprivileged dogs. During her first four months in business, she donated $3,000 to local animal shelters. To make every day a special day for you and your four-legged friend, head for Posh Puppy.

3021 Mallory Lane, Suite 120, Franklin TN
(615) 771-6363
www.poshpuppyonline.com

Funkie Forest

The idea for Funkie Forest, a cross between a pet supply store and a pet boutique, hit Catherine Kessinger on one of those weekends when she was driving back and forth to Rivergate to get food for her adopted dogs and cats. Why not do herself and the other pet owners of Springfield a favor, she thought, by opening a store in town where people could get their regular supplies as well as shop for pet gifts and toys? Since opening in 2005, Funkie Forest has made a lot of pet lovers and their pets very happy. Catherine and co-owner Tina Henderson are committed to keeping dogs and cats healthy by carrying holistic, all-natural pet foods. Just for the fun of it, they also stock everything for the pampered pet, from gourmet treats to jewelry and apparel. Catherine and Tina find encouragement in the number of customers who have come into the store and told them that Springfield really needed something like this. They are proud to be part of a revitalized downtown. For a store that will make cats purr, dogs wag their tails, and pet lovers say thanks, go to Funkie Forest.

606 S Main Street, Springfield TN
(615) 384-0091

Haus of Yarn

If you love texture and color, you'll find Haus of Yarn an inspirational wonderland. Owned by Carolyn Smith, the shop has quickly become a favorite shopping destination for knit and crochet fans both local and visiting since opening in 2003. Haus of Yarn's friendly staff has more than 250 years of combined knitting experience. Each welcoming staff member gladly answers questions and offers project suggestions and ideas. The shop features an inviting arrangement and an ample array of needles, patterns, books, accessories and yarn. Quality yarns carried at Haus of Yarn include Noro, Colinette, Lorna's Laces, Malabrigo and Koigu. Model garments created by talented staff members are on display throughout the shop as inspiration to patrons. The store also offers a wide variety of classes, as well as private instruction for all skill levels. Come in, get inspired and find what you are looking for at Haus of Yarn.

73 White Bridge Road, Nashville TN (615) 354-1007
www.hausofyarn.com

The Quilt Emporium

Located in an award-winning renovated building just off the square in historic downtown Lebanon, the Quilt Emporium features top-quality consignment quilts and quilting-related products. Exposed brick walls give the shop the look of a gallery and form a stunning backdrop for new and vintage quilts. Owner Sisi Wilson is living a dream that started more than 30 years ago when she first took quilting classes at Quilter's Haven in Bell Buckle. Many people who attended classes there are now nationally known quilting judges, teachers and master quilters, and Sisi considers the quilters whose work graces her shop to be the threads that hold the fabric of her organization together. The Emporium carries a colorful array of 60 brand-name fabrics as well as quilt-related gifts, such as needle art, handcrafted Amish baskets and jewelry. Long arm machine quilting is provided as a service in the shop, and Sisi donates fabric to the local quilt guild for its charity projects. The Quilt Emporium won the 2006 *Busy Bee Trader* readers' choice award for Best Quilt Shop. You'll be wrapped in cozy warmth the moment you step through the front door. And remember, you can eat chocolate here, too. For quilting classes, textile art and great browsing, visit the Quilt Emporium.

115 S Cumberland, Lebanon TN
(615) 453-9333
www.thequiltemporium.com

Historic Bell Witch Cave and Canoe Rentals

At the Historic Bell Witch Cave, you can get spooked by touring the cave and cabin and hearing some unforgettable history, or spend a leisurely day paddling down the scenic Red River. This is the site of the most documented case of the supernatural in American History. An unseen force known as the Bell Witch terrorized John Bell and his family for three years starting in 1817. Tour the 1800s log cabin, a replica of the Bell home where many of the hauntings occurred. If you dare, you can even arrange a special night tour of the cabin and cave. Tours of the Bell Witch Cave can chill the spine, as many visitors claim to feel the presence of the spirit still looming in the dark corridors. The cave also brings visitors to such famous formations as Eagle Rock and the Witch's Face. Even before the Cherokee Trail of Tears passed through this area, now known as Adams, this was home to many tribes, some of which now rest on the grounds above the cave. Archeologists estimate these graves to be 3,000 to 5,000 years old. A lone stone box grave also lies inside the cave. The farm is a launching point for canoe trips to Port Royal State Park. For a well rounded experience combining fun, history, fright and scenery, visit the Historic Bell Witch Cave.

430 Keysburg Road, Adams TN
(615) 696-3055
www.bellwitchcave.com

Miss Mable's Village

It must be true that one good thing leads to another, because Fay Davidson has created a shopping village where you can enjoy a proper tea and go skateboarding in the same day. This collection of family-owned shops began with Miss Mable's Tea Room, where tea and ceremony are served in a beautifully restored 1897 home. Although women are encouraged to dress up in old-fashioned hats and wraps, the men are comfortable here as well, thanks to hearty entrées, such as steaks, that accommodate larger appetites. At Mrs. Potts' Playhouse, youngsters dress up for tea parties in a whimsical castle setting. You can rent the playhouse for a special occasion and take part in such themed events as Cinderella Teas and Breakfast with Santa. The shop also carries gifts and clothing for children from infants to teens. Granny B's Quilt Shop offers 1,000 bolts of bright quilting fabric along with the books and notions you'll need to get started on your next masterpiece. You can take a class at Granny B's or share your passion at a Sit & Stitch session. Nellie's Antiques features glassware, furniture, linens and other treasures that make thoughtful gifts. For exquisite lace-trimmed cotton gowns and scented lotions, soaps, candles and potpourri, stop in at Miss Bubbles Bath Shop. The young daredevils in your life will want to check out New Creature Skate Shop for everything they need for better kickflips and tailslides. For a day of shopping that will appeal to every member of the family, visit Miss Mable's Village.

301 W College Street, Dickson TN
(615) 441-6658 (Miss Mable's Tea Room)
(615) 441-5288 (Mrs. Potts' Playhouse)
(615) 441-3884 (Granny B's and Bubble's Bath Shop)
(615) 441-6658 (Nellie's Antiques)
(615) 969-1759 (New Creature Skate Shop)
www.missmable.com/village.htm

Opry Mills

With more than 200 retailers under one roof, Opry Mills in Nashville is an essential destination for any serious shopper. The dynamic mix of manufacturers' outlets, off-price specialty stores and distinctive specialty shops guarantees something for everyone. All of the famous names are here, such as Bass and Saks Fifth Avenue for apparel, Off Broadway Shoe Warehouse for footwear and Barnes & Noble for books. Music lovers can shop for the latest releases at Tower Records, and the young ones can create adorable play pals at Build-A-Bear Workshop. At Gibson Bluegrass Showcase, visitors watch craftspeople make the company's famous mandolins, dobros and banjos. NASCAR fans get to feel the thrill of racing with the stock car simulator at Check Flag Lightning's NASCAR Speedway. When you are ready to take a break from shopping, live performers provide entertainment at Center Stage. The food court offers a dozen eateries, while Opry Mills' themed restaurants promise an unforgettable experience. You can dine in a tropical rainforest at the Rainforest Café or enjoy an underwater dining adventure at the Aquarium Restaurant. Twelve million visitors come to Opry Mills annually for the shopping variety, bargains and entertainment. For a marathon shopping spree, visit Opry Mills.

433 Opry Mills Drive, Nashville TN
(615) 514-1000
www.oprymills.com

Chaffin's Barn Dinner Theatre

One of the most enchanting ways to spend an evening in Nashville is to visit Chaffin's Barn Dinner Theatre. Nashville's first professional theatre started in 1967, when John and Puny Chaffin opened the doors of the MainStage theatre-in-the-round and dazzled audiences with live theater tours from New York and a magic stage descending from the ceiling. Their son John and his wife, Jane, continue the tradition of welcoming folks to a mouthwatering Southern-style buffet, complete with salad bar and homemade desserts. A friendly staff works to make your evening enjoyable, and a countryside setting adds to your pleasure. Chaffin's presents Broadway-style shows by some of the area's most talented performers on two stages—the year-round MainStage and the more intimate part-time Backstage, which also makes an excellent setting for private parties. Both theatres perform top-quality comedies, musicals and mysteries that appeal to a broad range of theatergoers. Artistic Director Martha Wilkinson makes sure the productions are first-rate, so you can sit back and be assured of a thoroughly enjoyable show. Come out to Chaffin's Barn Dinner Theatre, relax, and let the food and entertainment entrance you.

8204 Highway 100, Nashville TN
(615) 646-9977 or (800) 282-2276
www.dinnertheatre.com

Tootsie's Tours

You may not have a relative who can show you around Nashville, but you do have Tootsie's Tours. Tootsie's specializes in sightseeing tours of this vibrant and historical city. Relax in a 25-passenger minibus as an experienced, knowledgeable guide who embodies Southern charm shows you what Nashville has to offer. Tootsie's offers five standard tours that appeal to many interests and time schedules. The five-and-a-half-hour Historic Mansions tour makes stops at the Hermitage, Parthenon and the Belle Meade Plantation. Another popular trip is the two-and-a-half-hour Country Legends tour, which brings you by the homes of such fabulous entertainers as Kitty Wells, Roy Orbison and Johnny Cash. This tour boasts an added feature—it's conducted by the Man in Black's sister, Joanne Cash, and her husband, Harry Yates, a pastor from the Cowboy Church. Another tour drives through Music Row and stops at the Ryman Auditorium gift shop. Tootsie's even offers a Magical Mystery Tour that gets you off Nashville's beaten path. Customize your own tour with Tootsie's, rent a limousine, or let Tootsie's shuttle you to and from the Grand Ole Opry. If there's something you want to see in Nashville, Tootsie's will take you there.

422 Broadway, Nashville TN
(615) 207-3999
www.tootsiestours.net

The Nashville Palace

The Nashville Palace is a place where legendary members of the Grand Ole Opry share the stage with rising stars of country music. The live music continues from open to close, with Legendary Lunch kicking things off from 11 am to 1 pm. In the spotlight during these hours are the greats who helped make Nashville what it is today, legends such as Billy Walker, Jeannie Seely and Jimmy Dickens. Enjoy the music with a burger, ribs or catfish from the Palace's menu of hearty favorites. Nighttime is the time for Nashville hopefuls to shine. Here is your chance to play talent scout and predict which entertainer has the right stuff to be a superstar. Randy Travis, Alan Jackson and Ricky Van Shelton got started here. These days you might still find Randy and the others at the Palace, because Opry members often hang out at this Nashville hot spot before and after Opry shows. No doubt they appreciate the Palace's role in honoring the tradition of country music while providing a showcase for the next generation of performers. For an exciting day and night of live country music, check out the Nashville Palace.

2611 McGavock Pike, Nashville TN
(615) 884-3199
www.nashvillepalace.net

Sweet Dreams Cookie Company

At Sweet Dreams Cookie Company in downtown Franklin, owners Marnice and Bobby Smith cater to your every cookie whim, creating delicious cookies before your eyes exactly the way you like them. The shop's signature build-your-own cookie starts with your choice of a traditional or oatmeal cookie base. Next, add such fillings as toffee, macadamia nuts, chocolate or all three. One of the friendly employees will whip up the dough, bake it and then serve it to you fresh from the oven. The couple's five-year-old twin daughters, Jasmine and Madison, are one of the reasons the Smiths started Sweet Dreams online in 2004. They opened the storefront in 2006 and now their girls contribute to the business by handing out cookies and coupons that encourage new customers to stop by. Once you visit, the warm hospitality, the cookies, gourmet coffees and other sweet treats, such as cheesecakes, homemade ice cream sandwiches and Big Mama's butter roll, make it likely you will want to return often to sample the possibilities. If you find yourself unable to get to the store, you can do the next best thing and build your favorite cookies online, then have them delivered straight to your front door anywhere in the United States. The Smith family's cookies also make thoughtful wedding favors, and kids of all ages have a blast at build-your-own-cookie birthday parties. Come to Sweet Dreams Cookie Company, Where Your Cookie Dreams Become Reality.

111 Bridge Street, Franklin TN
(615) 599-5979 or (866) 455-2253
www.sweetdreamscookies.com

Burdett's Tea Shop & Trading Company

Stop by Burdett's Tea Shop & Trading Company to savor the atmosphere of an English-style tea shop with a Southern flair. Conceived by Sandra Ramsey and her daughter, Erin Whited, Burdett's has played a large part in the revitalization of Springfield's historic downtown area as a favorite luncheon and meeting place for locals and visitors alike. The shop, which is housed in the 1912 McCord and Harris Drug Store building, has been featured on *Tennessee Crossroads*, a highly viewed PBS travelogue program. Come by and sample the delightful selection of salads, quiches, sandwiches and homemade scones served with a cup of Rosehaven Quality Loose Teas. The friendly servers are always happy to answer your tea questions and to offer recommendations on teas that have been harvested from the finest gardens in the world. When in Springfield, head downtown to Burdett's Tea Shop & Trading Company for a cup of tea and scones that were complimented by the former Lord Mayor of London.

618 S Main Street, Springfield TN
(615) 384-2320
www.burdettsteashop.com

Scarlett's Garden Tea Room and Creative Accents

Scarlett's Garden Tea Room is named after everyone's favorite Southern belle, Scarlett O'Hara, who would certainly feel right at home here. A few years ago, owner Linda Morrison took a plain building and created a charming setting for lunch and tea. Scarlett's is modeled after a Southern mansion—a section of the dining area even looks like the front porch of the home in *Gone with the Wind*. There's nothing fictitious about the hospitality here, however. It's genuine, and the food has been generating quite a buzz around Mt. Juliet. "Everything we make is special," says Linda, "but the cornbread salad is what people say they come to taste." For those wishing to enter fully into the spirit of the place, there's Miss Scarlett's Chicken Salad Croissant, a family recipe of chicken breast, pineapple and toasted almonds. Another guest favorite is the Southern Hospitality Salad: crisp greens with a honey mustard chicken breast, fresh pineapple and caramelized pecans. With luncheon tea, guests enjoy tea sandwiches, pastries and fresh fruit. Creative Accents, the companion to Scarlett's Tea Room and located at the same address, offers *Gone with the Wind* collectibles as well as silk floral arrangements, candles and home accessories. A favorite place for Scarlett and Rhett fans as well as for anyone fond of special dishes from a Southern kitchen, Scarlett's Garden Tea Room and Creative Accents welcome you. Lunch is served Tuesday through Saturday.

12192 Lebanon Road, Mt. Juliet TN
(615) 773-5513
www.scarlettsgarden.com

Dawson's Sweet Cakes

Customer satisfaction has been job one for more than 20 years at Dawson's Sweet Cakes. With the assistance of talented and dependable employees, owners Joyce and Don Dawson consistently put out top-quality products. Dawson's Sweet Cakes uses family recipes to turn out beautiful baked goods, including breads, rolls and biscuits and such desserts as pies, cakes and cookies. The products taste as wonderful as they look and smell. Joyce and Don's considerable experience helps—Joyce worked for three other bakeries before starting her own business in 1991, and Don is a baker too. Other bakeries refer customers to the Dawsons when they have special requests that the other shops can't accommodate. Repeat customers make up more than 80 percent of the Dawson's business. Their biggest sellers include snicker-doodle cookies, fudge pie, and sweetbreads of all types, including strawberry, cranberry-orange and other holiday breads. They also create custom-designed and sculptured cakes for all occasions, especially weddings. Dawson's Sweet Cakes is regularly included in the local paper's 101 Best in Sumner County, and the Dawsons and their staff appreciate the community's support. Rely on Dawson's Sweet Cakes for top-notch customer service and scrumptious baked goods that taste as good as they look.

109 Old Shackle Island Road, Hendersonville TN
(615) 822-5459

The Frothy Monkey

Miranda Whitcomb, owner of the Frothy Monkey, strives for greatness. Miranda insists she will not serve anything at the Frothy Monkey she would not serve at home. Indeed, she does not consider the Frothy Monkey to be a coffee house; she calls it a coffee home. Miranda sells gourmet coffees from around the world but believes that serving world-class coffee is not enough. Miranda creates a place where people can relax with others and dine on great food that complements the outstanding selection of coffees. The Frothy Monkey serves breakfast, lunch and desserts. Where possible, Miranda uses natural and organic ingredients in everything she makes. The shop carries a wide variety of baked goods from Julie Simpson and Anne, local bakers who create tasty wares exclusive to the Frothy Monkey. The shop is located in a completely refurbished old house with cathedral ceilings, hardwood floors and a fireplace. A highlight is the exposed brick wall used to display selected pieces from local artists. The bricks were rescued from the nearby historic Community Baptist Church when it was torn down. French doors lead to a large deck with seating for up to 75 guests. Events at the Frothy Monkey have included acoustic concerts, chess tournaments, coffee tasting parties and other community functions. Visit the Frothy Monkey for great coffee and great food in a great place.

2509 12th Avenue S, Nashville TN
(615) 292-1808
www.frothymonkeynashville.com

Pickles & Ice Cream Maternity Apparel

Pregnant women with a craving for looking great are talking about Pickles & Ice Cream—Maternity Apparel, that is. Created specifically for today's expecting mother, Pickles & Ice Cream carries the latest in maternity fashions, the staples every wardrobe needs and the specialty items every woman loves. Pregnancy no longer means putting your days as a fashion diva on hold. You can get great clothes along with the extra-special service that a pregnant woman deserves. Because Pickles & Ice Cream is a locally owned and operated, the boutique's owners, Brea DeTray and Rebecca Lee, are on-site, constantly monitoring what their customers want and doing everything they can to keep them happy. They strive to make their boutique more than a maternity store. Pickles & Ice Cream provides an understanding environment, a helping hand when there are questions to be answered, and a place to have fun and feel beautiful at a time when everything around (and inside) a woman is changing. The shop promotes an atmosphere where women feel comfortable sharing their excitement or talking about the changes they are experiencing. Visit Pickles & Ice Cream Maternity Apparel for extraordinary service and clothes.

539 Cool Springs Boulevard, Suite 110, Franklin TN
(615) 778-1599
www.picklesandicecream.com

What's-in-Store

From Miss USA to country music stars LeeAnn Rimes, Martina McBride and Sara Evans, everyone's wearing What's-in-Store. This trendy accessories destination in Franklin with a unique, trademarked name offers up jewelry, handbags, sunglasses and other personal accessories that appeal to celebrity clientele as well as fashion-conscious locals. Owner Dena Nance and her creative staff travel the world to bring customers the latest in high fashion at reasonable prices. Her philosophy, that women should express a little of who they are on the inside by what they wear on the outside, is strongly reflected in customer service that provides personal styling and custom designs. The wares at the little boutique that Nance opened more than five years ago are now sold through a network of vendors in the USA and Canada. The Miss USA, Miss Teen USA and the Miss America pageants have included her accessories in their goody bags, as did the CMA Awards and the NBC Fan Fest with the cast of *Days of Our Lives* and *Passions*. A graduate of Ole Miss with a bachelor's degree in marketing, Nance also teaches fashion entrepreneurship at O'More College of Design and writes a fashion humor column for *Southern Exposure Magazine*. For cutting-edge accessories that will suit your style without busting your budget, stop in at What's-in-Store or check out its trendy website, because When It Comes To Accessories, A Little Excess Is Best.

407 Main Street, Franklin TN
(615) 794-7560
www.whats-in-store.com

Fallalary

Fallalary, a woman's accessory boutique in Franklin, prides itself on its variety of merchandise, with items for ladies at every stage of life. A 73-year-old grandmother can shop with her 53-year-old professional daughter and her 19-year-old granddaughter, and they can all find an appealing piece of jewelry, a scarf or a handbag here. The word *fallalary* means *fancy ornament*, which gives you some idea of the stylish yet affordable merchandise that fills the store. Fallalary offers hundreds of styles of costume jewelry, plus belts, watches and sunglasses to accent any wardrobe. All of it is attractively displayed and looks more expensive than its actual price. Owner Carol Cochran sees her store as an alternative to the chain stores found in malls, which typically cater to a single age group, often teenagers, and lack the kind of customer service found at Fallalary. Fallalary customers are welcome to open packages, try on items and ask the staff for advice. For an enjoyable shopping adventure for all the ladies in the family, Carol invites you to visit Fallalary.

251 2nd Avenue S, Suite 200, Franklin TN (615) 790-9112
www.fallalary.com

Mud Puddle Pottery Studio

At Mud Puddle Pottery Studio, Owners Ronnica Stanley and Sharon Ingram offer everyone a chance to play in the mud. They will teach you how to throw clay on the pottery wheel, sculpt or hand-build an original piece of art. Mud Puddle Pottery customers can pick up supplies and equipment from such companies as Laguna Clay, AMACO and Coyote Glazes. The work of local artists, as well as Ronnica and Sharon's own pieces, are showcased and sold in the gallery area. Learn the art of pottery through a workshop in hand building or pottery wheel techniques. The studio feels more like a gathering place than a classroom, and people tend to chat and socialize as they express their emotions through their artwork. The fun and relaxing atmosphere makes learning a pleasure. Potters jokingly call working with clay "the cheapest therapy around." Be sure to check out the holiday art opening and sale held each fall, where you can find amazing bargains on functional, sculptural and decorative pottery. Get there early, though, because people come from all over for the great deals. Come to Mud Puddle Pottery Studio and discover the thrill of playing with clay.

538 Highway 70, Pegram TN
(615) 646-6644
www.mudpuddlepottery.com

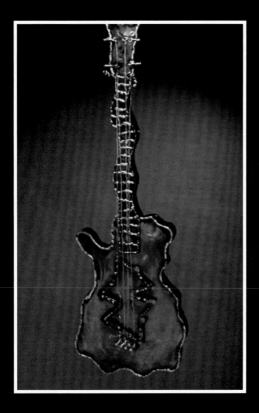

Twisted Sisters

Yes, they're really sisters, and yes, they do amazing things with copper, cast iron, steel, glass and found objects. Linda Levy and Debbie Graham, the Twisted Sisters, wield an oxy-acetylene torch, mig welder and plasma cutter to shape metal into one-of-a kind art pieces. Debbie previously worked in woodworking and marketing, and Linda in interior design and fashion, so creativity just bubbles up naturally in these two. Open-minded and self-taught, they delight in creating unique and functional, yet whimsical, works of art. They showcase sculptures, fountains and lighting as art on their website, where you'll also find information about their upcoming art shows, and they welcome both residential and commercial commissioned jobs. Among the charter members of WOW, or Women of Welding, their awards include the Cutting Edge award from the Woodlands Festival in Lexington, Kentucky and an award from the Virginia Highlands Show in Atlanta. Atlantis Restaurant in Nashville features their custom-made indoor lighting, and the sisters created more than 20 original lights for Nashville's Park Café. Their studio is located on property in Cheatham County that has been in their family for 150 years—they like to say that their granddaddy made moonshine, but they make light shine. Check out the Twisted Sisters and see for yourself. The energy, humor and creativity of their art pieces will light up your life as well.

4655 Pond Creek Road, Pegram TN
(615) 352-3535

The Milo Gallery

Artist Nikki Danby and her husband, Ron Twist, opened the Milo Gallery in Kingston Springs as a studio and showcase for Nikki's artwork. Nikki graduated from the Byam Shaw School of Art in London in 1983, and since that time has traveled continuously between Europe, Australia and North America. A world-class portrait artist, her portfolio includes not only traditional portraits of people but portraits of houses, landscapes and pets. Nikki never settles for a stiff, technically correct representation. Her work captivates and endures because she creates likenesses in oil and pastel that capture a subject's true essence. Collectors of her work include film actress Jacqueline Bisset, the Newman family of Perth, Australia and the Elliott family of Melbourne, Australia. Nikki's paintings have been shown in Europe, Australia and the United States, and she divides her time between painting for exhibition and commissioned portraits. She also teaches summer art workshops at the Renaissance Center in Dickson, as well as summer and fall workshops and courses at Cheekwood Museum of Art in Nashville. The gallery also showcases an eclectic mix of local artists' work, including fine art, photography, jewelry design and textiles. It only exhibits artwork that is original, handmade or hand-decorated. Come browse at the Milo Gallery, and discover riveting original art by inspired artists.

2304 Highway 70, Kingston Springs TN
(615) 952-9181
www.miloartgallery.com

Nikki Danby—*The Twins*
oil painting on linen canvas, 32' x 38'

Lyzon Art Gallery

Lyzon Art Gallery is Nashville's oldest gallery and frame shop, having served the area for more than 50 years. Ron King's exceptional frame-making skills have transformed what began in 1948 as a handcrafted furniture shop into one of the city's premier art galleries with craftsmen on hand to perform the most painstaking restorations to artwork and frames. The Lyzon Art Gallery exhibits an extensive selection of original contemporary paintings and fine handmade prints from Europe and America, including works by Sterling Strauser, Phillip Perkins, Red Grooms, William Edmondson, David Burliuk, Paul Lancaster, Svetlana Bellamy and Lowell Lotspeick. You'd have to search long and hard to find another frame shop offering this concentration of woodworking skills. From carving ornate rococo moldings to applying paper-thin gold leaf to specially prepared frames, every artisan at Lyzon has a specialty that has been perfected over time. Lyzon carries more than 900 different moldings, and craftsmen can carve the rest on-site. Specialists restore damaged or broken frames, from modern casting to painstaking re-carving, and Lyzon handles art restoration as well. Come to Lyzon for all your framing needs, or leisurely browse the gallery and pore over the profusion of exquisite artworks. Who knows what might be in store for you?

411 W Thompson Lane, Nashville TN
(615) 256-7538
www.lyzon.com

Origina Salon Spa

At Origina Salon Spa. you can rejuvenate the mind, body and spirit—and get a new look. Jackie McCall opened Origina as an Aveda Lifestyle Salon Spa for Nashville area in 2003. Origina is a full-service salon and spa that provides all types of hair services—including cuts, colors, perms, and relaxers—using pure, plant-sourced and organic Aveda products. Staff members begin by focusing on what defines you, your lifestyle needs, your sense of style and what you expect from the service. You are pampered and relaxed in a calm atmosphere with a complimentary scalp massage with every cut, mini-facials at the shampoo bowl and cosmetic touch-ups after any service. Origina also offers spa manicures and pedicures, Caribbean therapy hand and foot treatments, customized 30, 60 and 90 minute massages and a variety of facials. The new Skin Refiner Facial (as seen in *O, the Oprah Magazine*) delivers results that are comparable to microderm abrasion but without discomfort or irritation. Origina spa services are a perfect balance of scientific advances and ancient wisdom. These alternative approaches to total skin and body care are designed to restore your energy and revitalize your outlook. Jackie and her staff are dedicated to their clients' beauty and well-being, inside and out. Origina Salon Spa gives back to the community in many ways, and Jackie observes: "To us, having a business is not just about making money—it's about having prosperity with a purpose." Come to Origina Day Spa and you'll leave looking and feeling your best.

443 Cool Springs Boulevard, Suite 105, Franklin TN
(615) 771-9005
www.originasalon.com

Bear Creek Gardens

Bear Creek Gardens offers one-stop shopping for all your gardening needs. This full-service garden center offers an incredible selection of trees, shrubs, domestic and exotic flowers and hanging baskets, as well as Rumford gardening tools, mulch, paving stones and a wealth of other landscaping supplies. Owner Jason Daughrity and his capable staff can help you pick the perfect plants for your landscape, or design and plant it for you. Bear Creek's gift shop, housed in an historic farmhouse, bursts at the seams with goods that include Burt's Bees products, Garden Sloggers and gardening gloves. You can decorate your yard with fountains, bird feeders and statuary, or pick up smaller items such as wind chimes, candles and potpourri. Expect to find seasonal items as well, such as fat fall pumpkins, colorful spring flowers and fresh Christmas trees. Bear Creek Gardens makes customer service a priority. Knowledgeable employees will ensure that you find exactly what you need. It's easy to see why readers of the *Daily Herald* voted Bear Creek Gardens the best landscape supplier in Maury County in 2006. You can rely on the great selection, excellent customer service and experienced staff at Bear Creek Gardens. You'll appreciate the difference.

200 Bear Creek Pike, Columbia TN
(931)-840-0030
www.bearcreekgardens.net

ReCreations Furniture

ReCreations Furniture

When you walk into ReCreations Furniture, a boutique of fine home furnishings, you are sure to find yourself captivated by the exquisite selection. Since 1998, Tim Causey, Richard Epperson and Bedford, their cute dog, have pooled their energies, talents and resources to provide the ultimate in home accessories, custom silk floral designs and fine furniture. ReCreations offers a breathtaking collection of treasures from the far corners of the world. The enormous selection is quite affordable. Expect to find the finest-grade woods and hand-carved details along with sophisticated fabrics and luxurious upholstery. Anticipate the discovery of enchanting accessories and gifts. The expert staff at ReCreations will help you express your personal style of home design. ReCreations specializes in creating custom dried silk and preserved floral arrangements. One of the store's most popular services is Custom Christmas. After an in-home assessment, ReCreations will help you create a Christmas décor that suites your living space. Your Christmas decorations will look as if your home was built around them, not the other way around. Tim, Richard and Bedford have uncompromising standards, and stand behind their service. Delivery is an option. Enjoy a glass of wine while walking through ReCreations Furniture, a gallery of discoveries

4319 Sidco Drive, Nashville TN
(615) 834-0055
www.recreationsfurniture.com

Katydid's

If your home were just four walls and a roof, you wouldn't need an interior design store like Katydid's. But because your home is your castle, your investment and your statement of who you are, you will want to meet the caring staff at both of the Katydid's locations. Katydid's offers highly customized window treatments, unusual tapestries and imported fabrics. Did we say that your home is your castle? Thanks to owner Kaye Lockwood's connection with international book antiquarians in New York City, Katydid's can offer exact interior reproductions of the finest 19th century Parisian homes. It's possible to give your home a royal presence with drapery designs, bedding and wall coverings patterned after those in vogue during Napoleon's reign. "We even have instructions for the Empire Tent," says Kaye, "which was Napoleon's and Josephine's, with the actual carpentry outline for the wood structure framing plan and fabric patterns." Each of the two Katydid's stores fills a different need. Shop for open-stock fabrics in downtown Franklin or go to Long Lane and find exquisite items such as hanging beds and ornate tapestries, and save on discontinued fabrics from upscale suppliers. For home designs worthy of a king and queen, go to Katydid's.

1222 W Main Street, Franklin TN (615) 794-8465
4242 Long Lane, Franklin TN (615) 790-9965
www.katydids-interiors.com

Savage Gallery

Savage Gallery specializes in fine furniture, accessories and works of art. The gallery believes that pieces of furniture are more than functional items to make our homes comfortable. The things that surround us in our homes become a reflection of who we are and transmit a unique personal message to visitors. Savage Gallery understands the subtle nuances of home decorating, and fills its showroom with exceptionally crafted furniture, lighting and home accessories. The Nashville gallery boasts a coveted selection of art created by Jamali, one of the most collected artists in the nation. The list of other notable artists represented in the gallery is tight and impressive. It includes Murat Kaboulov, Zing and local artist Paige Moorehead. The gallery also has an enviable collection of acclaimed hand-blown holiday ornaments by Christopher Radko. Lillian Savage put her 35 years of service in the antique business to work in this brilliant endeavor, and Mark Savage contributes extensive management skills to help fill this streamlined gallery with pieces that can make a customer's dreams come true. Savage Gallery offers custom work. Craftsmen can work one-on-one with you to develop exactly the piece you envision. Beloved pieces you already own can be updated with slipcovers or new upholstery. Bring any idea to Savage Gallery and watch as it is translated into reality.

4012 Hillsboro Pike, Nashville TN (615) 297-5414
www.savagegallery.net

The Gallery of Belle Meade

A beautiful home environment can nurture you and express your essence in myriad ways. The focus of the Gallery of Belle Meade is to provide fine home furnishings at competitive prices while ensuring superior style and service. A talented staff of interior designers works to fulfill each client's desires by creating interiors that reflect the personality of individual patrons. They know that luxury is not a style, but rather a feeling that is conducive to physical comfort, a feeling that is sensuous and rich. "We believe that quality must be coupled with value," says owner Tim Gregory. With everyday discounts of 35 to 50 percent off manufacturer's suggested retail prices, the selection at the 15,000-square-foot showroom will make many dreams possible. The gallery is one of a very few American retailers to represent Rho Mobili d'Epoca, a furniture manufacturer specializing in handmade furniture with fine hand-inlaid features, like the fine antiques of the 1800s. You will find a diverse range of furniture styles, from the exquisite designs of the Italian Rho Mobili d'Epoca to traditional English and French lines. The gallery offers many hand-painted chests, armoires and bedside tables, while staff members blend fabrics, textures and colors for the right look. You'll find original art, decorative accessories and Nashville's largest collection of original oil paintings. Visit the Gallery of Belle Meade for a home environment that expresses your individuality.

4530 Harding Road, Nashville TN
(615) 298-5825

J.J. Ashley's

If you like to pick and choose eclectic, original designs for your home furnishings, then
J.J. Ashley's is the place for you. *Southern Living* and *Natural Home* magazines have
recognized this stylish store for its broad and varied selection of furniture and creative
displays. Consider a French-style acorn sofa, Asian cabinet or barrel-backed chair. Mix
and match light and dark woods, rustic and contemporary styles. You could furnish
your entire house at this store and no one would know that it all came from the same
place. The inventory changes daily, so you'll always find something new and unusual at
J.J. Ashley's. What you won't find is a complete bedroom or dining set in which every piece
looks alike. This shop is all about versatility, about combining different pieces together to
represent your personality and tastes to the fullest. The look is casually elegant, tasteful yet
spontaneous. Come to browse and be inspired by the finds and designs at J.J. Ashley's.

Harmony Home

Harmony Home is a home furnishings and gifts mall where you can make one stop and shop for anything in your home. The store is located in a historic house built in the early 1800s that is on the Historic Walking Tour of downtown Franklin. Owner Amy Simcik opened the business in 2001 with the premise of women helping women. Amy's shop, which offers dozens of furniture and home furnishings lines, as well as gifts for all occasions, makes up almost 10,000 square feet. She offers free decorating advice to anyone who walks in and is well-known for her customer service and reasonable prices. Recently added on is a garden section outdoors creating a bird-lover's paradise. The premise of Harmony Home is to create a harmonious home environment with the philosophy that harmony outside creates harmony within. Also carried at the shop is a broad selection of home accents, including artwork, lamps, pottery, florals and gifts for all occasions. A children's play area with a full-sized chalkboard wall keeps kids occupied while parents browse. As you are browsing, be sure to look for Sir William and Lady Madeline, the friendly shop cats. With new merchandise arriving daily, you can be sure each visit to Harmony Home will yield new treasures and a fresh look. Bring harmony to your home with artistic touches from Harmony Home.

236 2nd Avenue S, Franklin TN
(615) 791-0414

Greenhouse Gallery

With a breathtaking inventory of rare and unusual plants, plus the expertise in custom design to create beautiful landscapes, Greenhouse Gallery is a place Where Plants and Art Combine. The habitats that Greenhouse Gallery has added to the Nashville Zoo are so natural that the primates believe they are home in the jungle. If you visit the zoo, you can't miss the work this company has done, because it is substantial, beginning with the Gibbons Island at the Entry Village. You can thank Greenhouse Gallery for the landscapes at the macaw and tiger exhibits, too, and for the vegetation along the Meerkat and Bamboo Trails. These projects involved moving boulders and fully-grown trees, installing intricate irrigation systems and creating waterfalls. The good news is that the same attention to detail and artistic sense that the folks at Greenhouse Gallery bring to large commercial jobs is available to the homeowner. In fact, although big jobs like the Nashville Zoo grab the spotlight, owners Wesley and Jill Wall say that their focus has been residential since they started the company in 1998. If you are looking for a bonsai for your desk or a lovely plant to occupy a spot in your garden, Greenhouse Gallery is the place to shop. The gallery can also handle an entire landscape, complete with intricate brickwork and water features. For large or small plant projects that bring artistry into your environment, visit Greenhouse Gallery.

1415 ½ W Main Street, Lebanon TN
(615) 443-7756
www.greenhousegallery.net

Rustic Ranch Furniture Company

Until recently, shoppers in the Nashville area who were looking for home décor with a rustic flair faced a long drive to some other city. Today, Rustic Ranch Furniture Company can meet their needs. Owner Laura McMullen started the company in Texas and recently opened this second location. She offers specialty Western and lodge furniture, along with accessories and gifts suitable for home and office. You can set up a bar outfitted with playful cowhide barstools or choose the upscale flair of a bar with a marble top, alligator-embossed leather and a studded border. With 5,000 square feet of showroom, customers can expect to find items essential to creating the look they want, from aspen log beds to antler chandeliers. Rustic Ranch Furniture Company can also meet your need for customized furniture pieces. The store is a great place to turn for smaller gifts and accessories that complete your décor. Look for pictures, sculptures and fountains, along with dinnerware and lighting. Rustically styled switch plates and boot scrapers make perfect gifts for anyone who appreciates a Western theme. Ranchers aren't the only ones who appreciate the ease and beauty of rustic furnishings. Laura's store attracts schoolteachers, sports stars, corporate executives and interior design specialists. The store marries an Old West feel and Southern hospitality with many gift services, including gift certificates, a gift registry, a mailing service and a website for 24-hour browsing. Find the furnishings to match your country lifestyle at Rustic Ranch Furniture Company.

900 Conference Drive, Suite 10, Goodlettsville TN
(615) 851-7899 or 877-RUSTIC9 (787-8429)
www.rusticranchfurniture.com

The Kilgore Collection

The Kilgore Collection, a shop of home and garden accents, is the product of a passion that keeps growing. Beginning with one shipment of antiques, Joe K. Kilgore II turned his passion for home furnishings and interior design into a business. The merchandise now fills most of a 3,500-square-foot showroom. You'll find a broad array of items, everything from affordable European antiques to china and distinctive gifts. As long as there is room for more, Joe will be out looking for it, whether it be furniture and lamps or crystal, silver and pewter. Joe could not have grown the Kilgore Collection into a successful venture without help. The business is a two-person operation that not only depends on Joe's time and energy but that of his wife, Carroll. In fact, you could say that he is the finder and Carroll is the keeper. While he is out purchasing antiques and merchandise, she keeps the store running. If you are searching for something in particular, be sure to tell Joe, because he enjoys finding pieces that are on customers' wish lists. Eager to help couples, Joe and Carroll offer bridal registry and custom invitations. Stop by the Kilgore Collection and see what Joe is bringing in today.

120 W 7ᵗʰ Street, Columbia TN
(931) 540-8833
www.kilgorecollection.com

Loblolly Interiors Market

To help you decorate with originality, Ellen Gunn Calvin offers Loblolly Interiors Market, a small but exciting shop of personally selected art and antiques. Here you will find eclectic furniture and accessories that you can mix into your home, creating an element of surprise in every room. Indeed, Ellen uses the word *surprise* a lot when describing her ideal home. The warmest, most inviting homes avoid the predictable. They pique a guest's curiosity with well-chosen items that delight, surprise and tell the story of the people who live there. Ellen's love for English and French furniture is reflected at Loblolly, where you will also find English porcelain, Oriental rugs and architectural elements. Ellen orders nothing for her store. Instead, she prefers

to bring in items that she collects. She is very active in her collecting, so customers see something new every time they visit. Ellen has worked with antiques for many years and is also an oil painter. She can customize your chairs and tables with a hand-painted finish or artwork, turning them into fun and exciting pieces that fit your décor. Ellen calls Loblolly Interiors Market Columbia's smallest shop with the biggest surprise. Visit her there soon.

**810-A Walker Street, Columbia TN
(931) 388-4676**

Rooster Tails

If you like a little adventure with your shopping, then Rooster Tails is your kind of place. New and used furniture is the attraction, lots of it, sprawling over 10,000 square feet of indoor and outdoor space. In 2005 and 2006, readers of the *Busy Bee Trader* voted Rooster Tails the Best Place to Find Bargains. Find is the right word, because you might have to search for that antique door or rocking chair you need—but that's half the fun. Besides, you never know what you might discover along the way. Rooster Tails carries tables and chairs, as well as beds, bookshelves and entertainment centers. From kitchen islands and country hutches to tons of concrete planters and ornaments, Rooster Tails features furniture and accessories for every room in your home and for your garden. Do you like the rustic look of Adirondack furniture? Owners Wayne and

Pat Killebrew keep a large selection in stock in six different colors. Drop by Rooster Tails, and see why the *Busy Bee Trader* poll also named this store the Best Good Used Furniture Store in the area.

**4108 Columbia Highway, Franklin TN
(615) 794-7472
or (800) 984-7472**

Dumpster Divers Antiques

At Dumpster Divers Antiques, you won't be required to plunge into any smelly bins to search for treasures. Owner Ted Fridholm and his staff have done all the dirty work for you, making this architectural salvage store a great place to look for everything from antique hardware and stained glass to doors, furniture and ironware. Ted takes the best of what there is to grab from demolished buildings, an occupation that takes him throughout the country and to England, and hauls it all back to his shop in historic Leipers Fork in Franklin. If you know something about antiques, you could probably guess that old mansions, hotels and movie theaters are high on the list of likely sources for antiques of distinction. Churches are another valuable source, not only for their stained glass but, interestingly enough, for their pulpits. Ted says that the pulpits are popular with restaurants because they make good reception stands. Restaurants are among Ted's best customers, as are other businesses looking to decorate in a particular theme or style. No doubt Dumpster Divers Antiques has something nice for your home, whether it be a pedestal sink, a dazzling chandelier or anything Art Deco. For salvage items without the scrounging, go to Dumpster Divers Antiques.

**4158 Old Hillsboro Road, Franklin TN
(615) 591-3832
*www.dumpsterdiversantiques.com***

Vanderbilt Legends Club

Just 30 minutes from Nashville International Airport, Vanderbilt Legends Club is nestled in the beautiful countryside around Franklin. The club, which opened in 1992, features two 18-hole championship golf courses that were designed by pro golfer Tom Kite and renowned golf course designer Bob Cupp. The Ironhorse Course received its name from the railroad tracks that run along its eastern boundary. The Roper's Knob Course bears the name of the historic hill to its south that was used during the Civil War as a signal station. Club members enjoy a 19-acre practice facility along with a chipping and putting green. Known for its impeccably manicured greens, Vanderbilt Legends Club has hosted many golf tournaments, including the LPGA Franklin American Mortgage Championship. *Golf World Business* has voted the pro shop at Vanderbilt Legends Club one of America's Top 100 Golf Shops for six years straight. Meticulous service extends to the Legends Grille, which serves lunch seven days a week in a room with a massive stone fireplace and elegant chandeliers. The facility provides an ideal setting for corporate events, wedding receptions, rehearsal dinners and other special occasions. Whether it's a business meeting followed by a round of golf or a formal social gathering, Vanderbilt Legends Club can provide everything you need to make your event a rousing success.

1500 Legends Club Lane, Franklin TN
(615) 791-8100
www.legendsclub.com

Drakes Creek Activity Center

If you have lots of energy and are raring to go, you'll love Drakes Creek Activity Center (DCAC), where you and your friends and family can have the time of your lives. No matter what your age, DCAC provides excellent options, including nine batting cages suitable for all levels. A long, challenging 18-hole miniature golf course, replete with water fountains and castles, offers special lighting effects for an entirely different experience by night. Get your blood pumping with a game of aeroball, a combination of volleyball and basketball played on trampolines. The outdoor Laser Adventure combines the best parts of paint ball with indoor laser tag, using infrared light instead of messy projectiles. With games geared for ages seven to 80, the Laser Adventure makes an outstanding group or party event and is popular for corporate team-building events. If you'd prefer something more relaxing and scenic, consider a ride in a hot air balloon, or challenge the machines in the interactive game room. Half the fun is the soft serve ice cream and other great food items. With such a wide range of entertainment, everyone will have a ball at Drakes Creek Activity Center.

130 Cherokee Road N, Hendersonville TN
(615) 822-0232
www.funandenergy.com

The River Rat's Canoe Rental

The River Rat's Canoe Rental offers a day full of outdoor fun for the whole crew. This family-owned business provides all equipment needed to explore the beautiful Duck River, including quality Old Town canoes crafted in Maine. Whether you're a beginner or an experienced paddler, a leisurely trip down the river is a safe, easy adventure. The Duck River flows south of Nashville past Columbia and Chapel Hill and through Henry Horton State Park. Day trips on the river vary in length from five to nine miles, with no time limit. Another option is an overnight stay or a multiple-day adventure—up to a 29-mile, three-day trip. The scenic hollows and bluffs along the Duck River are shrouded with an abundant forest of oak, hickory, maple and tulip poplar, to name just a few species. Abundant river life shows that it is a clean, healthy watercourse. The Duck contains about 50 species of freshwater mussels, four times the number of species living in all of Europe. For good, clean fun, bring your scout troop, school or church group, or your entire extended family for a getaway in the great outdoors. It's easy to get your feet wet. Ernie Stewart founded the River Rat's Canoe Rental in 1979, and today it's operated by Bill Stewart. With a little help from The River Rat's Canoe Rental, everyone can make a splash in Tennessee's beautiful Duck River.

4361 Highway 431, Columbia TN
(931) 381-2278
www.riverratcanoe.com

Hermitage Golf Course

With greens ambling along the banks of the Cumberland River, Hermitage Golf Course, named for the stately residence of President Andrew Jackson, brilliantly combines challenging, playable layouts with natural wonders. As they celebrate Hermitage's 20th anniversary, owners Mike Eller and Ray Danner are proud of the course's history, which includes hosting the LPGA Sara Lee Classic and the Executive Women's Golf Association. With 36 championship holes, Hermitage is Tennessee's finest public access golf course. *Golf Digest* has awarded Hermitage a four star rating; *Golf for Women* and *Travel + Leisure* have also honored the course; and the state of Tennessee has twice honored Hermitage with soil and land conservation awards. The General's Retreat has a traditional look yet offers water hazards, courtesy of eight ponds and a lake. The new President's Reserve, noted for its well-bunkered fairways, natural wetlands and a monster par four 11th hole, was recently rated among the Top 10 in the State by *Golf Digest*. Hermitage offers professional instruction in its Golf School, where you can improve your game whether you are a beginner or an accomplished player. Frequent players earn points toward free lessons and equipment with every round. For convenience, you can book your tee time online. In Nashville's backyard, wrought from what was once two farms and a black walnut tree grove, the Hermitage Golf Course has everything you could want for an ideal day of golf, from blue grass and green grass fairways to a green philosophy. For a beautiful yet demanding golf experience, come to the Hermitage Golf Course.

3939 Old Hickory Boulevard, Old Hickory TN
(615) 847-4001
www.hermitagegolf.com

Cedar Creek Sports Center

Cedar Creek Sports Center owner Tom Schunk, a former vice president with Service Merchandise, set up the Mt. Juliet Sports Center for his retirement years, hoping to make a little profit while offering families affordable fun—and having some fun himself. He's been coming in every day for 15 years and says he still loves what he does. The 16 ½-acre family fun complex features two 18-hole Putt-Putt® golf courses and a go-kart track with Indy Go-Karts and NASCAR Rookie Karts. You'll also find a driving range, concession stand, indoor game room, private party room and plenty of parking. Family members can battle it out on bumper boats equipped with on-board water squirters or try their luck in the batting cages against pitching machines that can throw a ball at 80 miles per hour. The sports center, managed by Tom's son, Jim, draws ball teams, school and church groups. Cedar Creek hosts about 240 birthday parties each year, thanks to a package that includes the party room, drinks and special prices for all of the attractions. Lots of activity requires lots of food, and Cedar Creek obliges with such concession stand fare as hot dogs, corn dogs, pizza, pizza pockets, nachos and soft drinks. When you want affordable fun that engages the entire family, come to Cedar Creek Sports Center.

10770 Lebanon Road, Mt. Juliet TN
(615) 754-2774
www.cedarcreeksportscenter.com

Joey's House of Pizza

Picture perfect pizza, pasta and calzone will almost dance into your mouth when you visit Joey's House of Pizza. The authentic New York pizza and food is the specialty of the friendly Macca family, who treat customers like family, making sure they are well fed and content. You'll find yourself coming back time and again for the pizza. The dough, meatballs and sauce are made in the kitchen daily, with hand-shredded cheese and fresh pies. The artful presentation is a feast for the eyes as well as a treat for the taste buds. Know-how and great ingredients make every pizza worthy of your attention. For a hearty meal bursting with extras, try Joey's Special Pizza, piled high with homemade meatballs, fresh chicken and Italian sausage. The Maccas add breaded eggplant, artichokes and spinach, then finish it off with fresh tomatoes. They also make a scrumptious chicken parmesan sub, and a catering menu offers a copious choice of classic Italian dishes. The atmosphere at Joey's is family-friendly and relaxed.With two Joey's House of Pizza restaurants in metro Nashville, you can easily find a great Italian dining experience near you.

214 Ward Circle, Suite 400, Brentwood TN
(615) 661-0032
15 Arcade Alley, Nashville TN
(615) 242-7144
www.joeyshouseofpizza.com

Dotson's Pure Country Cooking

The residents of Franklin have a special place in their hearts for Dotson's Pure Country Cooking, which has been serving traditional Southern fare for more than 60 years. Choose one meat dish and three side dishes for one price at this community icon, where people from all walks of life come for the first, last and middle meal of the day. Some customers meet regularly for breakfast, an opportunity for eggs, pancakes, country ham and grits. Others eat all three meals at Dotson's and consider it a home away from home. For lunch or dinner, choose from such favorites as fried chicken, meatloaf and melt-in-your-mouth biscuits, along with delightful vegetable offerings. Save room for dessert, because you will surely want to try the Coca-Cola Cake after your meal. Chester and Clara Dotson opened the diner in 1943, with Chester in the kitchen and Clara up front. Today, owner Art McCloud faithfully continues the restaurant's reputation for reliable Southern-style food, ensuring Dotson's place as a community cornerstone. You never know who you will see here, but the signed pictures on the walls may give you an idea of the Country music stars that have visited, sometimes regularly. Make sure to visit Dotson's Pure Country Cooking, a beloved meat-and-three restaurant where Southern cooking and Southern hospitality are a cherished way of life.

97 E Main Street, Franklin TN
(615) 794-2805

Puffy Muffin, Inc.
Bakery and Restaurant

The Puffy Muffin has become more than a trusted place for delicious lunches, dinners and desserts. This 225-seat restaurant and bakery is a hub of the Brentwood community, a place where some of the same people gather day after day to enjoy the food while renewing friendships. After 20 years, Owner Lynda Scobey Stone still cannot believe the success of her business. Many of her customers have been loyal to the Puffy Muffin from her first year and are willing to drive 30 minutes for lunch each day. "I am blessed . . . Puffy Muffin is a gift from the Lord," says Lynda. In 2004, Lynda answered the popular demand for a Puffy Muffin cookbook and published *Memories in the Making*. Now the public can prepare such signature dishes as baked potato soup, amaretto chicken and poppyseed chicken casserole at home. Temptations from the bakery include the apricot nectar bundt cake, apple bread with caramel glaze and Jackson pie. In 1996, the Republican National Committee chose the Puffy Muffin to cater a luncheon for presidential candidate Elizabeth Dole. In 2003, the restaurant received the Williamson County Small Business award. *My Business*, a small business magazine, featured Lynda in an article about innovative management approaches to customer relations. Lynda credits her entire staff for the consistent growth of her business, saying "To me, they are all heroes." Drop by the Puffy Muffin and get the inside scoop on a true small business success story.

229 Franklin Road, Brentwood TN
(615) 373-2741
91 Seaboard Lane, Brentwood TN (Puffy Muffin in Cool Springs)
(615) 309-0703
www.puffymuffin.com

Famous Dave's

Here are two reasons why you aren't likely to forget the signature All American Feast at Famous Dave's. First, this is barbecue to die for. Second, it comes to your table on a trashcan lid. The uncommon serving plate is Dave Anderson's way of honoring his roots as an aspiring barbecue chef. He began his apprenticeship by sampling meats in a homemade smoker he built from a garbage can. Dave was born a seeker, but his obsession wasn't the Fountain of Youth or the Holy Grail. Before opening Famous Dave's, he logged 25 years visiting every rib shack, roadside joint and fancy supper club around, all in search of the most succulent meats, savory seasonings and lip-smacking sauces. Taste the fruits of Dave's love affair with barbecue at the five Famous Dave's locations in Tennessee. Famous Dave's is known for its hickory-smoked St. Louis-style spare ribs, which are flame-kissed on the grill just before being served. Other dishes, including the slow-smoked Texas-style beef brisket, spit-roasted chicken, spicy sausage and sweetwater catfish, contributed to the *Food Network* declaring Famous Dave's a Food Find. All meats are smoked daily, and the award-winning bread pudding and honey-buttered corn muffins are made from scratch each morning. For barbecue to remember, try Famous Dave's.

7086 Baker's Bridge Avenue, Franklin TN
(615) 778-1227
www.homeofthebigslab.com

Photos by David Schenk

Larriviere's on the Square

The Southern cuisine served at Larriviere's on the Square fits right in with the friendly family atmosphere and makes this one of the most comfortable restaurants in Gallatin. Rene and Amy Larriviere joined forces with Doug and Regina Dicke to create a winning team whose earnest efforts resulted in this cheerful home away from home on the town square in historic downtown Gallatin. Larriviere's bountiful menu features a collection of delicacies that are sure to please even the pickiest of palates. The restaurant serves a wide variety of breakfast, lunch and dinner choices that range from classic to Cajun. The seafood-stuffed mushrooms were featured on *Talk of the Town* in 2005 and the white chocolate bread pudding is some of the best, earning world-wide recognition. It is currently shipped all over the United States. In addition to its enticing menu, Larriviere's can put together an inspiring food tray to suit any appetite. The catering side of the venture is enjoying rapid growth—Larriviere's can accommodate any event. Catering packages include a choice of box lunches, chef on-site or a fully catered party plan. Wander in and satisfy your cravings at Larriviere's on the Square.

102 N Water Street, Gallatin TN
(615) 451-2772
www.larrivieres.com

Nick & Rudy's Restaurant and Piano Bar

Owners Nick Nikolaiczyck and Rudy Caduff like to say that if Frank Sinatra and his Rat Pack were still around, Nick & Rudy's is the place where they would eat in Nashville. Nick & Rudy's offers elegant dining on prime steaks, veal and seafood. Each guest is greeted either by Nick or Rudy. These two friends, proud and personable gentlemen with European backgrounds, met in 1979 while both were working at Opryland. They found that they had similar career paths in the club and hotel industry, as well as a joint passion for fine food and wine. The piano bar at Nick & Rudy's reflects another shared passion: their timeless taste in music. The lush sounds of the piano evoke the bygone days of movie stars and sophisticated evenings. The very air turns romantic under the influence of the piano. The owners say that it is atmosphere and the personal touch that separate their place from the big chain restaurants. Nick & Rudy's has earned a #1 from Citysearch. If you are looking for a restaurant in Nashville where the setting is as consistently pleasing as the food, let Nicky and Rudy help make your dining experience a special one.

204 21ˢᵗ Avenue S, Nashville TN (615) 329-8994
www.nickandrudys.com

Kalamata's Restaurant

Kalamata's Restaurant in the Green Hills area of Nashville has a dual focus: educating customers about healthful eating and providing nourishing dining options. Owners Maher Fawaz and Beth Collins believe they can make a difference by offering a wide variety of appetizing selections that tempt the palate and make the body healthier. Kalamata's generated a quiet buzz when it opened, and a growing number of food fans continue to discover this charming café. Fawaz opened his dream restaurant so he could partner with Beth to offer freshly prepared Mediterranean and Middle Eastern foods with a modern take on the classics of that region. You'll feel the cozy nature of the restaurant from the moment you walk in. A small dining area is separated from the cooking area only by the counter. Every item on the menu, with the exception of the baklava (which is created by a relative in Detroit), is made right in front of you and is sure to be a treat, even if you have experienced Middle Eastern cuisine in the past. "When you come to Kalamata's, you don't just get a meal, you get a show," says Fawaz. The succulent results are sure to prove memorable.

3764 Hillsboro Pike, Nashville TN
(615) 383-8700

Chaffin's Barn Dinner Theatre

One of the most enchanting ways to spend an evening in Nashville is to visit Chaffin's Barn Dinner Theatre. Nashville's first professional theatre started in 1967, when John and Puny Chaffin opened the doors of the MainStage theatre-in-the-round and dazzled audiences with live theater tours from New York and a magic stage descending from the ceiling. Their son John and his wife, Jane, continue the tradition of welcoming folks to a mouthwatering Southern-style buffet, complete with salad bar and homemade desserts. A friendly staff works to make your evening enjoyable, and a countryside setting adds to your pleasure. Chaffin's presents Broadway-style shows by some of the area's most talented performers on two stages—the year-round MainStage and the more intimate part-time Backstage, which also makes an excellent setting for private parties. Both theatres perform top-quality comedies, musicals and mysteries that appeal to a broad range of theatergoers. Artistic Director Martha Wilkinson makes sure the productions are first-rate, so you can sit back and be assured of a thoroughly enjoyable show. Come out to Chaffin's Barn Dinner Theatre, relax, and let the food and entertainment entrance you.

8204 Highway 100, Nashville TN
(615) 646-9977 or (800) 282-2276
www.dinnertheatre.com

Capitol Grille

The staff at Capitol Grille in Nashville guarantees the freshness of its Southern cuisine. They say that nothing served at the restaurant, except for ice cream, has ever been frozen. As for the ice cream, all of it is handmade. Black Angus beef, Nieman Ranch pork chops and Alaskan halibut put the emphasis squarely on quality. Add an elegant setting in the Hermitage Hotel, in what was originally the main dining room and then a private men's club, and you have the makings of the only AAA Five-Diamond restaurant in Tennessee. Executive Chef Tyler Brown has been the driving force behind the Capitol Grille's climb into the ranks of the industry's elite. During his tenure, the restaurant not only secured the Five Diamond designation but was voted one of the best new restaurants in the United States by *Esquire* magazine and one of America's best restaurants by *Gourmet*. As if the opportunity to dine at such a premier establishment were not reason enough to visit the Capitol Grille, patrons also enjoy ducking into the adjacent Oak Bar. It was here that the Francis Craig Orchestra pulled the longest running hotel gig on the books, entertaining Nashvillians from 1929 to 1945. Today, it offers a classy club environment that has often earned it the title of Best Bar in Nashville. When nothing but elegance and quality will do, choose the Capitol Grille.

231 6ᵗʰ Avenue N, Nashville TN
(615) 345-7116 or (888) 888-9414
www.thehermitagehotel.com

MAFIAoZA's

MAFIAoZA's arrived on the Nashville dining scene in 2003 with a simple goal of delivering authentic Italian food and a far-ranging wine list in a comfortable, welcoming atmosphere. It has succeeded on both fronts. The popular 1920s New York-style Italian restaurant features the finest stone-oven pizza in the southeast, and uses fresh, seasonal ingredients. Corporate Chef and Catering Director Brett Corrieri attended Rhode Island's prestigious Johnson & Wales University and has earned a solid reputation for his commitment to presenting flavorful dining experiences at MAFIAoZA's. This restaurant is a favorite among families, singles and members of Nashville's thriving music industry. Whether patrons are in the mood for authentic pizza and a few *piccolo morsi* (various Italian appetizers) or multi-course meals with accompanying wine, they find what they're looking for here. Co-owner and General Manager Lars Kopperud has assembled an impressive list of Old and New World wines with selections available for every taste and budget. Chef Corrieri is also the proprietor of Vinea Wine & Spirits, launched in Nashville in November 2006, and Corrieri's Formaggeria. Launched in Nashville in October 2005, it is home to some of the best artisanal cheeses, cured meats and specialty food items available in the Southeast. Chef Corrieri and Lars Kopperud, together with Gannett News Service columnist Barb Ford, have in the works a frank dining book, geared toward the dating set. The book, *Never Dine Alone Again*, is being billed as a cross between the controversial, best-selling *The Rules* and *Martha Stewart's Hors D'Oeuvres Handbook*, and is expected to hit bookstores in time for the 2007 holiday season.

2400 12th Avenue S, Nashville TN
(615) 269-4646
www.mafiaozas.com

The Loveless Cafe

Only a handful of restaurants are worthy of being called institutions. The Loveless Cafe has been in the business of serving down-home Southern food long enough to deserve such status. Since 1951, travelers along Highway 100 in Nashville have been stopping at the Loveless for heaping platters of its country ham, fried chicken and biscuits made from scratch. The television cameras have come here many times, filming for shows ranging from *NBC Today* and *CBS This Morning* to *The Home Show* on ABC. Al Gore and Princess Anne have eaten at the Loveless. Country music legend George Jones left praise in the guestbook for the biscuits, red eye gravy and ham, saying, "If you want to taste the best country cooking anywhere, you just need to go to my favorite restaurant, the Loveless Cafe." After passing from the original owners, Lon and Annie Loveless, to the Maynard family, it was then sold to the McCabe family and finally to current owner and Nashville native Tom Morales in 2003. Staff members working to satisfy the current generation of visitors include Carol Fay, the world famous Biscuit Lady, and Pit Master George Harvell, who makes all of the smoke house favorites. Sharing space with the Loveless Cafe are the former Loveless Motel Shops, now renovated and housing galleries, gift shops and the cafe's own Hams and Jams Country Market. For a taste of Southern cooking and culture that spans decades, stop at the Loveless Cafe.

8400 Highway 100, Nashville TN
(615) 646-9700 or (800) 889-2432
www.lovelesscafe.com

The San Antonio Taco Company

It could be hard to say "San Antonio Taco Company," when your mouth is full of a zesty chicken or steak fajita. Maybe that's why the locals call this casual restaurant, across from the Vanderbilt Library, Satco. By whatever name, it has been a popular gathering spot since 1983, not only for its Tex-Mex specialties but for its great music and cozy deck. Although you won't have to wait long for your meal, this is not fast food. Everything is cooked fresh. The San Antonio Taco Company even makes its own salsa, tortillas and cheese dip. If you are looking for more good reasons to eat here, you might want to consider the choice of 16 domestic and imported beers. Supervisor Robert Wilder, or Taco Bob, has been at Satco for 16 years. He heads an experienced management staff that is rightly proud of serving good meals in a fun atmosphere. For Tex-Mex food that's more than a mouthful, try the San Antonio Taco Company.

Omni Hut Restaurant

Pearl Harbor survivor James Frank Walls covered more than a million miles of travel as a United States Air Force pilot. Collecting authentic recipes during his travels to Hawaii, the Philippines, Hong Kong and the South Pacific, Walls founded the Omni Hut, a tiki-style restaurant, in 1960. The Omni Hut still features the same Polynesian and Chinese cuisines as it did in the 1960s, and the décor is virtually unchanged as well. Maori tribe wall plaques and the handmade tapa cloth wall covering add to the restaurant's South Pacific feel. From the netted hand-blown glass floats used as lights to the indoor waterfall, every element of the 1950s and 1960s tiki craze is in place. One of the four luau dinners is the best way to sample a little of everything Omni Hut has to offer. The Tahitian Feast, Omni Hut's most popular dinner, features a generous spread of 13 different items. Beginning with egg flower soup and Bora Bora (juicy pineapple chunks wrapped in bacon), the Tahitian Feast also features Omni Hut's signature Tid Bits. The luau continues with succulent pit-roasted pork ribs, basted in homemade Omni Hut teriyaki sauce that is thickened with honey and spiced with freshly grated ginger. After an array of finger food appetizers, muumuu-clad waitresses present you with steaming hot towels to wipe your hands. The feast concludes with chicken chow mein, shrimp fried rice and sweet and sour pork. For dessert, try the Flaming Volcano: a mountain of vanilla ice cream topped with chocolate lava and a flaming sugar cube. Memorable dining experiences begin at Omni Hut, Tennessee's first and one of the only remaining tiki-style restaurants with a charmingly retro atmosphere.

618 S Lowry Street, Smyrna TN
(615) 459-4870
www.omnihut.com

Mère Bulles

The stately Mère Bulles, a beautifully restored antebellum home, provides contemporary Southern cuisine with Asian influences and impeccable service in an atmosphere filled with charm. Signature dishes include shrimp and grits, phyllo-wrapped sea bass, Charleston She Crab Bisque and house-made carrot cake. Mère Bulles' cuisine emphasizes fresh, local ingredients presented with regional elegance. The restaurant tastefully accommodates you and your guests with everything from private rooms to exclusive use of various facilities, which makes the lush grounds and richly appointed rooms the ideal setting for a reception, bridal tea or rehearsal dinner. The professional staff can coordinate bed-and-breakfast or hotel accommodations, transportation and decorations. They are happy to arrange for entertainment as well, ranging from magicians to chocolate fountains. Mère Bulles offers full-service off-site catering for any occasion, including private dinner parties in your home. Mère Bulles, French for Ma Bubbles, was named for founder Rodney Wise's grandmother, whose effervescent spirit and fondness for champagne enlivened many gatherings. With an updated flair, Mère Bulles continues a Southern legacy of grand hospitality and satisfying meals in gracious surroundings. When your gathering of four or 40 calls for elegance and spirited good times, come to Mère Bulles.

5201 Maryland Way, Brentwood TN
(615) 467-1945
www.merebulles.com

Square Market & Café

Square Market & Café sits opposite the courthouse on the square in historic downtown Columbia. Square Market is definitely the place for downtown lunches, private parties and catering for area offices. Partners Liz Lovell and Debra Mann feature gourmet fare that's fresh, healthy and definitely unexpected, such as panini clubs, Polk's Roasted Pear Salad and tomato artichoke soup. The Tennessee Hot Brown, always a crowd favorite, combines sliced ham, turkey and bacon on white toast, topped with white sauce and cheddar cheese and then baked. For lunch, try one of the four melt-in-your-mouth Judges Square Steamers, meaty hot sandwiches with sauce and cheese on a hoagie bun. The dinner menu changes weekly, and includes baked salmon, steaks, chicken, fresh fish and pasta dishes. Square Market's beautifully tempting desserts include their towering strawberry shortcake and the three-layer Chocolate Confusion. The well-chosen wine list, candlelit ambience, impeccable service and beautiful décor ensure a wonderful experience. Special events include Songwriter's Night, normally the fourth Thursday of every month, when well-known Nashville songwriters perform. Artists have included such wonderful entertainers as John Knowles, John Ford Coley and Byron Hill, to name just a few. Reservations are required for this event. When you dine at the Square Market & Café, you'll see why local folks as well as out-of-towners are giving it stellar reviews.

36 Public Square, Columbia TN
(931) 840-3636
www.squaremarketcafe.com

Sunset Family Restaurant

One of the oldest family-owned restaurants in the area, Sunset Family Restaurant has become a landmark. It opened in 1959, and Lebanon's current mayor was the first dishwasher. Many locals call the Sunset their second home. Travelers frequently plan their vacations to include a stop here, while many customers drive from surrounding towns to enjoy a meal on a regular basis. The food has a reputation for excellence, and the local media have declared that the Sunset has the best meat, salad and burgers in Wilson County. *Tennessee Magazine* named Sunset Best for Country Cooking. This is truly a family owned and operated enterprise. The business changed hands in 1962 and again in 1967, but all the sales took place within a single family. Bob and Virginia Hodge initially formed a partnership with Bob's brother Bill and Bill's wife, Pat. Today, Bob and Virginia are the exclusive owners, but family remains as important as ever to this Lebanon institution. Bob and Virginia's four children, Jimmy, Debbie, Bobby and Meceia, have grown up working along side their parents and continue to do so, as do their spouses, Sheila, Tim and Tammy. Debbie's oldest son, Timothy, cooks with his Uncle Jimmy and on busy days, when an extra hand is needed, you might see some of the other grandchildren getting in on the action in their own fun ways too. Bob and Virginia are proud that some of their employees have worked at the Sunset for as long as 22 years. For award-winning food and legendary family traditions, visit the Sunset Family Restaurant.

640 S Cumberland Street, Lebanon TN
(615) 444-9530

Vittles Restaurant

While any business aims to be the best at what it does, owner John Craighead has set an even higher goal for himself at Vittles Restaurant in Hermitage. He strives to serve his guests country cooking that's as good as his mom's. "Mom provided a choice of main courses and more vegetables and side items than we could possibly eat," he recalls. "Everything she prepared was seasoned just right, delivering that down-home taste." Vittles applies the art of Southern down-home cooking to such favorites as catfish, beef pot roast and grilled or fried pork chops. As for the fried chicken, John claims his is simply the best this side of the Mason-Dixon Line. All dinners come with two or three side dishes, and the choices are many, everything from ambrosia fruit salad to black-eyed peas and potato salad. Vittles also serves burgers, salads and sandwiches. The irresistible banana pudding for dessert is made from scratch daily. In addition to its Hermitage location, Vittles has sites in Brentwood and Nashville, all of them popular with the locals for their carefully prepared food and friendly service. For food that mom could mistake for her own, go to Vittles.

3455 Lebanon Road, Hermitage TN
(615) 889-1819
4936 Thoroughbred Lane, Brentwood TN
(615) 371-2525
930 Lebanon Road, Nashville TN
(615) 254-3663
www.vittlesrestaurant.com

City Café of Brentwood

For one great price, the City Café of Brentwood will serve you one meat and three side dishes of your choice with a Southern down-home style that's been pleasing loyal customers since Jerry and Beata Cunningham opened the café in 1988. Service is fast and courteous, thanks to a cafeteria style where customers can view and choose from a lineup of delicious temptations, such as country style steak, turkey and dressing or fried pork chops, but the food is slow-cooked and nicely prepared. Table options also vary and include quiet private tables as well as a welcoming community table where you can make new friends or catch up with old ones. You can eat at City Café often and always find your favorites or something new to sample. Look for savory chicken and dumplings or a hearty squash casserole, fried chicken and sweet peas. Melt-in-your-mouth baked apples and homemade desserts are always popular. The employees love this café as much as the patrons, and many have been with the Cunninghams since the beginning. Some customers have been eating here on a daily basis for years. The café is a pleasant place to dine, with walls enhanced by fabulous paintings for sale by local artists. Make new friends, discover local art and find your favorite meat-and-three combination at the City Café of Brentwood.

330 Franklin Road, Brentwood TN
(615) 373-5555

Flying Horse Restaurant

Ride the trolley from downtown Franklin to Flying Horse Restaurant, where Southern specialties and music promise a relaxing visit with friends. The restaurant is one of an assortment of businesses in The Factory, a renovated factory complex that now holds art galleries, antique stores, eateries and even a farmers' market. The readers of Nashville's *City Scene* voted Flying Horse the number one restaurant in Williamson County in 2006. Wet your

whistle at the inside bar or upstairs at the rooftop Weathervane Lounge, which features live music each weekend. Flying Horse makes a great gathering place for large or small groups; it has an energetic atmosphere and a menu with options to please everyone. For lunch or dinner, try the sweet potato biscuits with ham or the Southern fried chicken and new potato salad. Sunday brunch is a feast of traditional favorites, including homemade baked goods, a smoked salmon platter and an omelette station. Flying Horse offers catering and can be rented for large events. Owners Katie and Gep Nelson will be glad to assist you with your plans. You can find the ambience you need in several large dining rooms and an outdoor patio. Next time you are visiting The Factory, take a break from shopping to enjoy the food and fun at Flying Horse Restaurant.

230 Franklin Road, Franklin TN
(615) 599-1957

H.R.H. Dumplin's of Franklin

H.R.H. Dumplin's is a lunch restaurant that has been a favorite of Franklin patrons for 16 years. Situated in a completely restored building, it's a place where repeat customers come to enjoy an extensive menu. Proprietor Sally G. Poe runs the place with the assistance of her sister, Betty Astleford. What stands out most about the extensive menu is that all items are homemade. The breads and rolls are extremely popular, as are the chicken and apple dumplings. Specialty salads include world-class chicken and tuna salads, a chef's salad, and the Briar Club salad, constructed with diced chicken, mandarin orange segments and other goodies. The sandwiches are all served on homemade bread along with the customer's choice of a garden or pasta salad.

For 50 cents more, customers can opt for a cup of chicken and dumplings or the soup of the day. The restaurant offers a small children's menu and several take-out selections. Among the desserts are the famous apple dumplings, meringue pies and a cake of the day. Beyond the salads, the health-conscious customer can find a healthy daily special and a low-calorie banana split. Visit H.R.H. Dumplin's for abundant lunch choices that taste like they came from mom's kitchen.

428 Main Street, Franklin TN
(615) 791-4651

Steamboat Bill's

When you dive into the tasty Cajun seafood at Steamboat Bill's, across from the Creekwood Marina on Old Hickory Lake, you may find yourself transported to bayou country, with its shrimp, gumbos, frog legs, catfish and fried pickles. Kids enjoy the chicken strips, grilled cheese sandwiches and popcorn shrimp, while everyone likes the friendly family atmosphere, the large portions and great prices. You can recreate the flavors found here with spices and cookware sold at Steamboat Bill's. You'll also find Zydeco music, T-shirts, books and bangles. In 1982, owner Kathi Bonamici left Chicago with her three young daughters and landed in the coastal community of Lake Charles, Louisiana with little money and no acquaintances. She went to work pedaling shrimp on the side of the road and, with brother Billy's help, obtained a shrimp

dock and buying plant. Next, Kathi met and fell in love with fisherman Bill Vidrine. The pair started three Steamboat Bill's in St. Charles, where readers of *Lagniappe Magazine* repeatedly honor the restaurant for the Best Seafood in Southwest Louisiana. The bayou got a lot closer for diners in Tennessee with the 2002 opening of Steamboat Bill's in Hendersonville. When you want a bit of the bayou, head to Steamboat Bill's.

248 Sanders Ferry Road, Hendersonville TN
(615) 264-8103
www.steamboatbills.com

The Hermitage Steak House

Visitors to President Andrew Jackson's mansion can add to the pleasure of their outing with a meal at the Hermitage Steak House, a neighborhood restaurant named after the Jackson home. For owner Ginger Turner and Manager Lisa Hulsey, the frequent visits of folks living in the neighborhood are the most heartening. The 36-year-old restaurant features certified Angus

steaks, a cozy log interior and the longtime service of such employees as Daphne Engles, a waitress at the Hermitage Steak House for 26 years. Recently, the restaurant added a lounge with live music. Steaks come in every cut you can imagine, including porterhouse, New York Strip, filet mignon and rib eye. You can count on portions tailor-made to your needs, thanks to specialized menus for children and seniors. With 40 fresh offerings, the salad bar is worthy of your full attention. The steak house also offers such seafood choices as New Zealand lobster tail and salmon filet. The original building was constructed in the 1960s using logs from old houses and barns. The beams over the salad bar come from a walnut tree on the property of Andrew Jackson's home. For first-rate dining, visit the Hermitage Steak House.

4342 Lebanon Road, Hermitage TN
(615) 872-9535
www.hermitagesteakhouse.com

The Cuckoo's Nest

Hidden on a side street off of West Main in Lebanon is a neat little nook where some folks come to eat three or four times a week. Located in an award-winning renovated cottage is The Cuckoo's Nest. Owners Debbie Harden and Joann Bohannon give Chef Linda Rogers a lot of the credit for the repeat customers. Creativity between Debbie, Joann and Linda has produced many signature dishes at The Cuckoo's Nest. Wonderful homemade bread is baked daily and served with orange honey butter. Sandwiches are served on the fresh bread or flavorful herb wraps. Dishes you won't find anywhere else include a layered strawberry salad and an Asian coleslaw. Linda can do very interesting things with chicken. Try the pineapple pecan chicken salad or the poppy seed chicken for proof. Fresh salads, generous sandwiches, creative entrées and vegetables and sinfully rich desserts all form a tempting menu sure to please everyone. Breakfast offers all your southern favorites, including French toast, pancakes, quiche and omelettes. The Cuckoo's Nest can accommodate private in-house parties for up to 50 people and offers full-service, off-site catering. When in Lebanon, don't fly by The Cuckoo's Nest. Drop in for some helpings of Southern cuisine with original flair.

120 N Greenwood Avenue, Lebanon TN
(615) 444-1398
www.angelfire.com/tn3/thecuckoosnest/
cuckoo.html

Caney Fork Fish Camp—Nashville

Photo by gail f548

Nothing says fresh fish like an old Southern hunting lodge, and Caney Fork Fish Camp in Nashville delivers the promise and the ambience of such a lodge. Catfish and trout are the stars in a lineup of made-from-scratch Southern-style offerings. Fresh fillets and the house cornmeal breading make a fine marriage that slides down real easy, especially when accompanied by slaw, thin-cut fries and golden brown hush puppies. Other regional dishes that promise satisfaction include meat loaf, baby back ribs and burgers, along with chicken and pot roast. Lighter fare includes sandwiches and salads, assuring a menu that will excite everyone. A spacious interior, separated by dividing walls, private dining space and a small cabin for larger parties, provides options for groups from 15 to 280. A lively waterfall cascading into a stocked fish tank amuses guests, along with many game mounts and a restored 1939 Dodge truck. The bar top is covered with more than a thousand fishing ads. In the spirit of the South, the service is as golden as the carefully breaded fish. For Southern tastes, comfort and hospitality, find your way to Caney Fork Fish Camp.

2400 Music Valley Drive, Nashville TN
(615) 724-1200
www.caneyforkfishcamp.com

Jo's Diner

True to its name, Jo's Diner in Nashville offers straightforward, unpretentious dining that will leave you full and satisfied. A life-size statue of a chef greets customers, who, just like in an old-time diner, have the option of taking a seat at the counter or in the dining area. The blue plate specials on this menu of values go by the regional name meat-and-threes. At Jo's that's a choice of roast beef, meatloaf, ham or the daily special with corn bread and three side dishes. Among the Southern comfort foods available as sides are turnip greens, fried okra and pickled beets. Other choices include coleslaw, mashed potatoes and cottage cheese. Local voters have named Jo's Diner best for meat-and-threes for three years in a row. Burgers, sandwiches

and salads round out the menu. The *Tennessean* praised the steak salad for its "big chunks of well-seasoned grilled sirloin on top of plenty of iceberg and romaine lettuce." A diner wouldn't be a diner without generous, tempting desserts, and Jo's delivers with a big, fluffy coconut cake that also earned a rave review, plus pecan pie and chocolate pie with meringue. Joy Gower, the mother of owner Monica Jo Gower, makes all of the desserts from scratch. For home-style food that satisfies, try Jo's Diner.

7040 Highway 70 S, Nashville TN
(615) 662-4700

Jackson's Bar & Bistro

The lighthearted, come-as-you-are atmosphere at Jackson's Bar & Bistro appeals to singles, couples and groups of all ages. Everyone fits in at this neighborhood mainstay. Likewise, everything fits on the impressive menu. You can go in several directions with the pastas, from Asian to Italian to Creole. For panini, you might try the Basque, with homemade tuna salad and cheddar cheese, or the Cuban, made with roast pork, ham, Swiss cheese, chopped pickles and mustard. Standouts among the bistro entrees include the steak frites, an aged sirloin with garlic butter and crisp fries, and coq au vin, a chicken breast simmered in red wine and bacon with mashed potatoes. In addition to lunch and dinner, Jackson's offers a late-night menu and weekend brunch that offers such specialties as twice-dipped French toast and a Monte Cristo sandwich. No visit is complete without sampling the cookie-dough egg roll, a decadent creation

of chocolate-chip dough flash-fried in an egg roll wrapper. The specialty cocktails are another reason for checking out Jackson's. Again, variety rules. Sip a dapper concoction, such as the Kentucky Cocktail with bourbon and pineapple juice, or go coastal with a Nantucket Sunset, shaken and served martini-style with vodka, cranberry juice, sours and Chambord. If you are looking for a place where everything and everyone fits together just right, try Jackson's Bar & Bistro.

1800 21st Avenue S, Nashville TN
(615) 385-9968

Stock-Yard Restaurant

You know a restaurant is serious about inviting you to dinner when it sends complimentary transportation to pick you up at your hotel. Hop aboard the Stock-Yard Restaurant's chauffeured vehicle and join the other passengers en route to dining excellence. Named one of the Top Ten Steakhouses in the United States by the International Restaurant and Hospitality Rating Bureau, the Stock-Yard proudly serves certified Angus Beef and cold water Maine lobster, as well as delectable pork, poultry and pasta dishes. The house specialty, the slow-roasted prime rib, is served blackened, grilled over hickory charcoal or with au jus. Appetizers get you started with a variety of interesting tastes. Try the crab cakes, served on a bed of lobster cognac cream sauce, or the Norwegian-style smoked salmon. The Stock-Yard's wine selection has won many awards, including the Award of Excellence from the *Wine Spectator*. Rooms that once were offices for Nashville's livestock trade industry have, since 1979, made up the restaurant's 17 dining rooms, including one with a stage and dance floor. Enjoy the guitar playing, strolling balladeer who entertains all of the groups that dine there. The restaurant can play host to a variety of functions, large and small. After dinner, relax on your ride back to the hotel and savor your encounter with fine food. For a truly uniquely Nashville experience, consider the Stock-Yard.

901 2nd Avenue N, Nashville TN
(615) 255-6464
www.stock-yardrestaurant.com

Mesquite Chop House

"If all steaks tasted this great, I might be tempted to eat steak every day." That's the conclusion *Commercial Appeal* food critic Leslie Kelly came to after sampling the filet at Mesquite Chop House in Southaven. Kelly also called the restaurant "the Holy Grail of red meat." Mesquite only serves prime, certified Angus beef from the top 12 percent of all cattle farmed in America. Whether it's a delicious rib eye or a Kansas City tenderloin, you can get your steak cooked exactly to your specifications. In addition to the tender steaks, Mesquite Chop House serves bison tenderloin, seafood, chicken and pork dishes. The elegantly decorated dining room features the work of local artists on its walls. The open kitchen provides a great view of how your food is made. Your taste buds get a jumpstart as the aroma of food cooked over mesquite wood wafts in your direction. If it's sweet sounds you're looking for, head to Mesquite's piano bar, which provides jazz on Friday and Saturday nights. The restaurant offers a special VIP program that allows members to enjoy special events such as wine tasting. The restaurant's shuttle can transport members to and from nearby Memphis. If you're looking for the Holy Grail of steak, seafood and fine dining, make the pilgrimage to Mesquite Chop House.

5960 Getwell Road, Southaven MS
(662) 890-CHOP (2467)
www.mesquitechophouse.com

Antique Art Animalia

Owner Lisa Robison's lifelong love of art and antiques blends with her love of animals to create Antique Art Animalia in Nashville. Featured are 19th century dog and equine objects from the world over, but mainly from Great Britain, which is known for its rich history of equine sports. Inventory includes antique oil paintings, drawings and photographs, as well as figures, books, jewelry and just about anything else with a horse, dog or sporting animal theme. Lisa takes pride in offering only authentic, original antique and vintage art and artifacts—no reproductions or modern copies. She welcomes out-of-town visitors who come to Nashville for a variety of horse-related attractions. The shop is conveniently located about 15 minutes from the horse show grounds at Brownland Farms. The Iroquois Steeplechase, the richest amateur steeplechase in the United States, is located about five minutes away at the Warner Equestrian Center. Antique Art Animalia is only two blocks from Belle Meade Plantation, the so-called Cradle of the American Thoroughbred Industry, home to the early foundation sires of modern horse racing. If you are unable to visit the retail location, you can browse the website, which is updated frequently. In addition, Antique Art Animalia is likely to be found at a variety of antique fairs and horse events locally and nationally. If you have an interest in antiques or animals, be sure to visit Antique Art Animalia.

5133 Harding Road, Nashville TN
(615) 356-3313
www.AntiqueArtAnimalia.com

Hastings Entertainment– McMinnville

Hastings Entertainment is a multimedia entertainment retailer committed to supplying its communities with an extensive selection of movies, music, books and games. Hastings settles in smaller cities, including college towns, and provides them with a diverse selection of new and used wares. The store provides all the games, books and movies you could hope to find with options for renting, buying, selling and trading. Hastings offers theme clothing, collectibles, and a range of media-related accessories as well. Hastings was one of the first stores to employ cross-merchandising, a concept boldly carried out by entrepreneur Sam Marmaduke. His vision resulted in an entertainment store that stands apart from the rest, with a high degree of community interaction and an abundance of merchandise. The McMinnville store strives to reflect the interests of the community, and like many other Hastings branches, initiates individualized programs for community involvement. Along with all of this, Hastings Entertainment is fun to visit. Come in and pull up a chair.

Northgate Shopping Center
231 Northgate Drive, Suite 500, McMinnville TN
(931) 473-0990
www.hastings-ent.com

The Livery Stables–Antiques, Gifts & More

The Livery Stables–Antiques, Gifts & More brings back to life a building that has been a part of Pleasant View for more than 140 years. Today, it houses a 4,000-square-foot mall full of antiques and new gifts, making it a great place to shop for everything from furniture and heirlooms to vintage women's clothes and homemade jams. Horses were once boarded and groomed here, and the building was large enough to house the community's first fire engine. Locals come by with tales of this old place on Main Street. They say that Main Street was a lively place on Saturday nights. That's why owners Tommy and Kelly Ellis try to plan something special every Saturday, whether it's live music on the front porch or an historical exhibit. "It is a joy hearing our local people," says Kelly, "and watching them chuckle once more over an experience they had back when." Kelly couldn't manage the antiques mall without the help of her uncle, James Alford, who has been in the antiques business for 30 years. For the place in Pleasant View where shopping meets local history, go to the Livery Stables–Antiques, Gifts & More.

1104 Main Street, Pleasant View TN
(615) 746-8992
www.theliverystables.com

Howard Rawlings Antiques

Go to Howard Rawlings Antiques expecting to find bargains on English imports. Just don't go there expecting to meet a dapper English gentleman named Howard Rawlings. Owners Betty Ann and M.A. (Joe) Henderson combined their mothers' maiden names to come up with the very English-sounding name for their business. Their customers don't appear to be upset over the deception. In fact, most go away ecstatic about the huge inventory, great prices, and friendly customer service provided by Doris, Brenda, Margie, Patty and Chuck. Customer satisfaction is what earned Howard Rawlings the *Busy Bee Trader's* Readers Choice award for the Best Place to Find Bargains in 2004, followed by awards for Best Antique Wholesale Distributor, Most Helpful Staff in 2005 and Best Wholesale Antique Distribution in 2006. The imports arrive at the store in large containers several times a year. Dealers snap up many of the items, but visitors still get to choose from between 200 and 300 armoires, dressers and cabinets at any one time. This is a great place to search for 19th century stained glass and for smaller items such as estate jewelry. The passion for scoring a great deal still burns in Betty Ann, even though she is mostly on the selling end now. When she stumbles across something nice while traveling with her husband, her "blood runs hot," she says, "and if the price is right, then I know I'm going to buy it." To experience the same thrill, drop by Howard Rawlings Antiques, but don't ask for Howard.

13693 Lebanon Road, Mt. Juliet TN
(615) 754-7457
www.rawlingsantiques.com

Hastings Entertainment– Murfreesboro

Murfreesboro is an agreeable blend of the historical and the contemporary. It's the home of a historic battlefield, a wetlands Discovery Center and a celebrated Jazzfest. But when locals and visitors want to find at-home entertainment, they turn to Hastings Entertainment. The philosophy that drives Hastings is based on fun. The atmosphere is lively, but you can still find a place to hibernate with a good book. When you're finished with books and magazines, the store has an impressive selection of unedited music, movies and games. Hastings offers the option to buy, sell, trade or rent, making it easy to expand your collection. Here you can also find storage solutions for your entertainment media. A variety of action figures, t-shirts, board games and miscellaneous accessories make each store a little bit different and also make it possible to assemble theme-related packages for customized gifts. Community involvement is important to Hastings, and it is reflected in store events and a recycled products section in the store. A helpful, friendly staff, massive variety and community conscience are all great reasons to make the Murfreesboro Hastings Entertainment superstore your stop for home entertainment.

1660 Memorial Boulevard, Murfreesboro TN
(615) 904-9755
www.hastings-ent.com

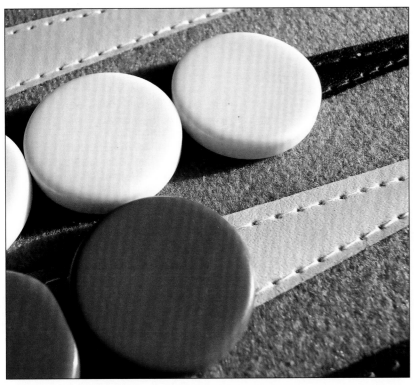

Hastings Entertainment– Clarksville

Clarksville draws a big crowd for its end-of-summer Riverfest, but for regular home entertainment, locals and visitors can always head for Hastings Entertainment. The superstore has a long history of supplying the community with a variety of multimedia entertainment. In a vibrant atmosphere charged by the Fish! Philosophy of fun in the workplace, Hastings offers a full selection of new and used media including movies, music and books and supplemented by board games, t-shirts, action figures, musical instruments and many related products. Hastings offers the option to buy, sell, trade or rent merchandise. The store is an upbeat combination of restful oasis and community gathering place. You can sit down and read a book or congregate with friends and family while you pick out what you need for a marathon movie or game night. Many events take place at Hastings throughout the year, such as book-signings that to allow customers the exciting chance to meet with their favorite authors in a comfortable setting. Shoppers enjoy the amenities of free gourmet coffee and CD listening stations. Hastings Entertainment provides a shopping experience as entertaining as the media products it provides. Go in and have some fun.

1600 Fort Campbell Boulevard, Suite A, Clarksville TN
(931) 906-1003
www.hastings-ent.com

Unique Flower Fashions and Décor

Whether you're looking for high-style floral design or a special accent for your home, Unique Flower Fashions and Décor is the place to come. The shop, located in Nashville's quaint Berry Hill neighborhood, is much more than a flower shop. It's also a treasure trove of antiques, lamps, artwork and gifts. Owner Linda Saunders and her friendly staff can help you beautify your home in many ways and look forward to putting their floral art to work for you. Unique Flower Fashions specializes in parties and banquets, and its award-winning floral designers can transform your special occasions with their know-how. They also create customized silk arrangements for homes and offices and assemble gift baskets filled with fruit and gourmet goodies. The shop offers prompt delivery of flowers, plants and gifts to the Nashville area and surrounding counties and can send flowers worldwide. Teleflora has honored Unique Flower Fashions with its Award of Excellence as one of its top 1,000 florists for more than 20 years. Remember Unique Flower Fashions and Décor for all your floral needs, and be sure to browse through the shop's extensive home décor selection whenever you're in the neighborhood.

2814 Bransford Avenue, Nashville TN
(615) 297-2092 or (800) 321-6691

Secret Garden Kids Consignment

Gallatin locals can't keep quiet about Secret Garden Kids Consignment. When owner Carla Howard lost her best friend Leslie in 2003, she opened the shop the pair had dreamed of owning—a joyful consignment store of children's clothing, toys and furniture. For the last several years Carla has run the business with the kind of thoughtfulness and attention you might expect from a best friend. Carla's customers leave knowing they received a bargain on high quality children's clothes, baby equipment and maternity outfits that will stand the test of time and wear. The store is superbly organized by size, from infant sizes to boys and girls sizes up to 14. The secure built-in play area entertains the little ones and frees up mom's hands to shop. Secret Garden is not your average consignment store—it purchases only the best from sellers and pays them on the spot for their clothing. The shop uses eBay to constantly rotate its inventory, which means customers always find something new. Secret Garden can even personalize some items, such as baby blankets and diaper bags, with embroidery. Remedy your children's boredom with fresh toys to occupy their busy hands. Visit Secret Garden Kid's Consignment. It's the best-known secret in town.

114 W Main Street, Gallatin TN
(615) 206-0027

Cuz's Antique Center

You should forgive Frank Buster when he can't remember where everything in Cuz's Antiques came from. After all, Frank has been at it for over 25 years, and his inventory fills four stores on the town square in Lebanon. The selection here is so vast and interesting that Citysearch named Cuz's among the best antiques stores in Tennessee for eight years in a row. Frank carries large lines of antiques, doors, stained glass and jewelry and a whole building full of wrought iron. Whether you are looking for a single piece of furniture or a complete bedroom or dining room set, you will want to check Cuz's first because of the enormous selection. Frank accumulates most of his antiques from auctions and from other countries, particularly England, Germany and Egypt. When Frank traveled to Germany in 1974, he met with the fellows that would produce his own brand of pocket knife, Fight'n Rooster. He has been producing Fight'n

Rooster pocket knives in Germany ever since; they too can be found inside Cuz's Antiques. Recently, he acquired five pieces from the estate of Johnny and June Carter Cash. Frank remembers and appreciates his store manager, Glenda Williams, who has been with him since the beginning. Another faithful employee is Assistant Manager Sterling Buster, who hopes to continue in the family business for years to come. For an extraordinary shopping adventure, visit Cuz's Antique Center.

140 Public Square, Lebanon TN
(615) 444-8070

Bellevue Antique Mall

At last count, the Bellevue Antique Mall housed 20 dealers under its roof, earning it a place on any antique lover's must-stop list. The business keeps expanding, so that number could change at any minute. Less than 10 years ago, owner Charlotte Evans was dealing antiques from a booth at another mall. Then her do-it-yourself spirit kicked in. "After about three or four months of being a dealer, I thought I could do this," she said. She was right. A retiree from a career in human resources and education, she put her experience to work in opening a 600-square-foot shop with six dealers. The Bellevue Antique Mall has only gotten bigger since then. Today, folks know to check here when they are looking for mahogany, oak or walnut furniture. Visitors also find lovely china, glass vases and porcelain ware. Each booth offers new surprises. Berenice Denton

is always adding items from the estate sales that she organizes from her business next door. No matter what your collecting niche, from books to dolls, Charlotte or the mall's manager, Diane Williams, can direct you to the right spot. The Cottage Cafe, located next door, offers homemade goodies prepared fresh daily for lunch and carry-out. If you love shopping for antiques, visit the Bellevue Antique Mall, where dealers neatly arrange items for your shopping pleasure.

158-160 Belle Forest Circle, Nashville TN
(615) 646-5828
www.berenicedenton.com

Hastings Entertainment–Tullahoma

Hastings Entertainment is an established multimedia entertainment retailer committed to supplying small and medium-sized cities with an extensive selection of movies, music, books and games. The store provides all the media selection you could hope for with options for renting, buying, selling and trading its wares. Hastings offers themed clothing and collectibles as well, making it possible to put together a whole package of related items for a customized gift. A full range of media accessories anticipates all your home and school media requirements. Hastings Entertainment was the first entertainment store of its kind, created to entertain and involve local residents with a diverse selection of cross-merchandising and community events. Hastings stores are configured to provide a comfortable environment for visiting shoppers. Each one is a little different. The Tullahoma store strives to reflect the interests of the community with programs and involvement. Take some time to get to know Hastings Entertainment in your town.

1905 Jackson Street, Tullahoma TN
(931) 455-4452
www.hastings-ent.com

Renaissance Gifts and Interiors

Norma Jones and Jennie Justice, the mother-daughter team behind Renaissance Gifts and Interiors, opened their store with a vision of making it the premier gift shop in the Robertson County area. That was in 2001. Since then, this business in the quaint New Orleans-style Memorial Plaza Shopping Center has earned a solid reputation for supplying customers with special gifts for their friends and family, suitable for all sorts of occasions. Norma, Jennie and their staff especially enjoy assisting brides and expectant mothers in selecting gifts that will help make their special occasions unforgettable. Distinctive gifts in every price range include china, crystal and flatware. Renaissance also carries jewelry as well as decorative accessories for the home, including original oil paintings by local artists. As part of its exceptional customer service, Renaissance offers bridal registry, baby registry and beautiful gift wrapping. Customers eagerly anticipate the Christmas open house, one of several special events that Renaissance hosts throughout the year. Judge for yourself how well Norma and Jennie have succeeded in realizing their vision. For blissful gift shopping, go to Renaissance Gifts and Interiors.

513 Memorial Boulevard, Springfield TN
(615) 382-4615
www.renaissance-gifts.com

Always in Bloom

Margie Dobler's dream blossomed into reality over a decade ago when she opened her floral shop, Always in Bloom, in historic Franklin. Always in Bloom offers fresh flowers and plants for any occasion, including special events and weddings, and gladly creates custom, permanent arrangements. Margie is a Tennessee-certified florist and has served as the president of the Tennessee State Florist Association. In addition to favorable reviews in magazines, Margie has received numerous awards, including the 2001 Tennessee State Florist of the Year award. Always in Bloom can also be found in the floral gallery at the Nashville Lawn and Garden Show, an annual, by-invitation-only event. It is a family business, employing Margie's son, Michael, and co-owned by Scott Dobler. You can order online, request delivery or visit Always in Bloom in person and let the staff take care of your floral and plant needs. When you want blooms that speak your sentiments for you, come to Always in Bloom for an original arrangement of live plants, cut flowers or silks based on your preferences.

306 5th Avenue N, Franklin TN
(615) 591-7990
www.alwaysinbloominc.com

Signature Transportation Services

Signature Transportation Services sets the standard for reliable, luxurious ground transportation. Owners Michael Dozier and Matthew Yorke maintain the largest fleet in Tennessee and have more than 15 years combined experience in the limousine business. Their clientele includes corporations, entertainers and private consumers, and their mission is to provide every client with a one-of-a-kind experience. Courteous reservationists can accommodate any special needs, or clients can make online reservations 24 hours a day through the company's award-winning website. Signature uses the

most advanced technologies available to the ground transportation industry, from real-time airline flight tracking to GPS vehicle dispatching and tracking. Their impeccably maintained late-model fleet offers a vehicle size for every need and includes Lincoln Town Cars, stretch limousines, SUVs and minibuses. Highly trained professional chauffeurs ensure prompt arrival at your destination and can describe the attractions in the Nashville area. From weddings and anniversaries to proms and nights out, they can enhance any occasion. Corporate clients will appreciate employee shuttle service and airport rides, and Signature can arrange complete transportation coordination for major corporate events. For service that consistently exceeds expectations, rely on Signature Transportation Services for all your luxury transportation needs.

1306 Antioch Pike, Nashville TN
(615) 244-LIMO (5466) or (877) 255-0033
www.NashvilleLimo.com

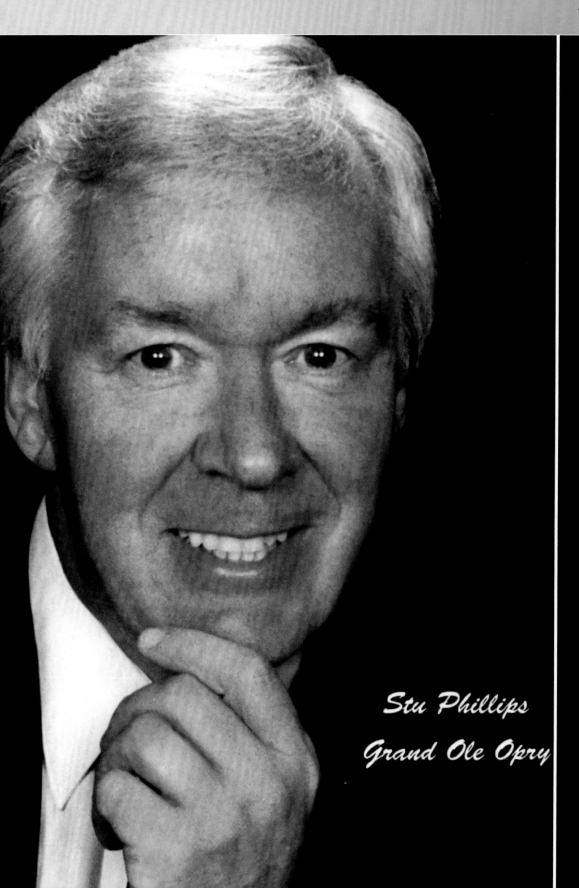

Stu Phillips
Grand Ole Opry

Long Hollow Winery

Music and wine are woven together to spell entertainment at Long Hollow Winery in Goodlettsville. Long Hollow is owned by Grand Ole Opry star Stu Phillips. Aided by his wife, Aldona, and by Joel, his vintner son, Stu has created an original Tennessee attraction in his winery with events, performances and a fun, personalized tour available by appointment. In true celebratory style, free tastings let you sample the superb wines, jellies and cheeses sold at the winery. A gift shop is next to the tasting room. Long Hollow wines run the gamut from dry to sweet and everything in-between. The favored, semi-sweet red Plantation label wine is made from an authentic west Tennessee plantation recipe, handed down to Phillips by a sharecropper many years ago. The South is immortalized in Long Hollow's ever-popular Blackberry dessert wine and the zesty-sweet Scarlet, an ode to the mistress of Tara in *Gone With The Wind*. A good choice for a dry red table wine is the mysterious Shackle Island, a French hybrid blend. The Chardonnay benefits from precise oak aging. This commendable dry wine is versatile and can be enjoyed with virtually everything. The winery is housed in a modern reproduction of a monastery that Stu visited as a boy and is only minutes north of Nashville. Take a detour to Goodlettsville and meet the star of the show at Long Hollow Winery.

665 Long Hollow Pike,
Goodlettsville TN
(615) 859-5559
www.longhollowwinery.com

Tootsie's Orchid Lounge

When Tootsie Bess opened Tootsie's Orchid Lounge in 1960, she made it a place people could come to have the time of their lives listening to favorites such as Willie Nelson, who got his first songwriting job after singing here. The lounge drew in customers such as Patsy Cline, Mel Tillis and Waylon Jennings. It's been popular over the years with other greats such as Roger Miller, Kris Kristofferson and Faron Young. With continuous live entertainment from 10 am to 2:30 am daily, Tootsie's continues to be one of Nashville's hot spots for both artists and tourists. Photos and memorabilia line the Wall of Fame, reminding the visitor of the musical triumphs that transpired within these walls. In 2002, Tootsie's launched Tootsie's Records to promote emerging artists. Two hundred artists with dreams of breaking into the recording business play at Tootsie's each week, which gives Tootsie's a splendid opportunity to discover new talent. In 2003, the lounge discovered a major talent in John Stone, who came through the door and tipped the band $10 for an opportunity to sing. John is a world-class musician, up-and-coming singer and songwriter and a knockout performer with a great future. He's on the Tootsie's label. Tootsie's is available for private parties. For hot new performers, good food and good times, stop by Tootsie's Orchid Lounge.

422 Broadway, Nashville TN
(615) 726-0463
www.tootsies.net

The Lipstick Lounge

Bringing people from different cultures, backgrounds and races together for the common goal of enjoying good times and good drinks is what the Lipstick Lounge in Nashville is all about. Owners Jonda Valentine and Christa Suppan are both committed to creating an enjoyable setting. The lounge is known for great entertainment and some of the best karaoke anywhere. Christa acts as general manager and bartender with a knack for knowing what everyone drinks. Jonda is much loved by customers for being funny, outspoken and willing to lend an ear. This popular hangout has something going every night. Look for Texas Hold 'Em Poker, trivia contests and dancing. The Lipstick Lounge is consistently recognized as a favorite by the readers of area magazines and newspapers. In 2003, it was the Girls Night Out winner at Nashville Citysearch. It's also been recognized for Best Karaoke in 2004 and Best Neighborhood Bar in 2005. The Lipstick Lounge is notable for its eclectic décor and subtle lighting, which draws the attention of many artists and photographers. *Playboy* has shot pictorials here, and country singer Pam Tillis shot her 2003 video, *So Wrong*, in this Nashville hot spot. Since 2002, the word is out that the girls who own the Lipstick Lounge have created an atmosphere that appeals to a broad cross-section of people. Get to know a whole new group of friends with a visit to the Lipstick Lounge.

1400 Woodland Street, Nashville TN
(615) 226-6343
www.thelipsticklounge.com

Station Inn

Tucked away on a nondescript block of downtown Nashville is the Station Inn, a club that bluegrass fans adore for its four-decade commitment to championing American roots music. A group of bluegrass pickers founded this venerable 200-seat venue in 1974, and for years they served as the house band, while welcoming other players to sit in and jam. When current owner J. T. Gray took over in 1981, he tried something new. Peter Rowan, well-known among bluegrass enthusiasts, moved to Nashville and started playing at the Station Inn on a regular basis. Rowan always brought along friends, who just happened to be some of the most respected names in bluegrass, folks like Bela Fleck, Sam Bush and Vassar Clements. The White family moved to town around that same time, and they, too, began appearing regularly at the Station Inn. The nature of the club had evolved from a place to jam to a place that hosts name performers from the world of bluegrass, acoustic and roots music. Today, seven nights a week fans from as far away as Russia, Australia and Sweden settle in with the locals for a delightful evening of music and performances by the best local and national luminaries of bluegrass, acoustic and roots music. If you love bluegrass, you can't leave Nashville without visiting the Station Inn.

402 12th Avenue S, Nashville TN (615) 255-3307

Long Hollow Jamboree

When you walk into Long Hollow Jamboree, you are immediately struck by the sense of history and the feeling that everyone here is like family. Since 1971, crowds have packed into this little nightspot to hear local musicians and more famous visitors, such as Bill Monroe, Earl Scruggs and Kitty Wells, perform traditional country music. Longtime customers go back to the opening days of Long Hollow Jamboree, so you are likely to see quite an age range when you're here. People travel here from all over the middle Tennessee hills of Sumner County to soak up the atmosphere and enjoy what some have called a small-scale Grand Ole Opry. Beyond music, this smoke and alcohol-free establishment features Southern meals, including barbecue options or catfish with all the fixin's. Eugene and Beverly Hardison opened Long Hollow Jamboree over three decades ago and it remains very much a family affair, with son Wally and daughter Sara serving in management positions. You can rest assured it will be part of the fabric of this area for years to come. Take a step back to a simpler time and enjoy a family atmosphere with great food, wonderful live music and a chance to join in the singing at Long Hollow Jamboree.

3600 Long Hollow Pike, Goodlettsville TN   (615) 824-4445

12th and Porter

For live music six nights a week and some of the best food you'll find anywhere, round up your friends and head for 12th and Porter. One of Nashville's top label showcase venues, 12th and Porter focuses on helping up-and-coming bands get record deals. Readers of the *Nashville Scene* recently voted 12th and Porter as second only to the historic Ryman Auditorium as Nashville's best place to hear live music. The main room holds 250 people and features state-of-the-art sound and lighting, and owners Jennifer Lee and Paula Willigar have developed the dining room into a loungy setting for acoustic music. The club features wonderful specialty drinks and a list of well-chosen wines. As an alternative, pick a Pomegranatini or a Wildberry Cosmo from the imaginative martini menu. Hungry? Try the ever-popular Pasta Ya-Ya, chicken and andouille in a spicy cream sauce over noodles, or sink your teeth into a fantastic pizza or burger. The club features two to five bands every night. Guests have included Velvet Revolver, Big'n'Rich and 3doorsdown. On one recent evening, the audience was surprised by a 45-minute solo set by Neil Young. You'll find every genre of music, from country and rock to alternative and R&B. Every evening is a special occasion at 12th and Porter, so grab your friends and head for one of the best live music hot spots in Music City.

114 12th Avenue N, Nashville TN
(615) 254-7250
www.12thandporter.net

Douglas Corner Café

Douglas Corner Café is to songwriters and aspiring musical artists what the world-famous Improv Club is to comedians. It all started in 1987, when owners Mervin Louque and Rick Martin decided to create a Nashville venue for showcasing new talent. Since its humble beginnings, Douglas Corner has grown into a well-established home-away-from-home for some of America's best-known music stars. When Trisha Yearwood needed a place to debut her new CD, *Everybody Knows,* she chose Douglas Corner Café as the place to do it. She was told she could hold the event anywhere and "I immediately said Douglas Corner," says Yearwood, whose producer, Garth Fundis, first heard Yearwood sing there. Douglas Corner is also where Garth Brooks chose to host his first fan club party. In 1989, MCA Records discovered Mark Collie at Douglas Corner and signed him up with an old-fashioned handshake agreement. The success stories of many musical careers have their beginnings in this place, where writers and performers still come together with the shared goal of creating and listening to great music. Visit the Douglas Corner Café to see current and future superstars take to the stage.

2106-A 8th Avenue S, Nashville TN
(615) 298-1688
www.douglascorner.com

Chateau Ross Winery

Don't let the awards that Chateau Ross Winery has won deceive you into thinking that this is a massive operation consuming hundreds of acres with an army of workers on staff. Chateau Ross is the only Tennessee winery to win the William O. Beach award three times for excellence in Tennessee wines, yet it is really just a two-person business. Ross and Deborah Proctor hand-cork and hand-label every bottle in their small boutique winery, which specializes in California and Italian-style wines. That means the focus is on reds, including the Big Bitch Red, which is the best seller. The name for this robust wine honors the Proctors' other love—dogs. If you are greeted by one or more large yet friendly canines as you pull into the driveway, you will know that you are in the right place. You must make an appointment before visiting Chateau Ross, because you will be entering the Proctor home as well as wine headquarters. The genius behind the wine, Ross, personally escorts guests through the barrel-lined tasting room in the basement. For a lesson in why smaller is better when it comes to wine, spend some time at Chateau Ross Winery.

5823 Fulton Road, Springfield TN
(615) 654-WINE (9463)
www.chateauross.com

George Dickel Distillery

Halfway between Nashville and Chattanooga, you'll find a genuine piece of Tennessee history. Since 1870, the George Dickel Distillery has handcrafted what may be Tennessee's smoothest whisky. Fresh, clear water from the Cascade Springs provides the main ingredient in every bottle of spirits. The recipe used today is the same one George Dickel used way back when. According to Master Distiller John Lunn, today the whiskey is chilled before it goes into the charcoal mellowing vats, inspired by George's custom of making the whiskey during winter months when the weather is colder. This process gives the whisky a very smooth, mellow taste. Time-honored traditions continue to serve the distillery well. In 2006, George Dickel Distillery won two gold medals at the tastings.com competition of the Beverage Tasting Institute. This was the first award for George Dickel Barrel Select and the fifth consecutive gold medal for George Dickel No.12. The distillery's Visitor's Center brings history to life with antiques, photos and memorabilia. Stop by the General Store for fleece pullovers, denim button-down shirts and umbrellas, all bearing the distillery logo. Drop a line to family and friends at the country's only working post office in a distillery. Take a tour of the George Dickel Distillery, where past and present blend together to create a delightful stopover.

1950 Cascade Hollow, Tullahoma TN
(931) 857-3124
www.georgedickel.com

Beans Creek Winery

"It began as a dream, no larger than a grape," muses winemaker Tom Brown, who made his first batch of wine about 30 years ago in his mother's pickle crock. These days, he pinches himself to make sure it's all real when he brings home medals for the grape and berry wines from his Beans Creek Winery. Friends and loyal local customers were already convinced that he turned out a highly drinkable product, but it wasn't until his wines wowed the judges at the Wines of the South Competition in 2005 that Tom knew that Beans Creek Winery had arrived. Going up against wine-making giants that have been pleasing the palates of discriminating wine lovers for years, Beans Creek won nine medals in all, including the gold for its blackberry wine and its Chambourcin Red. The winery had celebrated its first anniversary just a few weeks before the competition. Needless to say, there were big smiles and high fives in the tasting room for many days afterwards. You'll feel the joy still lingering when you drop by to sample the Chardonel Reserve, the Syrah or any of the delicious berry wines. Tom credits his friends and the eight other families involved (seven of which grow grapes for the winery) with the inspiration and encouragement that made this winery a success. Come and join the fun times in the tasting room at Beans Creek Winery.

426 Ragsdale Road, Manchester TN
(931) 723-2294
www.beanscreekwinery.com

The Legendary Exit/In

The legendary Exit/In is one of Nashville's premier live music venues. On the scene since 1971, the story of the Exit/In is a story about space, the people who helped to create it, the people who have performed in it and the people who have experienced it. Jimmy Buffet, fresh out of college, was one of the club's first acts. Other monumental performers followed, including Police, REM, Hank Williams, Jr., John Hiatt, Billy Joel, Linda Ronstadt, Steve Martin and Johnny Cash. On the Exit/In wall is a list of performers who have graced this stage. The old vibes from the Exit/In's start in the hippie era still echo, and an accumulation of images and mementos remind the visitor of the many magical nights and the sounds of legendary musicians. People remember the nights they spent at the Exit/In. The Exit/In has had many owners and many owners have gone down, but current owner Rick Whetsel has the business savvy the club needs. The place has outlasted many formidable contenders and as the oldest rock club in Nashville still brings in upcoming national talent. The famous rear door entrance gives the club its memorable name. Make your own vivid memory with a visit to the Exit/In.

2208 Elliston Place, Nashville TN
(615) 321-3340
www.exitin.com

The Mercy Lounge

A premier rock and roll venue in Nashville, the Mercy Lounge offers outstanding musical entertainment with different bands every night. The upscale yet comfortable bar offers pool tables and classic pinball machines. You can munch on casual eats such as sandwiches and wraps. The Lounge, on the second level of the historic Cannery Building, has a standing-room capacity of 500 and also features a luxury hospitality suite. The Cannery Ballroom, which occupies the ground floor of the building, boasts a standing room capacity of more than 1,000. Recently renovated, the ballroom features hardwood floors, large tiled bathrooms and one of the longest fully stocked bars in Tennessee. Like the Lounge, the Cannery Ballroom presents live acts, but it is also available for special events such as weddings, corporate events and private parties. The Cannery Building was built in 1883 as a flour mill. It acquired its modern name much later when the Dale Food Company began processing food at the site in 1957. The building became one of Nashville's prime music venues in the 1980s and 1990s, hosting acts such as Lenny Kravitz, Greg Allman and Iggy Pop. Today, the renovated Cannery Ballroom and Mercy Lounge, owned by Todd Ohlhauser and Clark Kinsolving, are the places to go in Nashville. Come enjoy the warm, inviting vibe.

1 Cannery Row, Nashville TN
(615) 251-3020
www.mercylounge.com

The Gateway to the Smokies—Gatlinburg, TN

East Tennessee

The Chattanoogan Hotel and Conference Center

Native cherry wood sets the tone for the contemporary luxury that is yours to bask in at the Chattanoogan, an upscale urban hotel and conference center. Views of downtown Chattanooga and picturesque Lookout Mountain are yours to enjoy from your room or suite. The Foundry, the hotel's bistro and lounge, serves up live jazz on the weekends to complement its menu of appetizers, salads and light entrées. The open kitchen at the cosmopolitan Broad Street Grille allows guests to watch as their Pan Roasted Salmon Roulade, House Made Duck Prosciutto Bucatini or other culinary delight is created before their eyes. Pop a complimentary bottle of champagne at the start of your Girls Just Want to Have Fun Getaway, just one of the hotel's packages that combine lodging with services at the Chattanoogan Spa. Museums, shopping and entertainment are within walking distance of the hotel lobby. When you aren't sightseeing, you'll enjoy wandering the park-like courtyard of the hotel, an urban forest of shrubs, flowers and nine varieties of trees. The 25,000 square-foot conference center accommodates up to 500 with the latest in audio and video technology. Clients have access to the newly expanded Chattanooga Convention Center and a Conference Planning Manager who helps you plan your conference from A to Z. Experience the cosmopolitan soul of Chattanooga at the Chattanoogan Hotel and Conference Center.

1201 Broad Street, Chattanooga TN
(423) 756-3400
www.chattanooganhotel.com

Vacation Rentals–Chattanooga

You will need several days at least to see Chattanooga properly, and you will need the team of Paula and Paula to find you a cabin, cottage or house that you can call headquarters during your stay. Since 1993, Paula has been fixing folks up in her hometown with Vacation Rentals–Chattanooga. Check her website to see some of the best vacation rentals in town. She points out that Chattanooga is second only to Orlando for family vacations in the United States. Whether you're in town to visit the Civil War museums and historical sites or to enjoy outdoor attractions such as Lookout Mountain and Ruby Falls, Paula has accommodations to suit your dream vacation. Do you fancy a comfortable luxury home on a quiet city block? Views of the Smoky Mountains? A romantic cabin on the river? Paula grew up in Chattanooga and knows everything it has to offer. Her small, family-run business offers the kind of personal service you won't find with big rental agencies. Give Vacation Rentals–Chattanooga a call to find your perfect vacation home.

Chattanooga TN (423) 886-6130
www.vacationrentalschattanooga.com

Creekwalk Inn at Whisperwood Farm

Located on 47 stream-bordered acres of green Smoky Mountain paradise, Creekwalk Inn at Whisperwood Farm is an ideal place for those looking to get away from it all without straying too far from some of Tennessee and North Carolina's biggest attractions. Owners Janice and Tifton Haynes have a deep appreciation for log cabin living. Janice grew up in Hemlock Lodge, which was handcrafted by her grandfather. One visit to this rustic bed and breakfast inn and you'll fall in love with it, too. It offers seven bedrooms, each with its own charm and private bath. Whether it is the cozy greens and reds of the Hannah Mountain room or the bright wood panel and gingham look of the Little Cataloochee room, you'll find the perfect place to rest. Many of the rooms have fireplaces, hot tubs or whirlpool baths. The Whisperwood Cabin was finished in 2006 offers two additional bedrooms (one is up a ladder in the loft). The inn is located on Whisperwood Horse Farm just a few miles from the Great Smoky Mountains National Park. It is ideal for hikers or horse lovers wanting to meet the resident horses, Dreamcatcher, Blaze, Tura, Sapphire, Buster and Spirit of the Smokies. Dining on one of the porches or by an open campfire make this a nostalgic place to visit. Tifton designed rustic pews for the chapel and built them on the farm with his master builder, Isaac. Groups can reserve the entire grounds for a wedding celebration or family reunion with Chefs Janice, Tifton and the family barbecuing split Cornish game hens on the seasoned black smoker. Three-course breakfasts and four-course dinners are also enjoyed by visitors. Cosby is just 19 miles from Gatlinburg, a pleasant excursion if the hammocks and library don't snare you into just staying put on the farm.

166 Middle Creek Road, Cosby TN
(423) 487-4000
www.creekwalkinn.com
www.appalachianweddingadventures.com

Oak Haven Resort

Nestled in the foothills of the Great Smoky Mountains, Oak Haven Resort offers guests all of the charm and beauty of a mountain setting along with luxurious log cabin accommodations. The Sevierville resort, which opened in 1996, features 100 acres and 90 new cabins. Those looking to commune with nature will appreciate the wild turkeys, deer, hawks and bald eagles that live in this lush countryside. The cabins combine rustic charm with modern amenities. Whether you are looking for a cozy one-bedroom cabin or a spacious seven-bedroom dwelling, you'll delight in such features as a large hot tub, jetted tub in the master suite, king-size beds, a gas grill and a large fireplace, as well as cable television, private laundry facilities and a well-equipped kitchen. Many of the cabins contain game rooms with pool tables, foosball, ping pong tables and arcade games. Each cabin sports a big old-fashioned porch with rockers and swings for enjoying the sunset over the hills. Those looking to keep a high-tech eye on the outside world will appreciate the free high-speed wireless Internet access. For still more relaxation, plan a visit to The Spa at Oak Haven, which offers massage therapy, facials, manicures, pedicures and luxurious body treatments. The resort is well-placed for visiting many area attractions, including the Dollywood theme park, several golf courses, and shopping, dining and entertainment venues. For all the charm of the mountains and all the conveniences of town, plan a getaway to Oak Haven Resort.

1947 Old Knoxville Highway, Sevierville TN
(800) 652-2611
www.oakhavenresort.com

Monteagle Inn

Monteagle Inn has become a preferred destination for guests who want to escape the busy world to relax and rejuvenate in peaceful surroundings. The inn's gracious staff members make guests feel at home—yet free from the responsibilities that would follow if they actually were in their own homes. A special retreat for couples and families, the inn has several areas where guests can enjoy quality time together. Monteagle Inn is a Select Registry member and has been featured in many regional magazines and newspapers. These publications have extolled the inn's romantic atmosphere, impeccably kept rooms and the beautiful gardens that supply the herbs, vegetables and flowers for the inn's mountain gourmet meals. The inn's Tuscan atmosphere is an ideal setting for the art and antiques that complement the comfortable yet casual furnishings. Hosting retreats for businesses and non-profit organizations is a specialty of the inn. Its location atop the beautiful Cumberland Plateau provides guests with the opportunity to enjoy hiking, waterfalls, mountain vistas, artist's studios, antique shops and fine dining, as well as visits to the University of the South in nearby Sewanee. At the end of the day, guests can enjoy a glass of wine on a private balcony, or on the patio, garden gazebo or the spacious front porch as they fall under the spell of one of North America's top country inns.

**204 W Main Street, Monteagle TN
(888) 480-3245**
www.monteagleinn.com

Carnegie Hotel

The crown jewel of east Tennessee, the Carnegie Hotel is a grand, 19th century-style, full-service hotel. The rooms are sublime, warmly inviting and tastefully appointed. Among the standard amenities are a 32-inch color television, double granite vanities and a full-size desk with ergonomic chair, to name just a few. Larger suites have one and a half baths and a fireplace as well. The hotel's five-star restaurant, Wellington's, has been featured in the *Wine Spectator* due to its superior wine list as well as the cuisine. Wellington's menu features contemporary fusion cuisine—for example, sugar-seared Atlantic salmon accompanied by a spicy Moroccan chutney. The Appalachian rack of lamb was featured in *Southern Living*. From appetizers to desserts, dining at Wellington's is an exquisite culinary experience. The hotel's Austin Springs Spa offers services for both men and women. The mission of the spa's staff is to make you beautiful, relaxed and rejuvenated as never before. Energizing body wraps, relaxing massages, soothing aromatherapy, revitalizing facials and exceptional salon services elegantly meet this goal. The hotel offers magnificent wedding facilities as well as a fitness center and large European-style pool. Whether you're traveling for business or pleasure, the Carnegie Hotel assures your stay will be an enchanting, luxurious and memorable experience.

1216 W State of Franklin Road, Johnson City TN
(866) 757-8277
www.carnegiehotel.com

Hidden Mountain Resort

More than 25 years ago, in 1981, Butch and Brenda Smith found a way to share their love of the mountains of East Tennessee with friends from around the world. In time for the nearby 1982 World's Fair, and relying on their faith, they opened Hidden Mountain Resort with just seven small cabins in the magical Smoky Mountains. Butch and Brenda feel that the resort is a testimony to God's faithfulness and love, because Hidden Mountain Resort now offers nearly 300 cabins, cottages and villas. With homes ranging from cozy one-bedroom romantic getaways to a stunning 14-bedroom lodge on the river, the serenity of both Hidden Mountain locations provides the perfect setting to inspire new marriages, strengthen family ties and create memories with your loved ones. Enjoy strolling along the paths or picnicking in one of the pavilions. Take pleasure in the view from a front porch swing or meet in the spacious conference lodge. Swim in one of the pools or just relax in the beautifully appointed cabins. Each home is constructed of the finest materials and decorated with an individual theme, ensuring an unforgettable vacation. If, like so many Hidden Mountain visitors, you decide you want a place of your own here, speak to the Smiths about real estate opportunities. Visit Hidden Mountain Resort to experience the quiet beauty of the Smoky Mountains and the Smith family's labor of love.

475 Apple Valley Road, Sevierville TN
(800) 541-6837
www.hiddenmountain.com

Carr's Northside Cottages & Motel

You'll find Carr's Northside Cottages & Motel at a place where scenic mountain views meet sheer tranquility. A quaint hideaway, Carr's is tucked away on eight acres of beautiful mountain landscape. When you first arrive, you'll instantly feel like you've returned to a time before cell phones and skyscrapers. Founded in the early 1940s by Leamer and Lucille Carr, the property is still in the family 65 years later. Now owned and operated by the couple's grandchildren, Carr's lives up to its original commitment to provide guests with comfortable, quiet lodging. Enjoy the privacy and peacefulness of the area by relaxing near the picturesque creek running through the property. If you're in the mood for a gourmet meal or just some window-shopping, downtown Gatlinburg is only a short walk away. Carr's offers a variety of accommodation options at very reasonable rates. Cottages, motel rooms and townhouses are ideal choices for your next family vacation or weekend retreat. The hilltop chalets are perfect for a more romantic getaway, and the Jacuzzi rooms appeal to those in need of some serious rest and relaxation. When planning your next escape, book your lodging at Carr's Northside Cottages & Motel and experience serenity at a whole new level.

421 Laurel Road W, Gatlinburg TN
(865) 436-4836
www.carrscottages.com

Valley View Lodge & Little River Lodge

In the shadow of the Smoky Mountains, the Valley View Lodge makes its home on 15 lush acres. Little River Lodge is across the street. The property sprawls along the border of the Great Smoky Mountains National Park, and only the chatter of squirrels and the trill of songbirds interrupts the solitude. Walking trails and gardens encourage visitors to explore the grounds, while a quarter-acre professionally designed play village caters to children. The Valley View is pet friendly. Guests enjoy two outdoor pools plus an indoor pool enhanced by waterfalls and Jacuzzis. Every room comes with a private balcony or terrace that provides dazzling mountain or river views. Some rooms have wood-burning fireplaces and some have in-room Jacuzzis. All have WiFi, refrigerators, microwaves and other appliances. The Lodge's convention center can accommodate 400. Affianced couples will appreciate the on-site wedding chapel. Guests who want to stay on the Little River can wander across the street to the Little River Lodge. This lodge's cheerful country-style rooms have full kitchens, king-sized beds and porches with rockers to while away the quiet parts of the day. Picnic tables and a fire pit entice guests outside, where the river is easily accessible for trout fishing, tubing and swimming. Come to Valley View & Little River Lodge, where nature is blended with all the comforts of home.

7726 E Lamar Alexander Parkway, Townsend TN (865) 448-2237 or (800) 292-4844
www.valleyviewlodge.com

Apple Valley Country Stores

Apple Valley Country Stores is one family's way of sharing with visitors the pleasures of a simpler era. In a region known as the Peaceful Side of the Smokies, the Maples family broke ground in 1992 for the first in what would become a small village of log shops. The original shop had a country store atmosphere and a smattering of old-fashioned foods and gifts. You could sample fried pies, fresh apple pies, apple dumplings with ice cream or hot cider and take home gourmet coffee, ham, jams and jellies, as well as quilts, candles and bath products. Two years later, Kevin and Jennifer Maples added a second log building to house the Apple Valley Café. The additional space allowed them to branch out into specialty soups and sandwiches, along with daily lunch specials and boxed picnic lunches for the many tourists who stop by on their way to Great Smoky Mountain National Park and Cades Cove. As the Maples found themselves requiring still more room for quilts and other home decorations, they built the third log shop for home décor. The shop, called Country Elegance, houses log furniture, local artwork and specialty items from such well-known lines as Heritage Lace and Homestead Lamps. Beyond bed quilts, the store carries quilted accessories, including luggage and purses. For an introduction to the charms of historic Townsend, plan to stop at Apple Valley Country Stores

Deerfield Resort

Deerfield Resort is an exclusive lakefront vacation paradise nestled between the Cumberland Mountains and the foothills of the Great Smokies. Located north of Knoxville, this resort has been attracting vacationers since the early 1980s. A gated community offers residential homes and condos in addition to nearly 100 vacation rental units that are exquisitely decorated and outfitted with modern amenities. Rent six nights and your seventh night is free. Golfers will appreciate the championship 6,800-yard golf course designed by Golf Pro Bobby Clampett, along with a golf shop for supplies and the Greens Grill for nourishment. Aviators will delight in the resort's 3,200-foot private airstrip and the home-sites that allow them to park right outside. The resort is located on a 1,000 acre peninsula on sparkling Norris Lake, a lake that is well known for fishing, skiing, boating and its crystal clear deep waters. Norris Lake is the largest and cleanest Tennessee Valley Authority Lake. Deerfield has four marinas as well as private docks. The resort is conveniently located near several Tennessee landmarks, including Cumberland Gap and the American Museum of Science and Energy. From restaurants and tennis courts to children's playgrounds, Deerfield Resort offers something for everyone. Whether you are looking for a permanent or second home or want to experience a luxurious vacation, make a reservation at Deerfield Resort.

1235 Deerfield Way, LaFollette TN

(423) 566-0348 or (800) 458-8455
www.deerfieldresort.com

Christopher Place Resort

Sometimes life demands a wake-up call, and sometimes you need to indulge in a schedule of your own making, with nothing more pressing than a swim in the pool and the company of a loved one. Christopher Place Resort was made for honeymooners and romantics. Rooms and suites offer terry robes and CD players; some feature fireplaces or whirlpools. You can choose between views of the Smoky Mountains or of a ridge that's part of the 200-acre private woodland. You can swim, play tennis, enjoy the exercise room or take a hike. For some, the pleasure of sitting in a rocking chair under the colonnaded veranda and taking in the panoramic view is enough activity for one morning or evening. Others choose to relax by the fire reading a best-

seller from the resort's library. If you opt for exploring your surroundings, you'll find Great Smoky Mountain National Park nearby, as well as Gatlinburg, Sevierville and Pigeon Forge. The resort, rated four diamonds by AAA, follows the bed-and-breakfast tradition with a complimentary full gourmet breakfast, then expands on the tradition with the option of a four-course candlelight dinner. For a setting that fosters romance, visit Christopher Place Resort.

1500 Pinnacles Way, Newport TN
(423) 623-6555 or (800) 595-9441
www.christopherplace.com

Blue Mountain Mist Country Inn

Sarah and Norman Ball built the Blue Mountain Mist Country Inn on land deeply rooted in family history. Their ancestors have inhabited this part of the Smoky Mountains since the 1700s. Many special family heirlooms are used in the décor of their inn. Entering Blue Mountain Mist is taking a step back to quieter and simpler pleasures. With plenty of spacious common areas for guests to enjoy, there is still a coziness which inspires total relaxation. Each of the 12 guest rooms in the main house are individually decorated with private baths, luxury amenities and some with Jacuzzis. For even more privacy and romance, five cottages sit in a wooded area not far from the inn. The big Tennessee breakfasts are served in the lace-adorned dining room, which looks out over the valleys, layered hills and mountains. In the evening, delicious

homemade desserts and beverages are waiting for you to enjoy by the fire or on the big wrap-around porch. For 20 years, the Balls have shared their love and appreciation of the Smokies with their guests. Norman and Sarah, along with sons Eric and Jason, invite you to soak up the peacefulness of the Smoky Mountains and let the luxury of the Blue Mountain Mist Country Inn create memories of beautiful moments which will remain with you for many years to come.

1811 Pullen Road, Sevierville TN
(865) 428-2335 or (800) 497-2335
www.bluemountainmist.com

New Hope Bed and Breakfast

Set amidst the foothills of the Blue Ridge Mountains, the New Hope Bed and Breakfast offers the comforts of home, the privacy of an inn and the amenities of a quality hotel. Built in 1891 and restored in 1995, this 3,800-square-foot, two-story Victorian is typical of the period architecture. You'll observe expansive ceilings, transom doors, a wrap-around porch and hardwood floors. Filled with antiques and aesthetic décor, this home offers you the best in bed-and-breakfast charm and hospitality. Innkeeper Joan Bentley entertains with ease and has created a family and small-pet-friendly atmosphere that draws visitors from around the world. The four guest rooms are named in honor of former owners and each has its own personality. All have private baths. The Andes Room is romantic with a gas log fireplace and a two-person Jacuzzi tub. The English-style Reynolds Room features a candle-filled fireplace and an extra-long claw-foot tub with separate shower. The Allen Room has electric logs to set the mood; the rich colors and iron bed in the Arnold Room are stately and serene. New Hope is just a half a mile from downtown Bristol and is near King College, Virginia Intermont College and the Bristol Motor Speedway. To relax or rejuvenate, reserve your room at New Hope Bed and Breakfast.

822 Georgia Avenue, Bristol TN
(423) 989-3343 or (888) 989-3343
www.newhopebandb.com

Sky Harbor Bavarian Inn

Nestled into Lookout Mountain and just a short walk to Ruby Falls, Sky Harbor Bavarian Inn is a quaint, German-style retreat. The inn features broad patios with dramatic views of the Tennessee River's Moccasin Bend and downtown Chattanooga. You will have a front row seat for city fireworks, starlight or lightning, depending on the night. Some years ago, Steve and Patsy Evans went in search of a business that would leave Patsy free to work from home while raising their kids. They bought the 1938 motel in 1995. Over time, they have improved the property, adding a heated swimming pool and updating amenities, while taking care to preserve its original character. Trip Advisor calls Sky Harbor a Lookout Mountain gem and gives it the highest score. The 11 units offer a variety of accommodations to suit your needs. The honeymoon suite includes a sitting room with a jetted tub, a kitchenette and balcony with rocking chairs. Families appreciate the two-bedroom, two-bath unit with an outdoor hot tub. Let the Evans family welcome you to Sky Harbor Bavarian Inn.

2159 Old Wauhatchie Pike, Chattanooga TN
(423) 821-8619
www.skyharborbavarianinn.com

Maplehurst Inn Bed & Breakfast

Staying in an 18th century mansion adds a stunning new dimension to any visit to Knoxville. The Maplehurst Inn is a 7,000-square-foot mansion that became a bed-and-breakfast in 1982. Sonny and Becky Harben own the mansion, which offers 11 uniquely decorated rooms. The Congressional Suite provides antique cherry highback double beds and a light, airy feel, while the Anniversary Suite treats guests to a canopy bed and a mirror-lined Jacuzzi. Those looking for the ultimate in luxury will find it in the Penthouse Suite, which occupies the entire top floor of the mansion and features antique cherry wood furniture, a writing desk and a Jacuzzi located beneath a skylight. Whichever room you choose, you'll have your own bathroom and an incredible view of the Tennessee River. Guests at the Maplehurst Inn often come together to swap travel stories in the mansion's parlor. Sometimes, a guest with a musical ability will perform on the 1913 Baldwin piano. Guests meet for breakfast in the Garden Room, where Sonny makes his delicious Maplehurst Casserole along with many buffet choices. The Maplehurst Inn places you close to the Great Smoky Mountains, Dollywood and the Knoxville Museum of Art. For a lodging experience that combines Old World charm with 21st century comfort, come to the Maplehurst Inn.

800 W Hill Avenue, Knoxville TN
(865) 523-7773 or (800) 451-1562
www.maplehurstinn.com

Whitestone Country Inn

Whitestone Country Inn offers romance and beauty on a 600-acre country estate that resembles a charming New England village. Owners Paul and Jean Cowell, who opened this AAA four-diamond inn a decade ago, are proud that American Historic Inns has named the Whitestone one of the 10 Most Romantic Inns in America. Each of the inn's six buildings offers pristine accommodations. Relax by the fireplace in your room or take a leisurely soak in a whirlpool tub. Enjoy stunning views of the Smoky Mountains as you walk the miles of maintained paths through natural wooded areas and landscaped gardens, or just lounge around on the hammocks and rocking chairs. Whitestone serves three gourmet meals a day, but no one will tell if you sneak a few of the freshly baked cookies. Watts Bar Lake and the surrounding wildlife refuge offer ideal opportunities for bird watching, fishing and water sports. The on-site wedding chapel is a stunning example of Carpenter Gothic architecture, and provides an elegant venue for your special day. If you dream of an outdoor wedding, choose from two romantic gazebos, each overlooking the lake. Stay at the Whitestone Country Inn, where you can experience the charm of yesteryear with all of the comforts of today.

1200 Paint Rock Road, Kingston TN
(865) 376-0113 or (888) 247-2464
www.whitestoneinn.com

Arrowmont School of Arts and Crafts

A shining achievement of the Pi Beta Phi Fraternity for Women was the founding of the Pi Beta Phi Settlement School in 1912. The school's mission was to provide an education to those who might not otherwise have had such opportunities. The mission continues through what is now a nationally known center for contemporary arts and crafts education, Arrowmont School of Arts and Crafts. The school draws people from all over to develop skills ranging from wood turning to weaving. The 70-acre campus enjoys state-of-the-art facilities and offers classes in every media imaginable. From fibers to photography, you will find something wonderful to explore. The intensive classes are one or two weeks or a weekend in length and taught by outstanding artists. Take the time to visit the five galleries that feature contemporary exhibitions that explore a variety of art forms by regional, national and international artists. You can also peer in on artists at work from the catwalk that runs above the studios. Visit the resource center and art supply store after you have been inspired to explore your own creative talents. Arrowmont also offers artist residencies, assistantships, work-study and scholarships throughout the year. The music of the Appalachians is often featured in the 250-seat auditorium, which contributes to the school's mission of enriching lives through art. Visit Arrowmont School of Arts and Crafts. It is a journey worth taking.

556 Parkway, Gatlinburg TN
(865) 436-5860
www.arrowmont.org

The Pattern Hutch

No matter what you want to make, if there is a pattern for it, the Pattern Hutch will have it. Owner Cindy Hutchinson has been a crafter for 30 years, in business for 10 and thoroughly enjoys what she does. The Pattern Hutch features one of the largest selections of patterns in the South, with more than 3,500 unique designs in stock. You can find the quaint woodworking patterns of Sugar Bucket, Heidi Markish and Plum Purdy, which make fun projects and great gifts. If you enjoy appliqué or want to try something new, check out Heart to Hand, Bloomin Minds and Caught up in Stitches. The shop also carries pearl cotton for all of your appliqué projects. You will find a project for every season or occasion. Quilters will find an enormous selection of patterns for both the beginner and the expert. The store also carries totes that are ready for you to add your own creative flare. Also available are high-quality Swarovski crystals, fully faceted and flat-backed. If you can't make it in, be sure to check out the full-service website where you can browse for hours. For a huge collection of top-quality quilting goods, be sure to visit the Pattern Hutch.

172 Old Mill Avenue, Pigeon Forge TN
(866) PATTERN (728-8376)
www.patternhutch.com

The Cherry Pit

Unlike many for whom quilting has been a life-long career, Jane Washington and her husband George wandered into the industry in 1998, when Jane began quilting with a friend. She ran a small business from her basement for three years before George found their current perfect location. Paying homage to George's namesake and distant relative, the first president of the United States, they named it the Cherry Pit. With 3,600 feet of inspiration, the shop quickly blossomed and has been named a top ten quilt shop by *Quilt Sampler Magazine*. Large and small models hang on the 1930 red brick walls. An extensive line of patterns, notions, fabulous fabrics and knick-knacks fill the inviting space. Many books are available to help you find that next quilting project. For those who want to start small, the shop has many wall hanging and quilt kits. Classes, taught by the friendly and enthusiastic staff, are available at every skill level and cover topics that include appliqué and wearables. The Cherry Pit also has an extensive Block of the Month club that draws mountains of interest. Jane, George and their staff want to share the art of quilting with others and invite you to let your creativity bloom at the Cherry Pit.

115 Bruce Street, Sevierville TN
(865)453-4062
www.quiltingatthecherrypit.com

The Gardens of Sunshine Hollow

Nestled in the Great Valley between the Smoky Mountains and the Cumberland Plateau, the Gardens of Sunshine Hollow are surrounded by 160 acres of unspoiled Tennessee forest. Here, native shrubs and wild flowers such as dwarf American buckeye, wild azalea, wild hydrangea and native ferns abound. At the center of the gardens, a spring feeds a two-acre lake that is surrounded by 4,000 linear feet of terraced flower beds. Over 1,750 varieties of Hosta, iris, roses, daylilies, dahlias, annuals and perennials make seasonal displays of bloom. Gentle trails allow visitors to do as much or as little walking as they wish. A major part of the gardens can be seen from the Luncheon Pavilion, so guests can enjoy lunch and homemade ice cream while soaking up the ambience. Groups of 10 or more can arrange guided wagon tours of Sunshine Hollow that recount its history and current projects. The site was basically a wilderness with no road or other improvements by the time Dave and Vicki Rhyne bought it in 1973. They made the gardens their life's passion and have worked steadily to preserve and improve the property. Today, Sunshine Hollow is one of the most visited private gardens in Tennessee. In 2005, *National Geographic* recognized it as one of the best places in the state to visit. While visiting, don't miss the Sunshine Hollow Bakery, where Dave and Vicki sell their homemade pecan fruitcake and their trademark Woozy Cakes. Call to reserve lunch or drop by to wander the Gardens of Sunshine Hollow. The gardens are open April through October, excepting August.

198 County Road 52, Athens TN
(800) 669-2005
www.sunshinehollow.com

Dolly Parton's Dixie Stampede

Known throughout the region as the Smokies' Most Fun Place to Eat, Dolly Parton's Dixie Stampede keeps you entertained with a wildly exciting horse show following your Southern-style meal. The kitchen crew prepares about 1,000 rotisserie chickens and 250 pounds of boneless pork tenderloin to feed the fun-loving crowd that packs the restaurant each evening. "Everything we do here is specially designed and state-of-the-art, from the way we cook our chicken to the types of seasonings we use on our potatoes," says John Shaver, general manager of Dixie Stampede. "In fact, we're rather protective of our cooking methods, which result in the juiciest chicken and tastiest pork in the business." After you have been well fed, you will be treated to the spectacle of magnificent horses galloping at breakneck speed. Riders thrill the crowd with daring feats of trick riding and competition. Ostrich races and the Dixie Stampede's famous racing pigs provide comic relief. There's live bluegrass music and comedy before the main show and patriotic songs and fireworks at the end of the evening. Despite all the gold records and the starring roles in Hollywood movies, Dolly Parton is still just a country gal at heart. Some of her fondest memories of growing up in these Smoky Mountains are of family gatherings where everyone would laugh and sing, engage in some friendly competition and feast on heaps of home-cooked food. You could say that the Dixie Stampede is an extension of those family events, only on a grander scale. Treat yourself to a night of thrills, laughs and good eating at Dolly Parton's Dixie Stampede.

3849 Parkway (Chapman Highway SE), Pigeon Forge TN (865) 453-4400 or (800) 356-1676
www.dixiestampede.com

Scottie Mayfield invites you plan a trip to Mayfield's Visitor Center in Athens, Tennessee

Mayfield Dairy Farms

Back in 1923, the Mayfield family started a dairy with 45 Jersey cows, spring water refrigeration and horse-and-buggy delivery. Over the next three generations, the Mayfields became important innovators in the dairy industry, bringing the latest processing methods to the Southeast and developing a full range of dairy products, including ice cream that *Time* magazine called the world's best in 1981. More than 100,000 visitors come to Athens every year to taste it for themselves. Visitors to the Mayfield Dairy Farms Visitor Center in Athens can retrace the family's history with a brief video presentation. Then, a guided tour provides a behind-the-scenes peek into how Mayfield's signature yellow milk jugs are produced and filled with Mayfield milk. Visitors will also see how Mayfield ice cream is packaged and prepped for distribution. After the tour, visitors can browse the charming novelty shop filled with collectibles and apparel. Ice cream fans can treat their taste buds in the ice cream parlor. With 35 different flavors to choose from, Mayfield is sure to please everyone. Visitor Center tours are offered Monday through Saturday, but be sure to call ahead for hours. Mayfield Dairy Farms Visitor Center is located four miles off I-75 (exit 52) between Knoxville and Chattanooga.

4 Mayfield Lane, Athens TN (800) 362-9546 *www.MayfieldDairy.com*

Creative Discovery Museum

The folks at Creative Discovery Museum know that what children learn through play sticks with them throughout their lives. At the museum, infants build motor function and social skills in the baby gym while toddlers tinker in a play garage or kitchen. Older children can build robots, launch balls into the air, watch rocks glow in the dark or excavate dinosaur bones. A budding artist can build a sculpture, play a musical instrument or ham it up at the Back Alley Theatre. The museum finds dozens of ways to stimulate creativity and natural curiosity. In fact, you will find multiple reasons to visit this Chattanooga treasure throughout the year, such as the temporary shows in the exhibition gallery. During the summer of 2007, youngsters were captivated by an Alice's Wonderland exhibit, where they crawled through a rabbit hole to play croquet with Alice and the Queen and visit the Mad Hatter's Tea Party. You can reserve the museum's Science Theatre at Northgate Mall for a birthday party that includes refreshments, a laser light show and an entertaining science show that rivals any magic act. The museum also offers an after-dark mystery adventure for kids, day camps and programs for the classroom on weather, geology, magnetic fields and electricity. For inspirational play, introduce your kids to the Creative Discovery Museum.

321 Chestnut Street, Chattanooga TN
(423) 648-6065
www.cdmfun.org

Photo courtesy of Hands On! Regional Museum

Photo courtesy Johnson City, Tennessee Chamber of Commerce

Photo courtesy of Hands On! Regional Museum

Hands On! Regional Museum

Offering more than 100,000 exciting participatory programs each year, Hands On! Regional Museum has drawn more than 1.3 million visitors from around the world since opening 20 years ago. Powered by a passionate philosophy of learning-by-doing, Hands On! keeps the spirit of discovery alive by providing some of the most impressive interactive displays in the Southeast. The moment you enter the museum, you sense energy and electricity as kids discover, explore and invent. They can crawl and slide through a coal mine, take a virtual flight in a real airplane, or report the news or forecast the weather in the WKID-TV studio. Centered in the museum, you find a giant ark filled with exotic real (stuffed) animals showcasing a collection from around the world. You can also discover what makes your body work, a kid-size grocery store, and live animals including the mascot iguana. Hands On! works closely with schools in the surrounding counties to provide programs in the arts, sciences and humanities that complement classroom education in accordance with Tennessee curriculum standards. The innovative Eastman Discovery Lab exhibit recently earned the prestigious Roy L. Shafer Leading Edge Award for Visitor Experience. Come to Hands On! and discover how much fun learning can be.

315 E Main Street, Johnson City TN
(423) 434-HAND (4263)
www.handsonmuseum.org

Knoxville Tourism & Sports Corporation

Let's face it. Although most visitors' centers can provide you with loads of useful information, they are not places where you want to hang out. An exception can be found in Knoxville. When the Knoxville Convention & Visitors Bureau joined forces with the Greater Knoxville Sports Corporation to create a welcome center, the partners had something more in mind than a nook with some racks full of maps and flyers. The concept was to introduce visitors to the city by immersing them in a distinctively local atmosphere. The Café Gourmet at the center serves coffees roasted by the city's own Goodson Brothers. Monday through Friday, local entertainers perform live inside the café during lunch, which is provided by one of the restaurants in the area. You can listen to the music or browse the Uniquely Knoxville Gift Shop, which carries arts, crafts and souvenirs from Knoxville artisans. What's more, the center houses WDVX, the community radio station of Knoxville, so you can watch and listen to the broadcasts as they originate from a booth in the corner of the café. By the way, you can also load up on those maps and flyers that will direct you to the most exciting Knoxville attractions. The center is at the corner of Gay Street and Summit Hill. Drop by and let the Knoxville Tourism & Sports Corporation welcome you to the local scene.

301 S Gay Street, Knoxville TN
(865) 523-7263 or (800) 727-8045
www.knoxville.org

The Historic Tennessee Theatre

It must be true that performers love coming to the Historic Tennessee Theatre as much as audiences do. Who wouldn't appreciate this beautiful entertainment palace, opened in 1928 and declared the Official State Theatre of Tennessee in 1999? A recent renovation installed many modern updates and added new sparkle and shine to the magnificent Spanish Moorish architecture, so now audiences find even more to love about this venue as they enjoy their favorite acts. Each season brings a busy schedule of musical entertainment, including jazz, bluegrass and pop, in addition to comedy and theatrical performances. Legends such as Johnny Cash and Ray Charles have awed audiences here, and the present lineup of performers is just as exciting as those in the past. During the 2006/2007 season, the Tennessee Theatre welcomed to its stage the nine-time bluegrass Entertainer of the Year Del McCoury and his band, as well as comedienne Lily Tomlin and the dazzling Ballet Folklorico de Mexico. Naturalist and television personality Jack Hanna shared his enthusiasm for wildlife in a captivating family show while performances by the Knoxville symphony and opera sated the city's appetite for the classics. The theatre also shows favorite movies from yesteryear during the summer and hosts a free organ concert once a month, played upon a mighty 1928 Wurlitzer organ. The future looks bright for this glorious facility. Take in a show this season at the Historic Tennessee Theatre.

604 S Gay Street, Knoxville TN
(865) 684-1200
www.tennesseetheatre.com

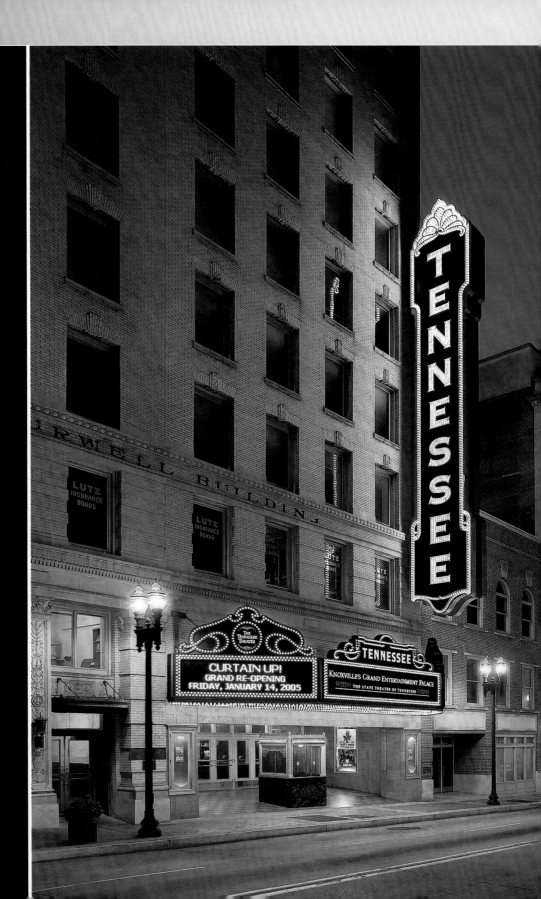

Tennessee Museum of Aviation

Ever since he was a small boy, Neal Melton had a passion for planes. He began collecting airplanes and aircraft memorabilia at a young age, and when his collection finally got out of hand, the Tennessee Museum of Aviation was born. What began as a small personal collection has now grown into one of the largest aviation collections in the state. The museum boasts the state's largest Warbird collection, including two flyable P-47 Thunderbolts out of only 13 in existence. The planes on display rotate often because most are airworthy and travel to air shows. The museum's new 50,000-square-foot facility is located right beside the runway of the Gatlinburg-Pigeon Forge Airport, so visitors are often treated to unexpected flight demonstrations by the vintage aircraft. One of the museum's special highlights is an ongoing lecture series where war veterans who actually flew these planes bring history to life through their personal stories. The museum stocks a variety of military artifacts, from uniforms to weapons. A 35,000-square-foot heated hangar features planes, jeeps and even one of Amelia Earhart's cars. Topics of the aviation history exhibits include: stages of technology advancement, women in aviation and impromptu historic aircraft flights. The museum is also home to the official Tennessee Aviation Hall of Fame. Don't forget to stop at the Flying Spirit Gift Gallery to browse through a wide variety of aviation gifts, from jackets to model kits to historic videos. An unforgettable experience for the whole family awaits you at the Tennessee Museum of Aviation.

135 Air Museum Way, Sevierville TN
(865) 908-0171, ext. 27 or (866) 286-8738
www.tnairmuseum.com

WonderWorks

Ever seen a building fall from the sky? The folks in Pigeon Forge see it every day. Visitors marvel at the façade of WonderWorks, which looks like a huge building crash-landed upside-down. It's so shocking that it still grabs the attention of locals every time they drive by. The attraction is based on the idea that a secret science institute in the Bermuda Triangle was blown sky-high in an experiment gone wrong, and just happened to end up upside-down in Pigeon Forge. Formerly the home of the Music Mansion Theater, the structure's wacky exterior matches the mind-boggling exhibits inside. WonderWorks is a family-friendly science museum with more than 150 interactive activities. Designed to be as entertaining as educational, WonderWorks is an amusement park for the mind. Although you won't find any roller coasters at this attraction, you can rip it up in a jet fighter simulator in the Space Zone and experience real hurricane-force winds in the Disaster Zone. Put your mind to the test with entertaining mental exercises scattered throughout, and brave the sights in the Far Out Illusion Gallery. Once dinner time rolls around, wrap your day up right with tickets to the hilarious Hoot 'N' Holler Dinner Show. With 55,000 square feet of family fun, you'll realize right away that a couple hours at WonderWorks is not enough. Whether you're a kid or just a kid at heart, WonderWorks is the spot for endless hours of fun.

100 Music Road, Pigeon Forge TN
(865) 868-1800
www.wonderworkstn.com

Hoot 'N' Holler
Dinner Show

WonderWorks has brought variety shows back in style with its hilarious Hoot 'N' Holler Dinner Show. Take a group of comedic entertainers, add a delicious multi-course meal and a heaping dose of audience interaction and what do you get? A guaranteed memorable night of family fun. Written by a senior writer for Disney, the Hoot 'N' Holler Dinner Show is staged daily in its own 300-seat theater. The theater is part of WonderWorks, an interactive family attraction in Pigeon Forge. Once your stomach starts grumbling, head to the theater, where you'll be greeted by tunes from Freddy, the resident piano player. Take your seat and get ready for a sidesplitting story about the adventures of four traveling entertainers in the vaudeville era. Don't get too comfortable, because you're likely to become a part of the ongoing shenanigans. Scraps, the cast's cook, does a fantastic job cooking up trouble with audience members. Enjoy the singing and dancing to classic melodies while putting away a scrumptious Italian feast. There's even strawberry shortcake for dessert. Beware of the serving staff—they do more than just deliver good food. Don't be surprised if they burst into their own comedic routine right in front of you. These folks go out of their way to make sure you and your family have an absolute blast. Enjoy a night at the Hoot 'N' Holler Dinner Show for a tummy full of food and a heart full of laughter.

100 Music Road, Pigeon Forge TN
(865) 868-1800
www.wonderworkstn.com

Photo by Chuck A. Rector

Tipton-Haynes State Historic Site

The eleven buildings of the Tipton-Haynes State Historic Site tell a story of Tennessee's history from early settlement to the Civil War era. Colonel John Tipton, who served in the Virginia Conventions with Thomas Jefferson, moved his family to what was then North Carolina in 1783 and into a log structure that he later renovated prior to his death in 1813. David Haynes purchased the Tipton farm in 1839 for his son, Landon Carter Haynes, who later served as a Confederate Senator. With such outbuildings as a smokehouse, joiner's shop, still house and large barn, the historic site fuels the imagination of visitors, who are invited to cast themselves back to an earlier time when self-sufficiency was essential for survival. Depending on when you visit, you may witness the tapping of trees to make maple syrup or the making of sorghum molasses. A cave on the grounds is the site for storytelling. Roast your own hot dog as you listen to a thrilling tale, perhaps one involving Daniel Boone, who according to tradition, camped in the cave. Famous French botanist André Michaux stayed as a guest of Colonel Tipton while exploring the trees and plants of the area. A trail through the grounds follows in his footsteps. You'll also find archeological artifacts from Native Americans of the Woodland period when you visit Tipton-Haynes, often considered Tennessee's most historic site.

2620 S Roan Street, Johnson City TN
(423) 926-3631
www.tipton-haynes.org

The Salt and Pepper Shaker Museum

Nostalgic, fascinating and artistically inspiring, the Salt and Pepper Shaker Museum is a delightful place to visit. The museum began almost by accident when owner Andrea Ludden was searching for the perfect pepper grinder. Having gone through several, she placed them on her kitchen window sill. When friends assumed she was collecting, she started to receive shakers and grinders as gifts, in droves. Today, the museum displays more than 19,000 salt and pepper shakers dating from 1400 to the present. There are an endless variety of forms from the whimsical to the ornate. Every medium is represented, from wood and plastic to the more unusual, such as bone and egg shell. The museum may inspire you to start or add to your own collection—you'll find a gift shop stocked with wonderful offerings. It stocks 130 different spices and spice blends to put your shakers to good use. Ludden family members also share their creativity through their jewelry line, Earth and Sky. Truly gorgeous, one-of-a-kind pieces are available. You will also find some of the most impressive travel photo art, by their son Alex. Come to the Salt and Pepper Shaker Museum and shake it up.

527 Cherry Street, Gatlinburg TN
(865) 430-5515 or (888) 778-1802
www.thesaltandpeppershakermuseum.com

Still donated by Donald & Elaine Gilliard

Floyd Garrett's Muscle Car Museum

If you could own just one car from Floyd Garrett's Muscle Car Museum, which bad boy would you choose? Would it be the '69 Camaro ZL-1? The purple '71 Cuda Convertible? Maybe it would be the 1970 Plymouth Superbird that was designed to race at NASCAR super speedways. Floyd, who describes himself as just a man who loves cars, has assembled a dazzling collection of over 90 cars from the golden era of the muscle car. You'll want to check under the hood of the 1970 Chevelle LS6. Its engine was the highest factory-rated horsepower to come out of Detroit in those years. Other highlights of the collection include Marilyn Monroe's Cadillac and Floyd's personal '67 Two Door Post Chevelle. Sorry, no joy rides allowed, though Floyd will let you pose for pictures beside the mighty beasts and dream. Besides the cars, Floyd has gathered together model train sets, a 1940s jukebox and a moonshine still donated by Donald and Elaine Gilliard. The gift shop is just as impressive in its way as the museum showroom. No car junkie can walk away empty-handed from the staggering selection of collectibles, T-shirts, car prints and die-cast models; approximately 18,000 items in all fill the 6,000-square-foot shop. Get revved at Floyd Garrett's Muscle Car Museum.

320 Winfield Dunn Parkway, Sevierville TN
(865) 908-0882
www.musclecarmuseum.com

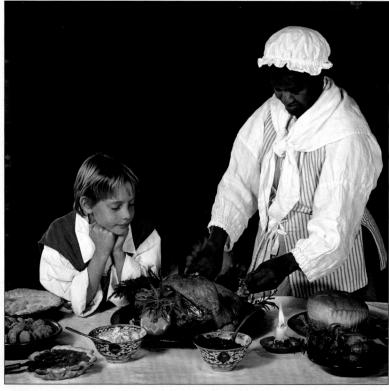

Rocky Mount Museum

As you visit the Rocky Mount Museum, men and women in period attire meet and greet you as friends and visitors to their homes. Before long, you'll think it really is 1791. You are but an arms length away from the hustle of 21st century Northeast Tennessee, but enjoying a slower and gentler lifestyle. As they shear sheep, strike the anvil and bake biscuits, the re-enactors will have you believing that they are the family, servants and friends of William Cobb, who built this two-story log house in 1772. His home served as the capital and seat of government for the Territory Southwest of the Ohio River from October 1790 until the spring of 1792. Before you look in on the re-enactors, you'll begin your visit at the Massengill Overmountain Museum, which explains the region's diverse cultural heritage. Then stroll from the barnyard and blacksmith shop to the weaving cabin and the bountiful gardens and marvel at the many skills that a frontier family had to master in order to provide its members with food, clothing and shelter. Life wasn't easy, though there was always time for a celebration, as you will see if you happen to visit during a festival day. In fact, each day at the museum is lived out according to its corresponding day in 1791, meaning that chores change according to the season and special events are frequent. Spend a day in the 18th century at the Rocky Mount Museum.

200 Hyder Hill Road, Piney Flats TN
(423) 538-7396 or (888) 538-1791
www.rockymountmuseum.com

Photo by Ernie Brown

Chattanooga Riverboat Company

Pick your preference in food and live entertainment, then add the romance of a riverboat plying the Tennessee River, and you've described the basic ingredients of a dinner cruise with the Chattanooga Riverboat Company. John Goldfine purchased the Southern Belle in 1998, when he added a variety of live entertainment to the boat's cruising repertoire. The dinner cruises depart from the boat's new Pier 2 dock for a two-and-a-half hour trip down the river. You can dine on slow-cooked prime rib prepared from a secret recipe or order the beloved Shrimp Creole while the Riverboat Ramblers tempt you onto the dance floor with your favorite tunes. Entertainment and meals vary depending on the night of the week. One night features gospel music and baked chicken; another, blue grass music and barbecued beef. Family night combines prime rib with spaghetti and a magic act. The Southern Belle is a modern boat that retains the graceful curves of her ancestors. You can board her for sightseeing or lunch cruises or use her for a wedding, where the Riverboat Chaplain would be honored to perform the ceremony. The Belle's docking facility harbors a stationary boat, suitable for large private parties. Let the river capture your fancy with an excursion from Chattanooga Riverboat Company.

**201 Riverfront Parkway, Chattanooga TN
(423) 266-4488 or (800) 766-2784**
www.chattanoogariverboat.com

Ijams Nature Center

A visit to Ijams Nature Center enhances your understanding and appreciation of the natural world. The center is a sanctuary and environmental resource and education center on the banks of the Tennessee River. Ijams instructors have programs for groups of all ages. At the site, you can explore 160 acres of protected woodlands, meadows and ponds by walking seven miles of nature trails. Will Skelton Greenway provides about four miles for scenic walks and bicycling. The River Trail boardwalk, built along a rock cliff next to the Tennessee River, provides close views of wildlife, including water birds such as great blue herons. The newly opened Mead's Quarry property features a picturesque 20-acre lake. The site's original Lotus Pond is host to frogs and turtles, and the surface is draped with aquatic red mosquito ferns that give the entire pond a red cast from a distance. The visitor center is earth-friendly, constructed with recycled building materials and sporting solar heating with the judicious use of natural light. Ijams Nature Center is a nonprofit organization that has gained wide public support for its ecological mission. It all began in 1910 with the Ijams family, who generously shared their wildlife sanctuary with the community. Let Ijams Nature Center inspire you.

2915 Island Home Avenue, Knoxville TN
(865) 577-4717
www.ijams.org

General Shale Museum of Ancient Brick

General Shale Brick is not just one of America's largest producers of brick. It also demonstrates respect for the history of its product at the General Shale Museum of Ancient Brick. The museum contains a fascinating display of more than 100 bricks, spanning millennia and gathered from around the world. Basil Shaffer, a longtime staff member, now retired, took it upon himself to single-handedly assemble this amazing collection, which represents 10,000 years of history. Over the past 33 years, with support from his employer, Basil obtained bricks from ancient Egypt, Jerusalem, Nimrod and Ur. You'll see bricks from Hattusa, the mountain

stronghold of the Hittites, as well as a perfect 2nd century Roman pilaster brick from the ancient bathhouse of Tripontium in Roman Britain. Also on display is a brick of sun-dried clay excavated by archaeologists from a settlement beneath the Biblical city of Jericho. Other treasures of the museum include bricks from the Great Wall of China, the Coliseum in Rome and America's original White House. Bricks that traveled to America on the Mayflower sit beside a brick from the saloon where Babe Ruth was born. The museum presents the story of brick, incredibly universal in construction, strength and lasting beauty. Visit the General Shale Museum of Ancient Brick and see the history of the humble and enduring brick.

3211 N Roan Street, Johnson City TN
(423) 282-4661
www.generalshale.com

Three Rivers Rambler

Lindy leads the way on the Three Rivers Rambler, an excursion train that takes passengers on a 90-minute trip along the Tennessee River. Lindy, the star of the show, is a 1925 Baldwin 2-8-0 steam locomotive that was rescued from storage in 2000 to begin a new life at the head of the Rambler. Passengers take seats on one of the 1932 coach cars or the 1940 open-air car. The journey starts at Volunteer Landing in downtown Knoxville, next to Neyland Stadium. You'll see plenty of scenic views as the train winds its way to its destination at the Marbledale Quarry. A stop on the historic trestle over the Holston and French Broad rivers is a thrilling highlight. The beauty of the turning leaves adds a special touch to the Autumn Express. Kids

are allowed to trick or treat on the Pumpkin Express in October. The Christmas Express features holiday food, storytelling and a visit from Santa. Sections of the train or the caboose can be reserved for parties. The train is also available for Railgate parties during University of Tennessee home football games. Be there when the Three Rivers Rambler blows its whistle to start its run.

Volunteer Landing, Knoxville TN
(865) 524-9411
www.threeriversrambler.com

American Museum of Science and Energy

From the frontier of Appalachia to the frontier of the nuclear age, the historical and scientific exhibits at the American Museum of Science and Energy span an exciting and important era. The museum opened in 1949, about 30 minutes after the gates opened at the top-secret World War II town of Oak Ridge, where scientists working for the government's Manhattan Project helped develop the atomic bomb. The secrets of Oak Ridge, a town not found on any map, make up the main focus of the museum, which details the race against the Axis Powers to develop the first atomic weapon. Exhibits range from nuclear weapons development to peaceful uses of nuclear power. View the AMSE Solar Array and encounter a hybrid solar lighting display. The museum also offers opportunities to learn about natural resources such as coal, geothermal, oil, natural gas and wind power. Visitors can take a new look at the world through hands-on exhibits that include laser pinball and a micro lab, or enjoy live demonstrations such as Atom Smashers, a hair-raising experience. The museum offers many educational opportunities geared to Tennessee educational standards. To get fun down to a science, allow two hours or more for the self-guided tour of two levels. Come to the American Museum of Science and Energy to uncover the secrets of the Atomic Age.

300 S Tulane Avenue, Oak Ridge TN
(865) 576-3200
www.amse.org

The Incredible Christmas Place

Christmas is one of the most magical times of the year, but sometimes that special spirit gets lost in the harried rush of shopping. The Incredible Christmas Place in Pigeon Forge strives to make your Christmas shopping experience as enchanting and spirited as the rest of the holiday. A cluster of quaint Bavarian-style shops arranged around a cobblestone square, this tasteful Christmas village radiates Old World charm. As you stroll the walkways through manicured gardens, beautiful window displays greet you at every turn, a miniature train whistles and smokes and a life-size cuckoo clock, complete with dancing wood-turned musicians, entertains you. Inside the shops are thousands of Christmas decorations of every imaginable variety, locally made crafts, collectibles and many other gift items. Visit the Personalizing Gallery to have artists transform your ornament selection into a personalized keepsake. The floral department designs wreaths and centerpieces in a variety of styles to match your home décor. Don't miss the Toys & Trains store with its life-like displays, or Mrs. Claus' Candy Kitchen, which offers some of the best homemade fudge in the South. Experience the magic of Christmas year-round at The Incredible Christmas Place.

2470 Parkway, Pigeon Forge TN
(865) 453-0415 or (800) 445-3396
www.christmasplace.com

Sevier County Heritage Museum

The Sevier County Heritage Museum began as the dream of long-time resident Rowena Schmutzer, who envisioned a place that would teach the children of the county about the wonderful history of their area. Through the support of County Mayor Larry Waters and the Sevier county commissioners, her dream was realized. Named after Tennessee's first governor, John Sevier, Sevier County has many stories to tell. An African American history exhibit highlights the strong cultural diversity of the area, which was relatively harmonious even during the time of segregation. Woodland Indian artifacts and farm implements from early settlers highlight the rustic pioneer age. Another display pays tribute to local veterans from the Civil War through World War II. Director Patsy Bradford works hard to keep the rich history of Sevier County alive for future generations. School visits are frequent, and kids can engage in a variety of history-related activities such as seeding cotton, dating arrowheads, scavenger hunts, and drying and shelling corn to take home. Whether you are a Tennessee local or just passing through, the Sevier County Heritage Museum offers visitors a perfect microcosm of American history.

167 Bruce Street, Sevierville TN
(865) 453-4058

Photo courtesy of Scott Fraker/Blonsagar Productions

Children's Museum of Oak Ridge

Believing that the world begins in one's own backyard, the first organizers of the Children's Museum of Oak Ridge placed a special emphasis on the cultural heritage of Southern Appalachia. Thirty-five years later, the Appalachian Heritage exhibit continues to teach children what life was like for their ancestors, who had to build their own cabins and churn their own butter. History comes alive in the Early Oak Ridge exhibit, the Native American Room and the International exhibit. Throughout the museum, children are prompted to use their senses for a truly interactive learning experience. The facility has grown since a local Girl Scout troop applied for and received a grant from *Reader's Digest* to fund a place where families could learn and play together. There's an award-winning rain forest exhibit now, and everything else from a child-size doll house to a World of Trains exhibit with a train garden and a real caboose. You'll find a music room, a puppet collection and fossil displays. Community contributions have been instrumental in providing Appalachian artifacts, natural history specimens and indigenous folk art. More is on the way, such as the vintage Oak Ridge fire truck that is being restored and will soon be the centerpiece of a hands-on exhibit. Excitement will fill the air at the Children's Museum of Oak Ridge for many years to come. Executive Director Mary Ann Damos invites you to be a part of it.

461 W Outer Drive, Oak Ridge TN
(865) 482-1074
www.childrensmuseumofoakridge.org

Great Smoky Mountains Heritage Center

Great Smoky Mountains Heritage Center, located in the peaceful gateway community of Townsend, celebrates the history of East Tennessee and the Smoky Mountains and is dedicated to preserving the region's unique culture. Through an assortment of artifacts dating from 3000 BC to the 1930s, visitors catch a glimpse of Native American culture and its pottery, hunting weapons, ceremonial dress and masks representing the Cherokee seven clans. Learn about both Native American and early settler life through three-dimensional displays, interactive exhibits, media presentations and a historic village including authentic log cabins, cantilever barns, a wheelwright shop, smokehouse and more. The center, just three-quarters of a mile from the entrance to America's most-visited national park, includes 10 historic buildings, two indoor galleries, a museum store, auditorium and classrooms. A 500-seat amphitheater offers a grand setting for teaching, storytelling, drama and music events. Festivals, day camps, music concerts and special events for children and adults are a significant part of the center's annual calendar. Visit the Great Smoky Mountains Heritage Center to see history and the spirit of the Smokies come to life.

123 Cromwell Drive, Townsend TN
(865) 448-0044
www.gsmheritagecenter.org

The English Rose

Any Brit who discovers the English Rose feels a bit closer to home after stopping in for a pot of tea and finger sandwiches or a hearty pub-style luncheon, such as a steak pie or Cornish pastie. The Chattanooga tea room belongs to Angela Becksvoort, who was born and raised by British parents in Zimbabwe, the former British colony of Rhodesia. Angela became a nurse in England and moved to the United States to work for a neurosurgeon. After moving to charming, historic Chattanooga with her husband, Angela began to seriously consider opening a tea shop like her friend in California owned. She found the perfect venue in the foyer of the former Grand Hotel, built in 1890. There Angela and her husband guided restoration work on the tea room, which opened in 1997. A thirst for an English theme took Angela from hot tea and freshly baked scones to the creation of an on-site gift shop, where you can purchase English china along with table linens and stationery. Angela also sells imported English grocery items, including teas, sweets, biscuits and sauces. The tea room has been featured in *Southern Living* magazine and gained *Tea Time* magazine's list of the top 20 tea rooms in the United States. Much of the staff is English and thrives in the tea room environment. Angela also takes inner city youth under her wing as staff. The tranquil atmosphere proves conducive to Angela's etiquette classes and seems to have a calming effect on children. For a sophisticated retreat into British customs, visit the English Rose.

1401 Market Street, Chattanooga TN (423) 265-5900
www.englishroseonline.com

The South's Finest Chocolate Factory

The chocolatiers at the South's Finest Chocolate Factory are obviously experts. The Factory hand-makes more than 100 varieties of creamy chocolate candies. Only the finest ingredients are allowed into the traditional favorites and new creations. Some of the candy is seasonal. The white chocolate Strawberries in Snow comes out in February, and the milk chocolate Strawberry Cordial is available from March to June. Confections can be brilliant combinations of taste. The Cashew Whisper consists of handmade caramel drizzled on select roasted cashews and coated with white chocolate. The Factory offers sugar-free candies for customers with special diets. Its gift packages bear the work of artists Marilyn Dwyer and Ruth Andrews, but you can also use one of your own photos to personalize the box. Visit the South's Finest Chocolate Factory, which opened in 1982.

8078 Kingston Pike, Knoxville TN (showroom) (865) 690-5454
1060 World's Fair Park Drive, Knoxville TN (factory)
(behind the Knoxville Convention Center) (865) 682-4449
www.chocolatelovers.com

Jim Gray Gallery

Housed in a century-old church, the Jim Gray Gallery showcases works in a range of different styles. When you first step into the gallery, you'll think you're looking at paintings by several different artists. In fact, Jim painted them all. From spectacular seascapes to scenes from Venice and Paris, Jim paints his travels rather than photographing them. He opened the gallery more than 40 years ago, becoming one of the founding fathers of the Great Smoky Arts and Crafts Community, an eight-mile loop in Gatlinburg with more than 100 craftsmen and artisans. By 1969, the demand for Jim's work was so great that he began offering signed lithographs that would be affordable to everyone. Much of the artwork is inspired by Jim's extensive travels throughout the world. Raised on the coast of Alabama, Jim moved to the East Tennessee mountains to make a home with his family. In addition to Jim's artworks, the gallery also displays the works of more than 10 potters from the surrounding area. For a preview of the gallery's works, visit the website, a virtual gallery to help you find the pieces you're looking for. In addition to the original gallery, Jim now has three more in Tennessee. Visit Jim Gray Gallery, where there's something for everyone in every price range.

670 Glades Road, Gatlinburg TN
(865) 436-8988 (office)
(865) 436-5262 (downtown Gatlinburg gallery)
www.jimgraygallery.com

Stegall's Pottery & Crafts Gallery

Stegall's Pottery & Crafts Gallery is filled with beautiful, handcrafted pottery and decorative craft items, gleaned from the best work of more than 75 local artisans. Owners Alan and Nancy Stegall carefully select each piece. You'll find a fine collection of both functional and decorative pottery along with various craft items worked in wood, metal, glass and clay. The gallery's 4,000-square-foot studio is a full production environment. Take a 30-minute guided tour through the production area, where you can see the gallery's craftsmen throw clay on a wheel and then extrude, press and build slabs. You'll also see the glazing and firing processes that complete the production. You'll be happily surprised at the reasonable pricing of these one-of-a-kind works of art. For group tours, just call ahead to reserve your date. You can order custom pieces as well. Watch Alan or Nancy as they begin the design process and make your work of art come alive. Beginning with a love for their art and a desire to work together, Alan and Nancy turned their one-time hobby into a full-fledged business more than 25 years ago. The studio now displays and sells its lovely wares in the finest shops all around the country. In Erwin, make Stegall's Pottery & Crafts Gallery a must-see stop for that most unusual pottery or craft item for your home.

200 Nolichucky Avenue, Erwin TN
(423) 743-3227

The Spa at Oak Haven

The Spa at Oak Haven, in luxurious Oak Haven Resort, offers customers spa services that smell as good as they feel. Spa Director Emily McBrayer and her team of professionals have prepared a welcoming environment in an area surrounded by mountain beauty. Among the spa's specialties is the Ice Cream Pedicure. You'll be treated to a delicious frozen dessert while your feet luxuriate in a spa version of an ice cream fizz. Following a sherbet exfoliation, you can select a firming foot masque in caramel, chocolate hazelnut or marshmallow. Next, it's a foot and leg massage with a hydrating body icing. Oak Haven's signature facial uses warm stones on the face, neck and shoulders to melt away your tension. The treatment continues with a warm stone massage to your hands and arms, finishing with a cup of tea. Revitalize your skin with a thermal body treatment in the DermaLife Spa-Jet, where you can choose from body masques and scrubs that detoxify the body and de-stress your mind. The Motherly Love spa package includes a Mommy-to-Be Massage, Almost Heaven Facial and Ice Cream Pedicure for the expectant mom. Remember that men enjoy pampering, too. The Gentleman's Retreat includes a deep-tissue massage, back treatment, essential manicure and pedicure, and a healthy lunch. For long-lasting relaxation, you can combine spa treatments with a stay in a beautifully appointed log cabin. For luxurious treatments in a peaceful environment, visit The Spa at Oak Haven.

**2042 Whispering Pines Way, Sevierville TN
(865) 453-6650 or (800) 368-6615**
www.oakhavenspa.com

Yarntiques

How big is the selection of yarn and knitting supplies at Yarntiques? "If we don't have it, you don't need it," says owner Candice Powell Baldwin, flashing the sense of humor that has helped win her scores of loyal customers since opening her business in 2003. Local knitters love hanging out in this shop, located inside a quaint Victorian house in the Historic District of Johnson City. It's a rare day when there isn't a group of seven or more sitting at the table knitting together while sharing tips, small-talk and belly laughs. Candice knits along with her friends, pausing to help folks who stop by to stock up on supplies. She sells yarn to women all over the country, who keep in touch long after visiting the store. They tell Candice that they can't find anything close to her selection where they live. Yarntiques also carries needlepoint supplies and offers a nice selection of antiques for sale upstairs. Relationships and laughter are the heart of her business, says Candice. Drop by Yarntiques to buy your knitting supplies, and perhaps make a life-long friend while you are there.

410 E Watauga Avenue, Johnson City TN
(423) 232-2933
www.yarntiques.com

Famous Dave's

Here are two reasons why you aren't likely to forget the signature All American Feast at Famous Dave's. First, this is barbecue to die for. Second, it comes to your table on a trashcan lid. The uncommon serving plate is Dave Anderson's way of honoring his roots as an aspiring barbecue chef. He began his apprenticeship by sampling meats in a homemade smoker he built from a garbage can. Dave was born a seeker, but his obsession wasn't the Fountain of Youth or the Holy Grail. Before opening Famous Dave's, he logged 25 years visiting every rib shack, roadside joint and fancy supper club around, all in search of the most succulent meats, savory seasonings and lip-smacking sauces. Taste the fruits of Dave's love affair with barbecue at the five Famous Dave's locations in Tennessee. Famous Dave's is known for its hickory-smoked St. Louis-style spare ribs, which are flame-kissed on the grill just before being served. Other dishes, including the slow-smoked Texas-style beef brisket, spit-roasted chicken, spicy sausage and sweetwater catfish, contributed to the *Food Network* declaring Famous Dave's a Food Find. All meats are smoked daily, and the award-winning bread pudding and honey-buttered corn muffins are made from scratch each morning. For barbecue to remember, try Famous Dave's.

7086 Baker's Bridge Avenue, Franklin TN
(615) 778-1227
www.homeofthebigslab.com

The Peddler Restaurant and the Park Grill Restaurant

The Peddler Restaurant and the Park Grill Restaurant are longstanding traditions in Gatlinburg dining. The Peddler Restaurant is constructed around the historic C. Earl Ogle log cabin. Its menu offers hand-cut, hickory-grilled steaks, seafood and grilled or pan-fried trout. The salad bar is top-notch. The hot blackberry cobbler and monstrous mud pie are dessert favorites. The full bar overlooks the river. Just down the road, The Park Grill Restaurant is housed in a majestic mountain lodge, with massive spruce timbers that complement the natural beauty of the Smoky Mountains. The Park Grill Restaurant specializes in mountain favorites, such as the award-winning ribs, grilled rainbow trout and its famous Moonshine Chicken. The restaurant provides mountain-sized portions and an outstanding salad bar. For dessert, try the Chocolate Ecstasy for a perfect ending to your meal. Both restaurants have great kid's menus. When in Gatlinburg, experience the beauty of the Smoky Mountains and a fine meal with a visit either to the Peddler or the Park Grill restaurants.

1110 Parkway, Gatlinburg TN (Park Grill)
(865) 436-2300
820 River Road, Gatlinburg TN (Peddler)
(865) 436-5794
www.peddlerparkgrill.com

Café Lola Bistro & Wine Bar

Hailing from New York City's eclectic Soho, Tara and Hunter Morrow bring a piece of the larger culinary world to Johnson City. Tara, a native of Thailand, has traveled widely and developed a passion for foods from around the globe in a lifetime spent in the restaurant business. After she and Hunter settled on Johnson City as an ideal place to raise a family and start a business, they pooled their knowledge of wine and international cuisine to create Café Lola Bistro & Wine Bar. Café Lola has quickly earned a place in the city's heart. It was voted Best Restaurant of 2006 in the *Johnson City Press* as well as Best Place to Meet for Lunch. It also got a nod for Best Panini Sandwich. One of its most popular features is the Passport Tasting Series, a monthly tasting tour that lets you travel the world through food and wine one country at a time. Tara is a graduate of American Sommelier Association, a prestigious wine school, and her knowledge of wine and food combinations is superb. The daily menu features panini with such distinctive ingredients such as chipotle mayonnaise, caramelized onions and homemade pesto. These are accompanied by creative salads and a special quiche of the day. For dinner, try the stuffed chicken with cranberry-walnut crust. Enjoy live jazz music every Tuesday evening. Come down to Café Lola Bistro & Wine Bar to discover flavors that transcends borders.

1805 N Roan Street, Suite B-1, Johnson City TN
(423) 928-LOLA (5652)

Ye Olde Steak House

Ye Olde Steak House racks up Best Steak House in Knoxville awards every year, but its fame extends far beyond the city limits. The owners say that on any given night there may be folks from 20 states in the restaurant, feasting on porterhouse, prime rib, sirloin strip or steak burgers. Bunt and Helen King began the tradition of serving the best Iowa grain-fed beef available back in 1968. Their three children, Nancy Ayres, Cheryl Wilson and David King, run the restaurant today. David, who cuts all the meat by hand, believes he has the best job in Knoxville. Steak combinations with shrimp, flounder or swordfish are popular. Signature side orders include baked sweet potato with cinnamon butter, broccoli casserole and hot buttered mushrooms. When you choose the baked potato, you get to load it to your liking at your table. All 13 desserts are homemade. Locals order whole cakes and pies and then carry them home. The steak house with its friendly, down-home atmosphere is especially well known to University of Tennessee football fans. Located just six miles from Neyland Stadium, it's on the list of the 100 Best Things about Tennessee Football. It has also made the list of the 100 Best Secrets of the Great Smoky Mountains. Don't leave Knoxville without eating at Ye Olde Steak House, a place that makes new fans every night.

6838 Chapman Highway, Knoxville TN
(865) 577-9328
www.yeoldesteakhouse.com

Dixie Barbeque

Dixie Barbeque is the real McCoy of Southern barbecue. It has a down-home, friendly atmosphere where you can roll up your sleeves and enjoy the substantial portions of genuine Southern barbecue with all the trimmings. As you enter, you'll see dozens of vanity license plates and sports pennants on the walls and a sailboat spanning the rafters. Owner Alan Howell is serious about his barbecue. He's cooked up his fall-off-the-bone-tender ribs, pork, beef and chicken for the last 25 years. He doesn't take shortcuts. The baby back ribs cook for four hours over smoldering wood, while pork goes for a full twelve. Alan's meats are prepared using traditions from all over the South. An avid sailor, Alan discovered his Anegada chicken sandwich recipe in the British Virgin Islands. This is a delicious spicy dish of cubed, marinated and lightly smoked chicken. The Brunswick stew is another local favorite. Dixie Barbeque offers sliced or pulled pork. Choose from eight homemade sauces to dress your meat. Local favorites include the Southern Carolina Gold, the Sauce from Hell and the Alabama White. For dessert, Dixie Barbeque offers Southern-style pecan pie and Grandma Ruth's homemade cakes. Kids eat for just $2.00. Take a trip to Dixie Barbeque for a delicious experience of authentic Southern barbecue.

3301 N Roan Street, Johnson City TN
(423) 283-7447
www.dixiebarbeque.com

Picasso's Fine Dining and Catering

Housed in a beautifully renovated century-old building with original wooden arches and brick walls, Picasso's Fine Dining and Catering offers fine food in a casual atmosphere. The walls are decorated with original art by local artists and jazz-themed posters. The restaurant is famous for its hand-cut Black Angus steaks. All of the breads and desserts are made fresh daily. To start your meal, try the crab-stuffed mushrooms, crawfish cakes or the signature fried green tomatoes. Classic entrées such as prime rib, shrimp scampi and chicken Marsala are some of

the delicious dishes that will tempt you. Picasso's Fine Dining and Catering serves a wonderful dish of shrimp and grits, as well as an excellent lasagna and nightly specials. When it's time for dessert, you must try the Death by Chocolate three-layer cake coated with Chambord liqueur and a dark chocolate ganache. The crème brûlée is another delectable favorite. The restaurant offers full catering services, both on and off site, for parties of any size. Each Monday and Friday evening, enjoy the lively and entertaining Tennessee Poker Tournament. The bar has a grand piano. With local accolades such as Best Dining Experience of 2006 and Best Fine Dining Restaurant in Northeast Tennessee, Picasso's Fine Dining and Catering is place to come see what the buzz is about.

400 Ashe Street, Johnson City TN
(423) 232-7499
www.picassosfinedining.com

Linebergers Seafood Company

Linebergers Seafood Company has been in the business of serving quality seafood for more than 50 years. The restaurant originally started in Gastonia, North Carolina, in 1947. A proud tradition continued when Andy and Teresa MacKinnon brought Linebergers to Gatlinburg in 1989. Their dedication to fine food and great service is evident from the first warm greeting. The restaurant is open and airy with high ceilings, large windows and scenic views both from upstairs and the main floor. Andy and Teresa spend a great deal of time making sure they obtain products of the highest quality, and that commitment is evident in every dish. Each meal is prepared from home recipes that date back to the restaurant's founding. As a starter, many diners love the fried blue crab claws, shelled claws fried to a golden brown. The appetizers, salads and soups, including the signature clam chowder, are delicious feasts on

there own, but be sure to save room for an entrée. From the generous platters to specialty dishes such as Alaskan king crab or the Atlantic swordfish, the menu is filled with must-haves. Linebergers also has a wonderful selection of steaks, all prepared to perfection. Try them blackened for a spicy change. Visit Linbergers Seafood Company once and you can't help becoming a regular.

903 Parkway, Gatlinburg TN
(865) 436-9284
www.linebergersseafood.com

Jane's Lunch Box

The popularity of her chicken and dumplings has earned Jane Myron the nickname Dumpling Diva. At her restaurant, Jane's Lunchbox, comfort foods such as meatloaf, chili and cornbread are the specialties. Jane's meals are prepared with a focus on health, so you won't find anything deep-fried on the menu. For dinner, you'll find Copper River salmon from Alaska. This salmon has one of the highest omega oil contents of any fish. "I don't believe it's shipped to anyone else in northern Tennessee," says Jane, who, as a commissioner for Johnson City, initiated a community health awareness program. She has fun nudging her customers toward something different, and there's always a surprise or two in her selection of homemade soups. Her cute

décor blends local art with antiques, including, of course, old lunch boxes. With 17 years of experience in the catering business, the Dumpling Diva is a seasoned kitchen pro who has created an everyday restaurant that serves nutritious and satisfying food. Let Jane prepare your lunch at Jane's Lunch Box.

1109 W Market Street, Johnson City TN
(423) 434-2665
www.janeslunchbox.com

Little Dutch Restaurant

A Morristown institution since the late 1930s, the Little Dutch Restaurant remains a favorite spot for families, individuals and tourists looking for good food and service in a friendly, down-home atmosphere. Owner George Angelos bought the restaurant with his brother Tommy in 1973 from the original owners, Frank and Mattie Lorino. The brothers had come to America from Greece four years earlier and were saving every penny to invest in a business in Morristown. Upon marrying, George assumed sole ownership of the business. He and his wife, Nina, are the head chefs, managers, waiters and official greeters at the Little Dutch. With the help of their five daughters, George and Nina have carried on the Lorino's reputation for fresh, wholesome,

quality food, while adding a few traditional Greek treats such as baklava and Greek custard pie. Under their ownership, the restaurant has undergone six major renovations, more than doubling its original dining space. "I want this Little Dutch to be a part of downtown history," George says. "I plan to see it last another 65-plus years." Grateful and civic-minded, the Angelos have contributed to the community as board members and major fundraisers for several local nonprofits. Accept their hospitality at the Little Dutch Restaurant.

115 S Cumberland Street, Morristown TN
(423) 581-1441

Sushi Blues

Voted the Best Sushi in the Mountain South for four years running, Sushi Blues is worth your attention when you're in Johnson City. The restaurant is casual and trendy, so you don't need to dress up, but you certainly may if you like. Whether you're coming for a family meal or treating your special one to a romantic dinner, Sushi Blues is perfect. Chef John McGowan offers something for everyone. Some of his signature dishes are the sushi burrito, tuna pizza and panko-crusted ahi sashimi. In addition to fine sushi, Sushi Blues offers tempura, soups, vegetables and fabulous salads, along with a full kid's menu featuring chicken and fries. The Yummy Roll is a local favorite, a delectable combination of tempura shrimp and crab meat. Lovely desserts entice you at meal's end, if you still have room to enjoy them. Try the tempura cheesecake, battered, fried and served à la mode. John received intensive training in sushi preparation with some of the finest sushi chefs in the country. His love of the art is reflected in his beautiful and perfectly prepared creations. Sushi Blues features a full bar and catering services for up to 30 people. Tuesday through Saturday, the restaurant offers nightly specials. The restaurant also sponsors the annual 5K Sushi Blues run. Stop in to Sushi Blues for outstanding sushi at reasonable prices.

1805 N Roan Street, Suite E-3, Johnson City TN
(423) 232-1289
www.sushiblues.net

Hastings Entertainment–Maryville

The city of Maryville is located between Knoxville and the Great Smoky Mountains. Maryville College is here, so the local Hastings Entertainment retail outlet benefits from diverse student contributions to the used merchandise. You can sit in a comfortable chair while you browse the new and used books or listen to a CD at a listening station. From games to movies, Hastings has you covered for personal entertainment. Watch those movies wearing a World Warcraft t-shirt from the Trends section of the shop. Acquire one of the classic board games, such as Twister or Clue, and throw a theme party or just get together with your family. Lines of collectible action figures feature Star War characters and a variety of Ghost Rider figures, as well as celebrities, both real and fictional, including Lara Croft and Kurt Cobain at his last public unplugged show. The store also has a stock of media accessories, including flash drives and compact disks, digital video disks and iPod covers. Hastings Entertainment is more than just a place to pick up your next CD or DVD. It's a community center, and takes its role as a sponsor of local events seriously. Stop by Hastings Entertainment regularly to stay in touch.

501 N Foothills Plaza Drive, Maryville TN
(865) 977-7111
www.hastings-ent.com

Book Heaven

For Vivien Ross, reading is a joy that's better when shared. A former teacher and librarian, she has always felt that there is nothing more important than turning a child on to reading. Book Heaven, the book store her husband Sherman bought for her when he retired, is the fulfillment of a life-long dream. Book Heaven's mission is to promote general reading by making it easy and affordable. Ninety-five percent of the books are used, keeping the prices modest, and trading is encouraged to keep books moving from hands to eager hands. Out on the covered porch, the shop offers a selection of particularly tattered books for free or for 25¢. Even when the store is closed, locals can come by and choose a book under the always-lit porch light, leaving their coin in the honor box. The strategy seems to work: In five years of business, the store's size has doubled as a result of local demand. Book Heaven also supports local authors by selling their new releases and provides donated or discounted books to schools in the area that lack the funding for extra books. The shop offers a storytelling hour for local children's groups. Come browse the stacks, meet the resident tortoiseshell cat named Nom de Plume, and settle on the porch for a good read at Book Heaven, where all good books go.

2640 Upper Middle Creek Road, Sevierville TN
(865) 429-9886

St. John Milling Company

The St .John Milling Company, the oldest business in Tennessee, has been owned and operated by the same family for 230 years. The mill is an astonishing example of workmanship, built of hand-chiseled stone and hand-hewn timbers by the original owner, Jeremiah Dungan, in 1778. Here's a thought: the mill is so old, it has paid taxes to four governments, beginning with colonial North Carolina. Originally, the mill ground corn and wheat for the local farming community. Today, St. John Milling Company is still milling grain with the same 16-foot high water wheel, but now its operations include selling feed and seed as well as locally produced jams and jellies and herbal remedies. You'll also find handmade quilts, craft items and an assortment of furniture, all locally made. Garden supplies, pet food and veterinary supplies round out the eclectic inventory. Seeds may be purchased by the scoop or bag. If you need advice on making your garden grow, the staff is happy to advise. While you're visiting the mill, check out the St. John quilt barn, so-called for local artist Ron Dawson's large, colorful quilt mural, *Little Dutch Girl and Boy*, painted on one side. Chosen as the kickoff location for the Tennessee 1996 Bicentennial celebration, the St. John Milling Company is one of the area's oldest historic landmarks—one you won't want to miss.

3191 Watauga Road, Watauga TN
(423) 928-5841

Evergreen Cottage Inn, Cottages and Cabins

Looking for the ideal place for an in-town experience of Pigeon Forge, yet a bit unusual? Maybe sitting in front of a roaring fire or sunning in a private garden under magnolia trees? Look no further than the Evergreen Cottage Inn. Located in picturesque Pigeon Forge, this by-appointment bed and breakfast offers peaceful stays in well-appointed fireplace suites with whirlpool tubs and vintage queen beds. If you are looking for a reception, wedding or event venue, the Haynes can entertain you and your guests here in town or on Whisperwood Farm in Cosby. Whether you're looking to exchange vows in front of a fireplace in Evergreen Cottage or outdoors in the tranquil garden, you'll be delighted in the beautiful surroundings. The main house is ideal for receptions, and features stone floors, a massive stone double fireplace and glass porch enclosure that makes for a spectacular dining area. A full breakfast is included in your stay. Reunite the family and enjoy private catering on the grounds with a picnic or formal affair. The small cottages on either side of the inn, the upstairs rooms and a central dining room keep the family together. You can almost imagine what Pigeon Forge was like in the early 1920s, when you walk to the Old Mill just a few blocks away from this historic cottage on the Little Pigeon River.

3416 Householder Street, Pigeon Forge TN
(800) 962-2246
www.evergreencottageinn.com

The Lily Barn

The Lily Barn is a pastoral paradise, perfect for vacations, weddings, meals or just wandering in a three-acre perennial garden. Owners Janice and Steve Fillmore give the visitor plenty of reasons to visit their transformed 100-acre farm in Townsend. Janice planted the namesake lily garden in 1996 as a gift to herself and the community, intending it as a free public garden. After friends started asking her to host weddings there, Janice realized how much more could be done with the location and added a giant pavilion with a massive fireplace and roll-down walls to chase away the cold. She also purchased a small chapel. Next, the addition of four cabins created an ideal vacation spot. The cabins range from the cozy Sarah's Meadow Cabin, which is ideal for honeymooners, to the Flame Azalea, which can accommodate 15 guests and offers an inside Jacuzzi, pool table and full kitchen. The Fillmores went on to add Miss Lily's Café and Miss Lily's Catering, which feature the delicious creations of classically French-trained Chef Chris Henderlight. You will find many delightful Southern creations, from fried green tomato sandwiches to fish and grits. A florist shop and gift store allow you to bring garden beauty into your life with fresh flowers or custom planters filled with wildflowers, ferns and shrubs. You can even get a specific day lily variety shipped to your home. Come wander among the flowers, plan a vacation or a big event at the Lily Barn, a facility devoted to beauty.

Mammoth Cave National Park, KY
Photo by Code Poet

West Kentucky

The Eloise B. Houchens Center

Most communities have a place where people can come together to celebrate, share and organize the towns' events and gatherings. The Eloise B. Houchens Center, three blocks from Bowling Green's downtown corridor, is just such a place. The building's brilliantly crafted inlaid wood flooring makes an ideal runway for brides, and the intricately carved fireplaces and mantles that grace each room are perfect backdrops for meetings, parties and ceremonies of all kinds. The Center is home base for more than 45 organizations and is the site of a wide variety of festive and educational community events, including musical concerts and reviews, home tours and day-long card tournaments. This historic dwelling was built in 1904 by Francis L. Kister, a mayor and co-builder of the historic St. Joseph's Catholic Church, which he designed with his father. In 1976, in response to the generosity of Mr. Ervin Houchens, the Eloise B. Houchens Center for Women was chartered and signed a lease in perpetuity. Under the terms of the lease, the Center restored the house and continues to preserve it as a cultural and educational center for the community. Discover kindred spirits while expanding your horizons at the Eloise B. Houchens Center.

**1115 Adams Street, Bowling Green KY
(270) 842-6761**

Four Season's Country Inn

Carole Smith has lived in Barren County since childhood, but it's only recently that the outside world has begun catching on to its charms. In 2007, *Progressive Farmer* named Barren County the Number-One Best Place to Live in Rural America. About 20 years ago, Carole was working in the office of a local factory when she noticed that the businesspeople who traveled in to see her lacked a comfortable place to stay. She and her co-worker dreamed up the Four Season's Country Inn to offer the kind of small-town hospitality she felt they deserved. The inn was built in the Victorian style to blend in with the local historic homes while offering all the modern amenities. At 21 rooms, it's big enough to offer the privacy of a boutique hotel with the personal attention you'd expect from a bed-and-breakfast. The rooms feature some four-poster beds, free HBO, temperature controls and refrigerators. Executive suits include kitchenettes. The honeymoon suite is charming with white wicker furniture and an iron bed, and includes a whirlpool tub for two, CD player and VCR. Continental breakfast features a cappuccino machine, fresh fruit and assorted pastries. Carole manages the property together with her husband and daughter. She has decorated the interior with local arts and crafts and makes sure to keep a fire burning on frosty mornings. Discover what Barren County is all about when you stay at Four Season's Country Inn.

4107 Scottsville Road, Glasgow KY
(270) 678-1000

Lighthouse Landing

The Land Between the Lakes National Recreation Area, a peninsula located between Kentucky Lake and Lake Barkley, is a haven for outdoors enthusiasts. Located at the northern entrance of the Land Between the Lakes, Lighthouse Landing Resort & Marina offers romantic cottage accommodations for arriving vacationers. The cottages offer one to three bedrooms with fully equipped kitchens, most with gas log stoves. All one-bedroom cottages for two have whirlpool tubs. The cottages overlook the picturesque harbor, with exceptional sunset views of Kentucky Lake from private decks. At the Ship's Store, you can browse gifts, souvenirs and a gallery of wildlife photography by Marty Colburn. Guests enjoy a private beach with fire pit, picnic tables and grills located below the 186 feet of lighted walkway that leads to the lighthouse. A panoramic view awaits at the lighthouse. Take a stroll on the boardwalk, and bring your camera! Lighthouse Landing, established in 1977, is known for sailboat sales, service, rentals and training. The sailing school has consistently earned top ratings from the American Sailing Association. If you rent a sailboat during your stay, Lighthouse will outfit you with a Colgate 26, a family-sized 26 foot sailboat which has an outboard motor and is safe, self-righting and easy to sail. Whatever your reason for visiting Kentucky Lake, you'll find scenic accommodations in a central location at Lighthouse Landing.

320 W Commerce Avenue, Grand Rivers KY
(270) 362-8201
www.lighthouselanding.com

America's Paradise Resort

An elaborate front entrance of boulders and fountains welcomes you to America's Paradise Resort, featuring Stone Harbor Condominiums. Located on Snipe Creek right off the main channel of Kentucky Lake, the resort has been a paradise to water-lovers for more than 50 years. Managers and previous owners Rob and Traci Markum raised their family here, serving fried green tomatoes and old-fashioned Southern hospitality to fishers and lodgers. In 2006, they sold the property to HMA Hotels, and the company has initiated major renovations. The centerpiece of the new resort is Stone Harbor Condominiums, available for rent or purchase. America's Paradise Resort has always been known for seclusion and spectacular views, and these condos are no exception, with large private decks overlooking the lake. They also include fully equipped kitchens, cable television, whirlpool tubs and fireplaces. If you're like many visitors to the resort, you won't plan to stay inside all day. Many come to fish in the lake, which is famous for crappie, bluegill, catfish and bass. Record numbers of largemouth and smallmouth bass have been caught in these waters. The resort is expanding its full-service marina to 100 slips. If you haven't got your own boat, America's Paradise has got you covered with a full fleet of rental fishing boats as well as pontoons for cruising. Enjoy the best of Kentucky Lake and come home to luxury at America's Paradise Resort.

1024 Paradise Drive, Murray KY
(270) 436-2767 or (800) 340-2767
www.americasparadiseresort.com

Green Farm Resort

Situated on the historic Green Farm, a 19th century homestead spanning 6,000 acres of timber and farmland, the Green Farm Resort provides a luxurious bed-and-breakfast and one of Kentucky's most outstanding golf courses, Lafayette. The course boasts 18 holes of championship golf in 250 acres of scenic wilderness. Four tees on each hole vary the course from 4,200 to 6,900 yards. The terrain incorporates many lakes and rivers. *Golf Digest* named Lafayette the number two course in the state in 2005–2006 and one of the best four-star courses to play in 2006–2007. Come to play or simply wander the lovely grounds at Green Farm Resort. You'll stay at the Green Farm Mansion in one of nine elegant bedroom suites. Owner Sam Ware has devotedly restored the house with period fixtures and furnished it with Austrian and Baroque antiques. The rooms feature elaborate mahogany beds, hardwood floors and fine rugs. If you fall in love with Green Farm, you can stay forever. The property is now the site of a new, gated resort community. Pick out a romantic home site with forest, river or golf course views. The sites follow the rolling contours of the land, harmonizing with the environment. Green Farm dates back to 1821, when Willis Green bought the land to build a mill on the picturesque Falls of Rough. His last direct descendant lived on the property until she died in 1965, but the old mill and other historic structures still stand. Find historic charm with up-to-the-minute amenities at Green Farm Resort.

55 Jennie Green Road, Falls of Rough KY
(270) 879-3486
www.greenfarmresort.com

Bee Spring Lodge

Bee Spring Lodge is oldest resort on Kentucky Lake owned and operated by the original family. George Onnybecker and his wife, Christina, who took over for his parents in 1999, can't imagine living anywhere else. Offering home-like lodging and cooking for fishermen and vacationers, Bee Spring Lodge is like a stay in a former era. The natural quiet and deliberate pace of life here allow for the kind of first-name hospitality that is all but extinct in today's commercial culture. It's a place where late-arriving visitors will find the porch light on and the keys to their room inside. At the grill, Christina will greet you personally and probably know your order. Widely known as the best breakfast on the lake, the Bee Spring grill serves pancakes and country ham with real red-eye gravy from Dorothy Onnybecker's original recipes. Folks come by car, by foot and by boat to sit at the counter or on the patio overlooking the cove. Lodging includes a dock and campground, two cottages and three motel rooms that sleep up to four. The vintage décor in the rooms includes 1960s Coco-Cola ads and yellowed antique maps of the lake and Marshall County. Bee Spring Lodge is a seasonal resort, open St. Patrick's Day through October. Stop by for an old-fashioned meal or stay awhile to experience what living on the lake is all about.

573 Bee Spring Road, Benton KY
(270) 354-6515
www.beespringlodge.com

Diamond Lake Resort

When you're driving through the lush farmland of Owensboro, stop at Diamond Lake Resort, an oasis of family fun with a variety of accommodations, dining and entertainment. You can hook up your RV under a canopy of trees set in a verdant grassy landscape. For creature comforts, the Diamond Lake motel offers non-smoking rooms with microwaves and refrigerators. Sleep will be the last thing on your mind when you see the five lakes spread across a picturesque, tree-dotted countryside and hear of the ice cream socials, bingo and monthly events that go on here. Let the kids enjoy the go-kart track, or join in and try to race your way to family vacation fame. If you're looking for a slower-paced vacation, you can enjoy a quiet morning fishing or hiking around the grounds. For dinner, head over to the Pit Stop Grill or to the lakeside buffet restaurant. Owners Brian and Janice Smith, and Joe and Laurie Meythaler took over Diamond Lake Resort in 2005 after relocating from the west coast. It was their desire to bring family-oriented recreation to their new home. Today, the resort is a place where locals and tourists gather together to enjoy music, family and the outdoors. Visit Diamond Lake Resort to enjoy non-stop action or simply lounge in the sun.

7301 Hobbs Road, Owensboro KY
(270) 229-4900
www.diamondlakeresort.net

Green Turtle Bay Resort

Green Turtle Bay Resort overlooks beautiful Lake Barkley at the eastern edge of the picturesque village of Grand Rivers. Your vacation gateway to the Land Between the Lakes Federal Recreational Area, the resort is a convenient destination for arriving boaters and anyone looking for a comfortable home-base from which to enjoy the abundant recreation of the area. Stay in one of over 70 independently-owned and decorated condominiums at the resort. Most of the rentals are freestanding, making them virtually like homes, and fully furnished with everything from teaspoons to towels. They offer one to four bedrooms, each with its own bathroom, making a complete suite for each guest. A community health club with indoor pool is coming soon. Walk to breakfast or lunch at Docker's Grill or dinner at the classy Commonwealth Yacht Club, which is built on the pilings overlooking the harbor full of colorful sailboats and yachts. Bring your own boat or rent one at the marina, which offers everything from small fishing boats and waverunners to houseboats. You can stretch out your sea legs by browsing the harbor shops for marine paraphernalia and resort fashion. Kids love feeding the nearly-tame turtles at the bay and enjoy special activities programs in the afternoons and evenings. Make Green Turtle Bay Resort your home-base for enjoying all that Lake Barkley has to offer.

263 Green Turtle Bay Drive, Grand Rivers KY
(270) 362-8364
www.greenturtlebay.com

Bellevue Beadery

Beading is a contagious hobby. Joanna Maehren passed it to her sister, Cathy Brookbank, by recruiting her to help prepare for an upcoming jewelry show. Within days, Cathy wanted to know if they could do this everyday. The sisters opened Bellevue Beadery together in 2003. At the shop, the sisters and their staff make it easy for visitors to catch the beading bug. They offer free classes in everything from basic jewelry-making to wire wrapping, knotting and peyote stitch. Even if you're just browsing, they'll walk you through the process of picking out beads you like and designing your own project. Of course, they also make beautiful custom designs, including wedding party designs. Joanna and Cathy tour all the bead shows to pick out the most enticing pieces for their shop, including semi-precious stones from around the world, Swarovski crystals and colored Czech glass. Bellevue Beadery is in the historic district of town, an area that attracts groups of women shoppers to its many craft stores. The beadery tempts them with girls-night-out parties that revolve around specific beading projects. Party guests only pay for what they make. This strategy seems to work: in just four years of business, the shop has already expanded twice. Find out what all the fuss is about when you visit Bellevue Beadery.

341 Fairfield Avenue, Bellevue KY
(859) 292-0800
www.bellevuebeadery.com

Staton's Art & Framing

Jim Monroe has been involved in the custom picture framing business since 1985 when a friend offered to sell his full-service decorating center and framing shop. Having done a lot of painting in his school days, Jim saw the opportunity to dust off his aesthetic sensibilities and put them to use. Over the next 20 years, Jim cultivated Staton's Art & Framing to become Hopkinsville's central destination for all things artistic and decorative. While professional framing and framed art remain the staples of the business, Jim makes sure to keep a stimulating collection of original local art and home décor items, such as clocks, mirrors, lamps and sculptures. He continues to scour new sources in search of things he hasn't seen before, like the Sid Dickens Memory Blocks—beautiful, one-of-a-kind decorative tiles that are not widely distributed anywhere, let alone Kentucky. Working with a local artist and with help from the county historian, he had

the idea to commission a series of nostalgic scenes of Hopkinsville 50-plus years ago, which are now available as limited edition lithographs. In 2005, Jim moved the shop to its present, gallery-worthy location, a 2,400 square-foot space with beautiful floors, vaulted ceilings, columns and a look uncommon to the Hopkinsville area. Come reap the benefits of Jim's taste at Staton's Art & Framing.

4259 Fort Campbell Boulevard, Hopkinsville KY
(270) 885-0501
www.statonsart.com

The Paint'n Place

At The Paint'n Place, creativity is the name of the game. Artists of all ages and skill levels are welcome to experiment with painting their own pottery, t-shirts, mosaics and other items. With materials provided by the friendly staff members, guests are free to create their own masterpieces without the hassle or clean-up needed when creating at home. Don't feel like you're ready to tackle an art project alone? No need to worry. The staff will be happy to provide instruction and even stencils to help you create that special something. With enough room for 36 people, The Paint'n Place is perfect for school outings, birthday parties for kids or grown-ups, girls' nights out, baby showers and special occasions of all kinds. For kids' birthday parties, The

Paint'n Place offers a special package that includes cake, paper plates, party invitations and a special gift for the birthday boy or girl. The family-friendly atmosphere lends itself to gatherings of all kinds, and is perfect for quality time with the people you love. If you want a customized order, that's no problem—each staff member is an artist and would love to create a special piece of artwork just for you. Stop by The Paint'n Place any time for a good time, and go home with something beautiful.

1243 Magnolia Street, Bowling Green KY
(270) 783-0830
www.paintnplacestudio.com

Quilter's Alley

Both Pat English and her husband enjoyed high-powered careers in Chicago, but after retiring and moving back to their hometown of Paducah, "We were kind of under each other's feet," she says. That's when Pat had the idea of opening Quilter's Alley. Back in 1989, quilting was not yet the multi-billion-dollar industry it is today. Even Paducah, which was already known as Quilt City due to the local National Quilt Museum, had no full-service quilt shop. There was a fabric warehouse on the edge of town, but nowhere to find the experienced, personalized help, the schedule of classes or tasteful selection that today's quilters expect. "We built this business on service," Pat says, "and we gradually layered inventory on top of that." Today, Quilter's Alley offers a complete inventory of quilting and sewing supplies, including as many as 6,000 bolts of fabric. Customers frequently compliment the fabric selection, which Pat and her staff of three pick and choose by committee. You can learn anything from heirloom sewing to the latest quilting trends at the store, which holds classes almost every day. If you survey the display quilts on the walls, you're sure to find design ideas. You can even ask Pat to make your quilt to order. Find a world of quilting resources at Quilter's Alley, Quilt City's own community quilt shop.

420 N 4ʰ Street, Paducah KY
(270) 443-5673
www.quiltersalleypaducah.com

Bobby Lyken's Woodworking

For beautiful custom-made cabinetry, furniture and even canoes, folks in Park City turn to Bobby Lyken's Woodworking. The community keeps owner Bobby Lyken busy almost entirely by word-of-mouth. They appreciate his deliberate, personalized work and the old-fashioned way that he oversees every step of the process, from the drying of the lumber to the finishing of the wood. Bobby works closely with clients in the design process and accommodates such elaborate requests as faux-antiquing and putting kitchen islands on carved legs. Every project is different, and he likes it that way. Bobby loves to be in his shop with the wood, "when it's quiet, and it's just me. I'm a craftsman, not a businessman," he explains. The 3,000-square-foot shop and showroom are situated on the pastoral farm where Bobby lives. Growing up, Bobby learned woodworking by fiddling with scraps in his dad's shop. His dad built houses for over 40 years. This year, Bobby Lyken's Woodworking celebrates its 30ʰ year in business. When you see Bobby's work, you'll keep him busy for many more years to come.

1729 Rick Road, Park City KY
(270) 678-4325

Borders Custom Framing and Fine Gifts

Maybe it was destiny that Joan Borders would grow up to put pretty borders on things. Joan began her apprenticeship in custom framing when she was all of 15 years old. She went on to learn everything she could of the wide world of framing. At Borders Custom Framing and Fine Gifts, she gives free rein to her talents, displaying creative and unusual framing techniques and an artist's eye for gifts. The store is full of inspiring examples of what framing can do: shadow boxes, fabric-wrapped mats and mats with cutouts to look like shutters. Joan does every frame job in-house and to her own high standards. Joan's retail selection brings together artisan furniture and gifts of a quality not often found in small-town Kentucky. Visit the shop in an artistic mood, because you will find art in many different forms here. Joan has a particular eye for woodwork because her husband is in the trade. She offers for sale beautiful wood jewelry boxes, mantle clocks and furniture pieces. Those with rustic tastes will be pleased by the log and twig furniture, antler accessories and ornaments made of real leaves and dipped in 24 karat gold. You'll also find stained glass, local fine art works and one of the largest collections of fine art prints in the state. There are thousands in the sale group alone, offered at $10 or less. Enjoy the privilege of owning beautiful artwork and unusual gifts from Borders Custom Framing and Fine Gifts. Remember, its reputation hangs on your walls.

1226 Main Street, Munfordville KY
(270) 524-4387

Reed, Ribbon & Silks

An Owensboro fixture since 1997, Reed, Ribbon & Silks keeps the traditional crafts of basket weaving and cane furniture making alive in Kentucky. Jade Duncan, a longtime basket weaver, bought the establishment two years ago when the previous owner, Jan, decided to relocate. "I went to buy discounted inventory but I ended up buying all of it," said Jade. Jan taught Jade the ins and outs of running the business, and together, they kept the resource alive for Owensboro. Over time, Jade learned to tailor the store to meet the most current needs of her clientele. Today, handmade baskets, reeds, cane strips and ribbon make up about a third of the store. Jade teaches basket-weaving classes and her aunt, an all-purpose crafty type, teaches specialty classes, such as knitting. Craft fans in general will find much to divert them at Reed, Ribbon & Silk. Jade's aunt makes a fun assortment of paraphernalia—most recently, decorated wine bottles lit inside with Christmas lights, as well as clasp bags and decorative pin cushions. Customers also come regularly for the gourmet coffee and tea. Join the coffee club and you'll get a free pound for every 10 you buy. A pot is always brewing, so you'll smell the aroma as soon as you enter the store. You'll also find gourmet Kentucky-made foods, sauces and dips. Visit Reed, Ribbon & Silks for a traditional Kentucky experience.

1724 Sweeney Street, Owensboro KY
(270) 685-4093

James D. Veatch Camp Breckinridge Museum

An unexpected diamond from a rough piece of American history, the James D. Veatch Camp Breckinridge Museum is painted all over with murals by WWII prisoners of war. The building is the last of three service clubs, recreation stations for army soldiers, that once belonged to Camp Breckinridge, an infantry training camp from the 1940s through the 1950s. A place for dining, drinking and dancing, the building is marked by an enormous wrap-around balcony and contains dining rooms, a bar and a ballroom. In 2000, the local government received a grant to restore and preserve the historic building and its 32 murals inside. During WWII, more than 4,000 POWs lived at Camp Breckinridge. Many were talented young European men who had been drafted to the war when Germany took over their country. These artists were commissioned to paint scenes of their homelands, resulting in an extraordinary tour of Europe throughout the building. Visitors will also find a genealogy center and an exhibit of army memorabilia at the museum, including uniforms, maps, photos and weapons. A guided tour details the history of the camp and the daily life of the soldiers who lived there. Ever wonder how they all found dance partners to make use of that great ballroom? They sent buses out to neighboring counties, naturally. Take a journey into a little-known piece of American history at the James D. Veatch Camp Breckenridge Museum.

Claira M. Eagle Gallery at Murray State University

The Clara M. Eagle Gallery at Murray State University is a dramatic and exciting multi-level exhibition space. An integral part of the Department of Art, the gallery houses about 1,200 permanent artworks, from photography to sculpture, that provide a visual library for research. The permanent collections feature artists Andy Warhol, Jim Dine and Claes Oldenburg, among others. The Eagle Gallery has also hosted temporary shows that featured contemporary art, African art, woodworking and tapestries from Spain. Artists from Michoacan in Mexico and from Korea have been represented. The gallery is named after Claira M. Eagle, former chair of the Art Department, who initiated the permanent collections. Eagle Gallery is the home of two national juried shows—the Magic Silver, a biennial photography competition now in its 28th year, and the Kentucky National, which emphasizes new media. It is also the site for the annual spring student art exhibition. In fall 2008, a special show will feature faculty works, including those of Becky Atkinson, director of university galleries. Together with an exhibition area at the student center, the Eagle Gallery provides 8,292 square feet of exhibition and support space. Visit the Clara M. Eagle Gallery to experience fine art first-hand.

Wrather West Kentucky Museum at Murray State University

The primary mission of the Wrather West Kentucky Museum at Murray State University is to promote an understanding of the social, cultural and economic development of West Kentucky and the Jackson Purchase (Kentucky west of the Tennessee River). Acquisitions, exhibits and special programs support this mission. Both permanent and changing exhibits are open to the public at no charge. Major recent exhibitions include the Hal Riddle collection of Hollywood memorabilia. An alumnus of the school, Riddle accumulated more than a thousand items in his 50-year movie career, many of them extremely rare, and donated them to the museum. The Wrather Museum is located in the University's oldest permanent building, built in 1924. In the early years of the institution, the building was used for campus classes, chapel, pep rallies, debates and plays. It also housed the bookstore, post office, a dining room, science laboratories and the administrative offices. Listed on the National Register of Historic Places, the facility was extensively renovated and dedicated as the Wrather West Kentucky Museum in 1982. It was named for Marvin O. Wrather, a long-time and much loved staff member at the school who was three times its acting president. For an entertaining and educational experience, visit the Wrather West Kentucky Museum at Murray State University.

Wrather Hall, Murray State University, Murray KY

Mayfield, KY

The city of Mayfield lies a short journey from Paducah down the scenic, four-lane U.S. Highway 45. Tree-lined country lanes and one-lane bridges over wandering creeks signal your arrival. A place of Western Kentucky charm, historical Mayfield is draped with the trappings of old-fashioned Americana. The entire commercial district is listed on the National Register of Historic Places. Downtown you'll find antique stores, small boutiques and restaurants, antique street lights and brick sidewalks. You can pick up a map of historical sites from the Mayfield Tourism Commission, located in the stately Edana Locus Mansion. Perhaps Mayfield's favorite attraction is the Wooldridge Monuments, a collection of statues at the tomb Henry G. Wooldridge in the city cemetery. Dating from the late 19th century, the statues represent Wooldridge with several of his relatives, dogs and horses. They are nationally known from the television show *Ripley's Believe It or Not* and the movie *In Country* starring Bruce Willis. The Mayfield courthouse is the site of a prominent Confederate memorial, an obelisk with a built-in fountain, dating to 1917. Mayfield puts on a big bash on the main thoroughfare for the Fourth of July. If you visit in August, you can catch the annual Arts in the Community show, a community-wide exhibition of visual and literary arts. September brings the annual Gourd Patch Festival, a fun outdoor event featuring vendors, craft workshops and entertainment. Experience America in Mayfield.

Edana Locus Mansion: 201 E College Street, Mayfield KY

South Central Kentucky Cultural Center

Situated in the heart of downtown Glasgow, the South Central Kentucky Cultural Center, also known as the Museum of the Barrens, is dedicated to the preservation and interpretation of the history and culture of the barrens. Because early explorers observed open areas of grassland and a lack of major waterways, the area came to be known as the barrens. Today the barrens refers to present day Barren County and portions of Allen, Hart, Metcalfe and Monroe Counties. Exhibits touch on the life and history of this area, beginning with the Paleo exhibit. Other exhibits take visitors on a simulation of the Archaic, Early Cave Explorers, Woodland, Mississippian and Historic Periods. Life in the 1800s is represented by displays ranging from an 1854 sewing machine to a log cabin outfitted as was common in the early part of the 19th century. A military exhibit on the second floor begins with the Civil War and continues on to Desert Storm. On the same floor, view a doll collection, a one-room school, a 1940s kitchen, general store and more. Genealogists will find the research room filled with a variety of records and a large collection of regional newspapers. The center is housed in the historic 1928 Kentucky Pant Factory, a 30,000-square-foot building. At the Art and Antique Gallery, located adjacent to the Center in the old JC Penney building, you will find 25 dealers selling antiques and collectibles plus local artists displaying their art. Explore regional history at the South Central Kentucky Cultural Center.

**200 W. Water Street, Glasgow, KY
(270) 651-9792**
www.cityofglasgow.org/sckcc

Riverview at Hobson Grove

As regal and grand as any Victorian aristocrat, Riverview at Hobson Grove is a stately reminder of a bygone era filled to the eaves with stories and lore. Construction began on the Italianate home in the late 1850s but the Civil War halted the workers in their tracks. The Confederates used the abandoned project as a munitions magazine while they held Bowling Green during the long winter of 1861 to 1862. Atwood and Juliet VanMeter Hobson, the owners, completed the home in 1872 and took possession. Today the elegantly renovated Riverview is a living museum where students, families and groups can gather to peer into the past and learn about the dreams, trials and triumphs of those who came before us. The historic estate, open from February through December, offers tours along with a variety of engaging events throughout the year. Riverview has both a membership and a volunteer program and additionally houses a gift shop filled with treasures from the past and present. Spend a part of your present exploring the past with a visit to the Riverview at Hobson Grove.

1100 W Main Avenue, Bowling Green KY
(270) 843-5565
www.bgky.org/riverview

The Ben E. Clement Mineral Museum

Kentuckians are proud of their land, but not all of its riches are well-known. Dig a little below the agricultural surface and you'll find a whole new layer of riches. The Ben E. Clement Mineral Museum showcases a dazzling collection of minerals and gemstones from around the world, but mostly from the Western Kentucky Fluorspar Region. Thousands of colorful fluorite deposits were unearthed during a brief but potent period of fluorspar mining in the first half of the 20th century. Foreign competition eventually overwhelmed the local industry, but not before Ben E. Clement became acutely aware that he and his contemporaries in the Flurospar Region were making history. He began collecting period journals, photographs and mining tools as well as

Photo by Ron Stubblefield

minerals—a collection that is now considered one of the finest in existence. You'll see shelves of brilliant fluorescent specimens displayed under ultraviolet lights, faceted fluorite pieces of all colors and two collections of carved gemstones. There is also an extensive display of petrified wood and the coal plant fossil lepidodendron. You can retrace the history of the mining industry through documents, photographs, artifacts and audio tapes of miners at the museum. Discover a colorful new facet of Kentucky at the Ben E. Clement Mineral Museum.

205 N Walker Street, Marion KY
(270) 965-4263
www.marionkentucky.us/clementmineralmuseum

Jefferson Davis Monument

The Jefferson Davis Monument was conceived in 1907 at a reunion of the Orphan's Brigade— the First Kentucky Brigade—of the Confederate Army. They were called orphans because the state of Kentucky never seceded from the Union. The Orphans elected to build a monument to show their ongoing loyalty to Jefferson Davis, the President of the Confederate States of America during the Civil War. They conceived an obelisk in the image of the Washington Monument

Photo by Bailey Visual Life

and construction began in 1917. Rationing of building materials during World War I lead to a break in the construction, but the monument was finally completed in 1924. At 351 feet, it is the tallest concrete structure in the world and the third tallest obelisk. The concrete is completely unreinforced by steel. Its base is of limestone quarried from the site. Visitors can take an elevator to an observation room high on the monument. In 2004, a new visitor's center was unveiled. The center includes a gift shop featuring Kentucky handcrafts, souvenirs, books and Civil War memorabilia. You can also watch a video describing Davis's life and the construction of the monument. The monument sits in a 19-acre park with open and covered picnic areas and a playground for kids. Stop for lunch, a great view and an interactive history lesson at the Jefferson Davis Monument.

US Highway 68 E, Fairview KY
(270) 889-6100

Photo by Mike Johnston

Lake Cumberland State Dock

Lake Cumberland is the houseboat capital of the world, with most houseboats built within five miles of the lake. For cream of the crop, though, travel no further than Lake Cumberland State Dock, the country's largest houseboat rental company. With over 80 houseboats in its fleet, State Dock has models to suit every budget, but luxury is its point of pride. If you've never rented a houseboat before, you'll be amazed at the amenities you can enjoy on the water: satellite tracking television, satellite music, great stereo systems, waterslides, outdoor grills and hot tubs. Perhaps the county's premier rental boat, the Mega Cat, is 87 by 22 feet and includes a two-story tube slide, 15-person hot tub, third level sun deck and top-side bar. Each of the eight bedrooms has its own television and DVD player and the kitchen is equipped for the gourmet. State Dock offers complimentary operating instruction for all its vessels and full-time radio access to customer service so even inexperienced boaters can have the lake vacation of their dreams. The 450-slip marina is located inside a state park, offering more vacation possibilities than any other location on the lake. When you feel the need to stretch your sea legs, you'll find tennis courts, swimming pools, horse back riding, hiking trails and golf courses. Back at the lake, 1,200 miles of shoreline, an astounding waterfall and countless secret coves await you. Set out in style to explore the treasures of Lake Cumberland from Lake Cumberland State Dock.

6365 State Park Road, Jamestown KY (270) 343-2525 or (888) 782-8336
www.statedock.com

Photos by Diane Eubanks

Janice Mason Art Museum

Located in the tiny rural town of Cadiz, the Janice Mason Art Museum draws up to 6,000 visitors a year with an impressive variety of local and international shows. Tourists headed for the Land Between the Lakes National Recreation Area and Cadiz's antique row are delighted to find art worthy of a major city with no admission fee. A dedicated committee of volunteers operates the museum and chooses the exhibits, which change every four to five weeks. Recently the staff was thrilled to present the art of Bhutan, a little country tucked between China and India. Bhutan was closed to visitors until 1978, and the exhibit at the Janice Mason Art Museum was one of the first of its kind in the United States. Other exhibits have included the work of a local sculptor, the art of the Trigg County Quilter's Guild, a Christmas tree-decorating show and work from the Best of Kentucky Watercolor Society. The museum holds its own juried art competition every other year. Founded in 1998 in a historic former post office, the museum's supporters so impressed the area with their civic enthusiasm that local resident Janice Mason endowed its renovation, beginning in 2000. Dedicated to presenting art in all its forms, the Janice Mason Art Museum produces a community play every summer. Volunteers offer arts and crafts classes in everything from painting to soap making. At the gift shop, you'll find hand-painted Christmas ornaments, jewelry and pottery made in Kentucky. Come see what Kentucky artists and artisans are up to at the Janice Mason Art Museum.

71 Main Street, Cadiz KY (270) 522-9056
www.jmam.org

Rose Hill Lyon County Museum

The Rose Hill Lyon County Museum protects, preserves and displays the cultural and historical heritage of Lyon County so that understanding is passed down to following generations. The museum vividly tells the story of Lyon County, Eddyville and the surrounding region through pictures, artifacts, information and displays. The house in which the museum is located was built by Robert Livinston Cobb, grandfather of local humorist and author, Irvin S. Cobb. The Cobbs and 11 other families were led from Vermont to Eddyville by a man named Matthew Lyon. Cobb and Lyon were trained ironmasters, drawn to the abundant iron ore deposits in the area. Together, they developed an iron industry in the county. One of the attractions in the museum is an automated iron furnace, built to scale, that nearly fills the room. One push of a button removes the top so you can see how it operates. The 19th century brick home, built circa 1832, overlooks Lake Barkley in the shadow of the Kentucky State Penitentiary, often called the Castle on the Cumberland. The two structures are the last remnant of Old Eddyville—Eddyville and Kuttawa were relocated when the Cumberland River was impounded and the lake was formed. The house has changed hands through the years and is now owned by the Lyon County Historical Society. The Rose Hill Lyon County Museum is open afternoons from mid-May to mid-October, Wednesdays through Sundays, and by appointment for escorted tours led by volunteers. Come explore the past of western Kentucky.

Old Eddyville Historic District, State Highway 730, Eddyville KY (270) 388-7322

Kentucky Opry

There is only one true purpose for the Kentucky Opry—to put on a fun show that keeps the customers tapping their feet, clapping their hands and having a good time. The family-oriented country music variety show features a dozen entertainers beside beautiful Kentucky Lake for regular crowds of 600. They've come a long way. The first show was performed at the junction of Highway 68 and 641 on April 25, 1988. In those days, crowds were small. One night there were seven customers, the only show the Opry performed with more people on stage than in the audience. Word-of-mouth advertising brought growing crowds. By the end of 1988, the little Quonset building was overflowing and plans were made for a bigger building. Within the year, a new, 520-seat theatre was constructed and the first show opened to a crowd of more than 600. The theatre on the hill in Draffenville has been Kentucky Lake's most popular live show for the past 20 years. Clay Campbell, with his wife, Barbie, and their sons Clayton, Cody and Casey have put together one of the most exciting, fast-paced music shows you'll ever have the opportunity to see. The Kentucky Opry hosts many special events throughout the year, including the Largest Talent Show in the Midwest, 1950s and 1960s Rock & Roll shows and Grand Ole Opry Stars. For a fun cultural experience, don't miss the Kentucky Opry.

88 Chilton Lane, Benton KY
(270) 527-3869

Kenlake State Resort Park

Enjoy a resort atmosphere without all the crowds at Kenlake State Resort Park, a lakefront hotel, restaurant and recreational facility. You can take advantage of many activities in and around the resort. A challenging 9-hole golf course and a marina with rental boats offer golf and

fishing aficionados close proximity to their favorite sports. The outdoor amphitheater plays host to several large Kentucky attractions annually, including the Kentucky Lake Bluegrass Festival and the Hot August Blues concert. An elk and bison prairie offers pastoral charm, while an 1850s working farm depicts the agricultural life of the 19th century. Kenlake is also within two miles of a pristine forest with 200 miles of hiking trails, a nature station and planetarium. After a day of sightseeing and sunbathing, enjoy fine dining at Aurora Landing Restaurant with breathtaking views of the lake and gardens. The hotel offers 48 rooms with modern amenities. Fully equipped cottages, complete with kitchens and living rooms, are perfect for the entire family. Spend your next vacation at Kenlake State Resort Park and discover your new favorite Kentucky destination.

542 Kenlake Road, Hardin KY
(270) 474-2211

Museum of the American Quilter's Society

The Museum of the American Quilter's Society, (MAQS), offers a modern view of an old tradition in the largest quilt museum in the world. From contemporary art to antique and traditional quilting, more than 150 quilts are always on display. Traveling exhibits from around the world make each visit a new and exciting experience. Stained glass windows based on specific quilts grace the lobby area and a hand-carved wooden quilt hangs in the Conference Room. The Museum Shop offers handcrafted pottery, jewelry, blown glass and wood work by regional and national artists as well as over 1,000 different quilt-related books. Life-size statues of the Lewis and Clark Expedition on the front lawn connect MAQS with local history and

provide accessible outdoor art. Education is an important aspect in the MAQS mission. The museum hosts workshops for adults and children as well as Gallery Talks by exhibitors and book signings by authors in the gift shop. Guided tours range from a 15 minute introduction to an in-depth 40 minute tour of all exhibits with time to ask questions. Hands-on activities are also available for prescheduled groups. Learn much more about MAQS when you pay them a visit.

215 Jefferson, Paducah KY
(270) 442-8856
www.quiltmuseum.org

Photo Courtesy of the
Paducah-McCracken County Convention & Visitor's Bureau

RiverPark Center

In 1992, Tony-nominated Broadway producer Zev Buffman was on tour with one of his productions in Louisville when the theater director asked him if he had heard about the "miracle out west." He hadn't. Was some new theater renaissance taking place in California or Washington? No—the miracle was the new, state-of-the-art RiverPark Center in Western Kentucky. With a 1,479-square-foot main auditorium that could host even the most ambitious national productions, the center was pumping new life into the culture of the region. Buffman was so intrigued that he decided to visit. When he saw the sparkling new civic landmark overlooking the Ohio River, he knew it was something special. Years later, Buffman returned to RiverPark Center as its president and CEO. First on his agenda was to produce an annual Broadway series. But Buffman also understood that the center was a great resource for building new productions. Owensboro offers all the necessary amenities for producing plays at half the cost of the bigger cities, plus Southern hospitality. Word-of-mouth spread through the industry, and today new productions pump millions into the local economy. This year, Buffman inaugurated the first annual International Mystery Writers' Festival, dedicated to discovering new mystery plays. Other annual events at RiverPark include the Winter Wonderland, a month-long celebration of the season including ice skating, a carnival, Santa and holiday movies. RiverPark Center hosts more than 1,000 events a year. Make plans to visit the miracle out west.

101 Daviess Street, Owensboro KY Box office: (270) 687-ARTS (2787)
www.riverparkcenter.org
www.newmysteries.org

Pinecone Art Gallery

A showcase for young and emerging artists, Pinecone Art Gallery is part of a booming arts district that is drawing tourists and relocators from all over the nation. Visitors to Lower Town, Paducah might be surprised to learn that just seven years ago, the historic neighborhood was in critical condition. The city and Paducah Bank implemented a revolutionary Artist Relocation Program to bring new cultural energy to Lower Town, selling established artists home and studio space in the grand old Victorians of the district. Char Downs, a neo-expressionist artist of mixed media, relocated to Paducah from the west coast of California. Most artists in Lower Town operate personal galleries and studios—there are more than 40 of these, to date—but Char's Pinecone Art Gallery is one of only a few that gives significant space to other regional and international artists. She rotates exhibits every two to four months, displaying a wide variety of media from mosaic to glass art, ironwork to jewelry, quilts to furniture in addition to her own paintings. With broad tastes and a respected name, she's never had to look far for exciting artists to exhibit, and she's already booked through the next four years. Char's own work uses watercolor and acrylic paint, pens and pencils to illustrate myths, legends, songs and women's stories. A onetime art teacher, Char divides her time between murals, sculpting and private commissions out or her studio. Char and her husband, Jay, wrote the book on Lower Town, Paducah for Arcadia's the popular Then and Now series. Pick up a copy online, at bookstores or when you visit Pinecone Art Gallery.

421 N 7th Street, Paducah KY
(270) 443-1433
www.artgallerypinecone.com

Rooti Patooti's Art on a Whim

One of Greenville's best-kept secrets, Rooti Patooti's Art on a Whim lies down an intriguing tree-lined drive. Here Lucinda Humphrey Scharf exhibits her vibrant artwork throughout her historic, plantation-style home. The house, originally built in the 1850s, belonged to the Armstrong family for more than a century. Famous horse jockey Sherman Armstrong kept a horse farm here. Lucinda and her husband bought the 50-acre property four years ago, where guests can stroll country gardens and about 70 percent of the house, with its many fireplaces and antiques. The main attraction, of course, is the constantly changing display of some 300 paintings by Lucinda. She works primarily in soft pastels—raw, undiluted pigments that make for incomparable intensity. A lively personality unites the paintings, which range from botanical to nostalgic themes. "I get on these whims," Lucinda explains of her diverse subject matter and the name of her gallery. You will see huge, intricate birds and flowers and antique photos given new life in full color. Several local towns have commissioned Lucinda to paint its historic landmarks to help raise funds for restoration projects. You can purchase prints and cards of the artwork along with original paintings in her in-house gift shop. Make an excursion and find something unexpected at Rooti Patooti's Art on a Whim.

2284 State Route 973, Greenville KY
(270) 338-2855
www.rootipatooti.com

The Gallery at 916

Artistic inspiration meets gift-giving paradise at the Gallery at 916, State Street's new hot spot. Lynn O'Keefe and Melissa Walblay are the masterminds behind this inspirational new shop on historic Fountain Square. The Gallery at 916 offers a full spectrum of masterfully crafted fine art paintings, sculptures and jewelry, as well as custom textiles and functional art pieces. The shop features the work of many local and regional artists working in a variety of media, including glass, pottery, mixed media and silk design. The Gallery even carries select antique pieces, which nicely round out a color-filled, eclectic inventory. Just for fun, the Gallery exclusively stocks Matilda's Candies. The Gallery at 916 hosts several artists' events throughout the year, such as new artist introductions and receptions. Invest in the arts while picking up the perfect gift or décor item for your home with a trip to the Gallery at 916.

916 State Street, Bowling Green KY
(270) 843-5511
www.thegalleryat916.com

WellSprings Institute

As a practicing dermatologist, Evelyn M Jones, M.D. has had the privilege of meeting with many patients and hearing their stories about life and health issues. These experiences and her personal passion for promoting wellness inspired the WellSprings Institute, Dr. Jones' comprehensive skincare treatment center. Dr. Jones believes that dermatology is more than skin deep. Highly trained medical skincare specialists partner with spa technicians and even a staff dietitian in an effort to meet the patient's needs in one convenient location. Underlying the success of WellSprings Institute is Dr. Jones' commitment to the education of her clients and patients. Seminars and workshops detail the benefits of specific treatments, topicals, nutritional counseling and stress management. Cosmetic concerns are fully addressed at the institute with laser treatments, Botox Cosmetic, which is a registered trademark, fillers, microdermabrasion and facials. Spa services are both cosmetic and therapeutic. Glycolic and Jessner's Peels dissolve surface debris from the skin while tightening, toning and evening the color. The menu of massages includes not only relaxation and deep tissue, but also a treatment to meet the special needs of pregnant women and cancer patients. The WellSprings boutique stocks physician-strength skincare systems, Jane Iredale mineral makeup, bath and body gels, candles and gift items. Treat your body well at WellSprings Institute.

2341 New Holt Road, Paducah KY
(270) 554-SKIN (7546)
www.wellspringsinstitute.com

Queen City Riverboat Cruises

Looking for a new favorite pastime? Take an enchanting moonlit dinner cruise or a fun family jaunt on the mighty Ohio river with Queen City Riverboat Cruises. Queen City offers some of the highest quality dining, entertainment and special occasion accommodations in the area, plus a variety of cruises, each tailored to fit your vacation, outing or celebration. Private and public charter cruises are available and can include continental breakfast, hot or cold lunch or a formal dinner. Each meal is carefully prepared with fresh produce, tender meats and served with Queen City's own special blend of coffee. Take a lunch cruise and enjoy bingo or captain narration. Try the sightseeing cruise or one of the dinner and cocktail cruises. Themed cruises include Monte Carlo night, Hawaiian luau and all-American grill out. Queen City's boats are also available for school tours, senior groups and non-profit organizations at a discounted rate. If you're looking for an amazing place to hold your wedding, reunion or anniversary, let Queen City Riverboats take you and your guests on a special occasion ride. Enjoy the crisp warm breeze and be surrounded by sparkling indigo water and a dedicated staff making sure every moment is perfect. Whether you have a group of 50 or a party of 10, Queen City Riverboats has the menu, entertainment and expertise to show you the Ohio river and its surrounding communities with style. Come aboard and experience stunning views from a whole new perspective.

303 Dodd Drive, Dayton KY

Stranded Cow Café, Catering and Gifts

In Paducah, the so-called Cow House on 6th Street is legendary. During the 1937 flood, the house was the refuge of a stranded cow named Bossie, who lived on the second floor balcony. The Coast Guard came by daily to milk and feed her. A photo in the June 1937 issue of *National Geographic* forever immortalized Bossie on the balcony. But it took Grace and Bernie Hebert, newcomers through the Paducah Artist Relocation Program, to rescue and restore the Cow House. The whole town turned out for the grand opening of the Stranded Cow Café, Catering and Gifts. The artist community of LowerTown donated the décor—cow portraits in every medium and style imaginable. Grace and Bernie themselves are artists of many talents and have worked in fibers and jewelry. The also have solid backgrounds in food service. The Stranded Cow combines their abilities. It offers excellent food and an ever-changing array of arts and crafts for sale. You can dine indoors or outdoors on homemade soups, salads, sandwiches and breakfasts. Of course, no meal is complete without a brown cow or purple cow dessert. Grace likes to play with cake recipes, so you may be lucky enough to try something original when you visit. Catering menus are tailored to your event and budget. Gifts include painted pottery, decorated crosses and original jewelry designs. If you see something you like, snap it up, because these artists never make the same thing twice. Don't miss this local landmark, the Stranded Cow Café, Catering and Gifts.

527 N 6th Street, Paducah KY
(270) 575-0020
www.thestrandedcow.com

Brickyard Café

Leaving the troubles of Yugoslavia for new lives in the United States, restaurant owner Robert Stupar and his partner Zeljko "Jake" Simic have used their skills and experience to create an exceptional restaurant. Featuring Italian and Mediterranean cuisine, the Brickyard Café offers attentive service, freshly prepared dishes and a welcoming atmosphere that encourages a leisurely pace. The wines are fabulous. The restaurant's full selection of traditional Italian dishes include spinach fettuccine, spicy seafood linguine and the Brickyard's own lasagna made with Bolognese sauce. Other favorites include the restaurant's flavor packed pizzas and sandwiches, made from scratch and piled high with quality ingredients. For the flavors of Yugoslavia, the goat cheese pizza is tasty and the baklava makes a wonderful dessert. In addition to the Bowling Green location, Robert and Jake have expanded into Franklin, where they have renovated a 1900s hardware store. Both locations embody the spirit of the Adriatic Sea, where you'll find perhaps the world's most beautiful coasts. Turn your next meal into a true gourmet getaway with a trip to Brickyard Café.

1026 Chestnut Street, Bowling Green KY
(270) 843-6431
205 W Cedar Street, Franklin KY
(270) 586-9080

Detroit Joe's Restaurant

If you gravitate towards comfort foods when you eat out, you'll want to visit Detroit Joe's Restaurant, a popular neighborhood establishment that regulars rate a cut above the rest. It's the little extras that make Detroit Joe's special, according to Polly Campbell, food critic for the *Cincinnati Enquirer*. "The cheeseburgers have at least an extra half-inch of thickness," she reports, "the salads have a better grade of lettuce, wings come with hot towels and the dessert menu offers plenty of homemade desserts." She could have added that the popular Hawaiian chicken salad comes not with just a few bites of chicken but with a whole tower of chicken breast in a honey Dijon yogurt dressing. Detroit Joe's is family-owned and operated by Mark and Marla Sandfoss,

who do Kentucky proud by using local products whenever possible. Enjoy the flavor of Kentucky's favorite distilled beverage on your dessert of apple bread pudding with bourbon cream sauce. Mark and Marla are so picky about what goes into their foods that they even cook their pasta in bottled water. Their restaurant is open for lunch on weekdays and for dinner on Fridays and Saturdays. For food that's both familiar and exceptional, try Detroit Joe's Restaurant.

115 E 9th Street, Newport KY
(859) 261-5637

The Cellar Restaurant & Wine Bar

The upscale Cellar Restaurant & Wine Bar is a haven for wine aficionados and those who appreciate an elegant, candlelit dinner. With menu items such as the Moroccan Lamb Kabob,

a marinated leg of lamb flame-grilled and served with curried couscous salad, and the tangy Cajun Jambalaya Pasta, you're sure to find your new favorite dish. Tempting starters such as Belgian cheese fondue and Alaskan salmon cake will be sure to wet any food-lover's whistle. The spicy Brazilian empanadas are a local favorite, made with Latin American beef turnover and filled with olives, carrots, raisins and cumin. The multi-ethnic menu makes Cellar a popular destination for tapas and drinks. The extensive wine list offers wines from all over the world, including South Africa, New Zealand, Australia, France and the Pacific Northwest. These exquisite wines are the theme of the restaurant, and with its fine wood interior, you may feel that you are dining inside a fine wine cellar. Expect classy ambiance and expert food and wine pairings at the Cellar Restaurant & Wine Bar.

937 College Street, Bowling Green KY
(270) 781-7891
www.thecellarbg.com

Frances BBQ

When five-year-old David Arms stood on a soda crate at Frances BBQ to take orders, he didn't imagine that he would one day inherit the family business, turning it into one of the most successful barbecues in the area. Second only to the tantalizing menu is the down-home atmosphere and the family welcome everyone receives at Frances BBQ. David says that since his mother, Frances, opened the restaurant, she hasn't met a stranger. David is a storyteller at heart, and the only thing bigger than the meal portions are the laughs and sincere warmth radiating from David, his wife Jennifer and the family of staff. Frances BBQ is famous for its pork steak, made with a fresh Boston bacon center cut and grilled by hand, lathered with the restaurant's secret sauce. The 100-year-old, vinegar-based barbecue sauce seeps into the pork, creating such a tender, tangy dish that it's almost addictive. David and his good friend, country singer, John Anderson, invented the sauce, and you won't find it anywhere else. Of course, you can't leave without trying one of the six different types of chicken and delectable barbecue ribs. Stop into Frances BBQ and take a bite of that Southern flavor.

Highway 163 and Highway 216
(270) 487-8550

Patti's 1880's Settlement

Although Grand Rivers is a small town, Patti's 1880's Settlement thrives. Visitors from the surrounding area come here for a great meal, a variety of activities and a relaxed atmosphere. However, the settlement's current size has humble roots. In 1977, Patti Tullar, her husband Bill, and son Chip, opened a small hamburger stand called Hamburger Patti's. The restaurant included a six-unit motel. Due to success, the motel units were eventually transformed into dining rooms. CEO Michael Tullar, Patti's son, says one of the restaurants first milestones was in 1990 when the operation expanded and the settlement began. "We had log cabins, which we turned into gift shops, there were gardens, streams and an animal park," he explains. Today, there are three restaurants: Patti's 1880's Restaurant, Mr. Bill's Restaurant and Miss Patti's Iron Kettle. "We are famous for our two-inch thick charbroiled pork chop," Tullar says. "We serve about 100,000 pounds of pork chops in a town of 350 people." Patti's is known for its homemade desserts and has about 15 varieties of pie on-hand every day. The bread is baked in clay flower pots and served warm with regular or whipped strawberry butter. Patti's also draws visitors to its attractions. The grounds are home to miniature golf, gift shops, gardens, a chapel, wedding gazebo and animal farm. There is also a rock-climbing wall and remote-control boats. "Every year, we try to do something different and create a new attraction," Tullar says. Patti Tullar's philosophy was to treat each guest like a visitor in the home. Today, that approach remains a top priority. Patti's is located between Kentucky Lake and Lake Barkley's dams at the northern entrance to the Land Between the Lakes. Visit Patti's 1880's Settlement, one of the largest tourism attractions in Western Kentucky.

1793 JH O'Bryan, Grand Rivers KY (270) 362-8844 or (888) 736-2515 www.pattis-settlement.com

August Moon

The artistic, contemporary design at August Moon makes an outstanding setting for its fresh and exciting Chinese cuisine. In addition to a daily buffet, you'll find such exotic specialties as Crystal Chicken, lightly battered chicken strips sautéed in a powerful sweet garlic sauce, and Festival Shrimp, sautéed with fresh house greens in white wine sauce. The bold diner will find fiery flavors expertly blended in the hot and sweet Fire Cracker Chicken. Health-conscious guests will be happy to know that the restaurant does not cook with any trans fat oils. The menu offers interesting tidbits on the cuisine, such as the origin of the Egg Fu Young, a Chinese omelet shaped to resemble the Fu Young flower. Local diners and surrounding communities have embraced August Moon for its consistently fresh and flavorful Mandarin wok cooking, available for dining in or carry out. In return, August Moon is a faithful supporter of the community through donation, fund-raising and charity events that support the Murray fire and police departments, Rotary Club, boy and girl scouts, Relay for Life and the American Heart Association, among others. The restaurant's three private dining rooms can accommodate groups of 20, 40 or 60 people. Reservations are accepted for large parties. Come to August Moon and see for yourself why it was voted Murray's Best Chinese Restaurant four years in a row.

1550 Lowes Drive, Suite F, Murray KY
(270) 759-4653
www.augustmoonmurray.com

Cecilia's Pizza

When you eat at Cecilia's Pizza, don't be surprised if everyone at your table orders their own large pizza and finishes it in one sitting. These fresh-baked, handmade pizzas have an irresistible aroma and heavenly taste that make you want to eat until there's nothing left. Owners Kevin and Cecilia Fulkerson and a friendly staff run this popular dinner destination with a flair for inventive recipes and outstanding service. Each pizza is made with homemade dough, a spicy sauce and fresh ingredients. In addition to offering some of the best carry-out and delivery pizzas in the area, Cecilia's Pizza has calzones, fresh salads, and sandwiches made-to-order. Choices of toppings include a wide variety of items such as peppers, onions, pepperoni and tomatoes as well as garlic butter, nacho cheese, bacon, hamburger and pepper rings. Inventive patrons are welcome to mix and match toppings to create their own pizzas or choose from the original Cecilia's Pizza menu. The Adam Bomb sub, a fully loaded dish with Philly steak, chicken, bacon, onions, green peppers and mushrooms, is said to explode with flavor in your mouth. Come in and try it, or one of the other delectable dishes, and find taste that goes beyond the ordinary at Cecilia's Pizza.

6530 US Highway 231, Utica KY
(270) 729-5700

Coe's Steak House

A family-owned and operated restaurant, Coe's Steak House started out in 1972 with 14 coffee cups and a few Southern home recipes. George and Geneva Coe now own one of the most popular steak houses in the area. Serving over 200 steaks in a single weekend, the Coes are busy feeding the small town of Russell Springs. Stepping into this homey country restaurant is like walking into Mom's kitchen, where the warm friendly atmosphere is second only to the delectable meals. Be sure to sample one of Kentucky's favorite dishes, Icelandic catfish, prepared with a closely guarded family recipe. In addition, the steak options are endless, and served to each customer's specifications. Whether it be super-rare or crisply well done, each steak is a juicy, mouth-watering phenomenon. Find out what all the fuss is about when you dine at Coe's Steak House.

2961 E Highway 80, Russell Springs KY
(270) 866-9980

Mandolin

Nermin and Rosa Kusmic have taken the classic Italian restaurant and elevated it to a new level with the creation of Mandolin. You'll cast off the present as you walk through the doors of the 140-year-old home, furnished with beautiful handmade art and woodwork, that hosts the restaurant. Mandolin takes you on a culinary journey that leaves you enraptured from the first taste through the last. Upon arriving in Bowling Green, the couple decided almost immediately

that this was the perfect town for the restaurant of which they dreamed. The Kusmics expertly meld quality ingredients using Old World recipes to create exquisitely savory, flavorful dishes, such as Mediterranean chicken and pork *saltimbocca*, as well as traditional favorites such as cheese ravioli and shrimp scampi. For dolci, or dessert, wrap your tongue around Mandolin's signature Italian cream cake, a smooth and dreamy delight that will have you smiling with every bite. In addition to an excellent word of mouth following, Mandolin has been named the town's Most Romantic Place by the *Bowling Green Daily News*. Savor fine wines, remarkable cuisine and a touch of old country ambience at Mandolin.

712 Chestnut Street, Bowling Green KY
(270) 901-0875

Unique Gifts

What better place to shop for unique gifts and get great ideas than Unique Gifts, a family-owned business that has been serving Kentucky for the past 11 years. Owners Rickey and Jackie Nuckols take great pride in making this a true adventure. This multifaceted shop is divided into different sections in a charming 60-year-old house, dubbed the white house with a red roof. Step onto the front porch and see the latest outdoor designs, such as wind chimes, flower pots, buckets, whimsical signs and yard stakes. One room features a candy case with over 25 different truffle selections to put a smile on your face. This room also includes Crabtree & Evelyn bath and body products, and Catstudio glasses, tea towels and Kentucky pillows. There is also a section filled with University of Kentucky, University of Louisville and Western Kentucky University memorabilia and kitchen accessories. Unique Gifts has a bridal and baby registry, and a large room filled with china, stemware and flatware patterns along with pottery, pewter, candles and acrylic. The baby room features Bunnies By The Bay, Three Marthas and Ty, plus Webkinz, Lamaze baby toys, children's jewelry, banks and books. Another room is filled with stationery, clocks, Vera Bradley and Brighton jewelry. You will even discover Waterford Crystal, Byers Choice carolers and of course, a horse section. Upstairs brings a large room filled with Christmas all year long. Call ahead for hours or visit the website for the latest updates. Let the gift giving experts offer you a helping hand when you come to Unique Gifts.

1101 Cleveland Avenue, Glasgow KY
(270) 651-6882
www.uniquegiftsinc.com

Treasure Nook Garden Gallery

Treasure Nook Garden Gallery is a friendly, come-as-you-are environment. The deceptive grey metal building hides a breathtaking garden paradise of floral, home décor and gifts. Jewelry and Crocs footwear are included in the delightful panopoly. Items such as the Yankee and Colonial candle products can add a festive ambiance to a home, while Willow Tree sculptures by Susan Lordi lend a touch of grace. The latest addition to the store features a 40-by-60 foot garden with a brick floor leading you on a garden stroll through lifelike flowers, greenery, small fountains and a waterfall pool. Large framed pictures and mirrors reflect the serene displays. All year, Treasure Nook is the source for holiday décor, ornaments and Christmas trees. The Treasure Nook's story is a tale of imagination and courage. Sisters Kathie Conn and Karen Hopper dreamed up the business on their parents porch. In one week, the dream became a reality. As business grew, they bought the current building, but almost gave up with the loss of one of their children, Brandi. Support of their friends and family and faith in a higher power gave them the courage to go on. Presently, upcoming additions to the family just might inspire a nursery in the next expansion. Treasure Nook Garden Gallery is within minutes of Lake Cumberland, Wolf Creek Dam and the new National Fish Hatchery.

212 Steve Drive, Russell Springs KY
(270) 866-8999

Miss Martha's Antiques

After seven years of renting spaces in a Jackson antique mall, Martha Price drove home from her job in Paris, Tennessee on a hot summer day and told her husband, Bill, "It was really hot in the traffic today; I think something might be wrong with the air conditioner in my car and by the way, I stopped in Hazel and bought a building on my way home." With these words, the future of Miss Martha's Antiques was born. For 25 years, Miss Martha's Antiques has been garnering a reputation as a solid, full-line, general antiques shop for the public. The staff is helpful and friendly and prices are reasonable. Miss Martha's is located in the small town of Hazel in the far western corner of Kentucky, but celebrities such as Bruce Willis, Demi Moore, Molly Sims and David Letterman, and many country and western music stars visiting from

Nashville have still managed to find them. The antiques showroom on Main Street is in a 1923 building that served time as a grocery store, laundry, pool hall and HUD offices before having its six rooms transformed into 3,300 square feet of resplendent antiques. Martha and Bill Price own every item. They have one rule: they never buy anything that they would not want to live with. Plan on making several trips to collect the items you want to live with. Everyone is welcomed at Miss Martha's Antiques.

403 N 18th Street, Murray KY
(270) 753-7346

Strictly Country Antique Mall

A love of history and antiques runs in the family at the Andrew Jackson Hampton homestead: Tripe Pine Farm, where Sherry Ford and her daughter Cindy run the Strictly Country Antique Mall. The mall offers shoppers an authentic setting in which to browse among the antiques, country furniture and advertising collectibles. Sherry acquired an interest in vintage items in her childhood, when she often accompanied her parents on antique excursions. One day they visited the Andrew Jackson Hampton homestead, which is listed in the National Register of Historic Places because it is one of few working farms in the state with its original 19th century outbuildings still intact. The owners invited Sherry's family for a personal visit. It was then

that she made up her mind to own a similar homestead someday. Sherry and her husband Wendell purchased the Triple Pine Farm in 1975. In 1984, the inspiration struck them to share a bit of history by opening an antique shop on the property. The barn was renovated, and the first visitors were welcomed. You'll also see a replica of 19th century pioneer log cabins built by Cindy's husband, Paxx, who specializes in vintage replicas and restorations. Soak up the ambiance of the old south at the Strictly Country Antique Mall, located on Highway 31-W North.

5945 Bowling Green Road, Franklin KY
(270) 586-3978

Brass Lantern

When a friend told Kelly Wilson about a restaurant available on Kentucky Lake, Kelly, who has a passion for fishing and 20 years experience in restaurant management, found it too appealing to pass up. He placed himself in the kitchen of the Brass Lantern as head chef and head dishwasher, and enlisted his wife, Bertha, to set the mood in the dining room as hostess and decorator. The Brass Lantern is an anomaly in its region, a restaurant that appeals equally to locals and tourists with two menus and a variety of themed rooms. It was the first restaurant in West Kentucky to earn the Mobil 3-Star rating and is recommended in both the AAA and Exxon guides. The gourmet menu boasts such fineries as lobster tail, roasted duck and the best prime rib around. Fresh pastas and signature sauces, all made from scratch, complement the selections. The Locals Lite menu takes local mainstays and kicks them up a notch—for example, fried catfish becomes jalapeño polenta-encrusted catfish. Appetizers such as stuffed mushrooms and French onion soup in a bread bowl are both fun and fine. You'll see everything from casual to formal wear, and a lot of parties. During December, it's best to call ahead, because the Brass Lantern hosts about a hundred Christmas parties in season. Its three rooms are decorated with locally-made art and crafts, including antiques. Many of these are available for purchase. Find local and world-class flavors at the Brass Lantern.

16593 U.S. Highway 68 E, Aurora KY
(270) 474-2773
www.brasslanternrestaurant.com

Yesteryear Antiques & Collectibles

Nestled in the heart of Western Kentucky is the town of Madisonville, named after President James Madison, with its 20,000 great people and lots of great places. Ruth Morrow grew up near here as a coal miners daughter. After 36 years of raising and showing AKC Chihuahuas nationwide, she decided to slow down and make another dream come true, the dream of owning and operating an antique shop. In 1999, with the help of her niece, Pat Duarte, she opened Yesteryear Antiques & Collectibles. The charming glass-front store located downtown on Main Street on historical Highway 41, has an inviting atmosphere with orderly displays of country glass and crockery from the 1930s to the 1970s, and pink and green glass from the era of the Great Depression. You will see tabletop décor, collectible plates, tea pots and cups, and highly sought after patterns, such as Fenton, Carnival Glass and Blue Willow, and other collectible items distributed tastefully among pieces of antique furniture. Glass is Ruth's first love, and she and Pat are always checking out flea markets, auctions and moving sales. When you are traveling through Western Kentucky, be sure to stop in Madisonville, where the sign will welcome you to the Best Town on Earth. Visit Yesteryear Antiques and other antique shops for a taste of Madisonville tradition and a trip down memory lane.

52 S Main Street, Madisonville KY
(270) 825-3776
www.yesteryearantiquecollectibles.com

A lonely pine on Indian Fort Mountain
Photo by Code Poet

East Kentucky

Jailer's Inn Bed & Breakfast

It was 1988 when the McCoy family bought the historic Bardstown jail at auction. The jail, originally built in 1819, had closed just one year earlier. The Jailer's Inn Bed & Breakfast offers an extraordinary way to do time in Bardstown for those who enjoy history, regional character and atmosphere. Guests enjoy beautiful accommodations in one fully renovated building of the jail with a complimentary tour of the unchanged second building. Visitors can also stop by just for the tour. You'll hear a full history of the jail and, if you ask, a number of ghost stories as well—one reason why Travel Channel. com named Jailer's Inn one of the Top Ten Spookiest Places in the country to visit. To really soak up the atmosphere, book the Jail Cell, one room in the inn that retains many of its jail cell features, including two original bunk beds. Other rooms bear little or no sign of their original purpose. The charming Victorian Room is covered in pink floral wallpaper and decorated with family heirlooms. Paul and his innkeeper, Lisa, offer a full breakfast in the flower-filled jailhouse courtyard. Plan a visit you'll never forget at the Jailer's Inn Bed & Breakfast.

111 W Stephen Foster Avenue, Bardstown KY
(502) 348-5551 or (800) 948-5551
www.jailersinn.com

Butler-Turpin State Historic House

This fine country home, built in 1859, is a place of remembrance to one of Kentucky's foremost military families from Colonial times through the American Revolution, the War of 1812, the Mexican War and the Civil War. The living house museum embodies life at the confluence of the Kentucky and Ohio Rivers and interprets the contributions of the slaves that lived and worked on the Butler family farm. Built in the Greek Revival style, the house is a three-bay two-story structure with a commanding a view of the Kentucky River Valley. The personal effects of military documents, furniture and objects bring to life a family steeped in military history.

1608 Highway 227, Carrollton KY
(502) 732-4384 or (866) 462-8853
www.parks.ky.gov/findparks/
resortparks/gb

Acorn and Fox Inn

A romantic getaway off the beaten path, Acorn and Fox Inn sits in the piney woods on the cliffs above Lake Cumberland. Deer, fox and a wide variety of birds frequent the 10-acre property. Wide wraparound decks offer tranquil views of the lake through the trees. A large roofed and screened porch with white wicker furniture makes a perfect place for lingering. This newly built bed-and-breakfast opened in 2004. Innkeepers Myrna and Al Noble say that the inn is really an excuse to store their antiques, many of which were handed down within their families. In addition to antique décor, all rooms have private entrances and baths, king-size beds and views

of the lake or the woods. Three of them have Jacuzzi tubs. Just outside Somerset and Burnside, the inn is convenient to three marinas and a wide variety of lake activities. Cumberland Falls, a 35-minute day trip, offers a special treat for anyone visiting on the full moon: a lunar rainbow appears over the falls each month. Plan your escape to Acorn and Fox Inn for a cozy and quiet respite in nature.

85 Noble Oaks Drive, Bronston KY
(606) 561-7755
www.acornandfoxinn.com

Historic Boone Tavern Hotel & Restaurant

Located where the rolling bluegrass horse farms of central Kentucky meet the beautiful foothills of the Appalachian Mountains, a magnificent building with pristine white columns greets travelers with Southern hospitality and gracious charm. Named after the early Kentucky explorer Daniel Boone, the Historic Boone Tavern Hotel & Restaurant has always been owned by Berea College and is located on the college campus. It was originally opened in 1909 to accommodate visitors to the college. Today, the rooms, restaurant and grounds are maintained by the students themselves, who take pride in this distinctive piece of local history. Become part of the unique Berea lifestyle where a tradition of quality blends with Southern hospitality and youthful vigor of the college campus. Spend the night in one of the inviting guest rooms where the quaint elegance of handmade furniture is enhanced by the modern amenities. Plan your wedding at Boone Tavern and experience an elegantly decorated event that will take you back through time. Choose between a formal sit-down dinner and a reception of light hors d'œuvres from Boone Tavern's award-winning restaurant. The menu takes a fresh approach to traditional Southern cuisine. Sample the spoonbread and enjoy the rich heritage and community at the Historic Boone Tavern Hotel & Restaurant of Berea College.

100 Main Street, Berea KY
(859) 985-3700 or (800) 366-9358
www.boonetavernhotel.com

Golden Pond Resort

Steve and Kathryn Allen relocated from Michigan after falling in love with the Lake Cumberland region. It's easy to see why when you visit their Golden Pond Resort, a constellation of picturesque, tree-shrouded houses near the lake. Spread across the Mississippian plateau and the Eastern Kentucky coalfields, the resort is local to major historic parks and abundant outdoor recreation. Camping, fishing, horseback riding and several marinas are a few of the attractions that draw thousands of tourists to the lake each year. The resort offers a variety of comfortable accommodations, including cabins, condos and deluxe vacation homes, all with two to five bedrooms. Some homes are equipped with washers, dryers and dishwashers and many have hot tubs and game rooms complete with pool and foosball tables. Some units boast private decks onto the fishing pond, which the Allens keep stocked with bass, crappie and bluegill. You'll find no shortage of entertainment at the resort, which includes tennis, volleyball and basketball courts, a swimming pool and a play area for kids. If you've come for boating, you'll find launch facilities two minutes away at the Fall Creek public access area and boat rentals and a large launch area at Conley Bottom Marina, five minutes away. For day trips, Cumberland Falls and several scenic railways are also minutes away. Stay at the center of it all and feel like you're in a world of your own at Golden Pond Resort.

110 Golden Pond Road, Monticello KY
(606) 348-7663
www.goldenpondresort.com

Lakeview Point
Bed and Breakfast

Dot Dunn grew up in the Burgin area around Herrington Lake. It was quiet and a long commute to her factory job, but worth it. When she read an article about the possibility of the lake area becoming a state park, it occurred to Dot that there was no lodging on the lake. Thus the Lakeview Point Bed and Breakfast was born. This is a place to come for tranquil respite and easy access to surrounding historic attractions such as Old Fort Harrod State Park, Constitution Square and Shaker Village. Guests love the bluff-top gazebo overlooking the lake and on-site massages by request. The bed-and-breakfast includes an in-ground pool and hot tub and a game room with a pool table, books and 50-inch widescreen television. The quaint, country-style rooms include CD players, in-room snacks and thermostat controls. The best room in the house, the View Room, offers a private balcony overlooking the lake, a fireplace and a king-size bed, as well as such extra amenities as a refrigerator, cable TV and DVD player. Dot, a onetime bakery manager, sets a delectable breakfast table including famous sweet potato biscuits and such original entrées as hash brown casserole and caramel French toast. Let her introduce you to an undiscovered paradise at the Lakeview Point Bed and Breakfast.

166 Lakeview Point, Harrodsburg KY
(859) 748-8359
www.thelakeviewpoint.com

Edgewater Resort

You'll be right at home when you stay at Edgewater Resort, the only resort development along the pristine shores of Taylorsville Lake. Each cottage is fully furnished and exquisitely decorated with the warm colors and personal touches you'd expect to see in your family home. With spacious great rooms, hot tubs, stone fireplaces, and details such as custom-made draperies and decorative pillows, these carefree two and three bedroom cottages have everything you'll need. Enjoy the peaceful lake by canoe and explore the woods that surround it by hiking or biking. For a truly relaxing escape, stop by The Village Spa, which features indoor and outdoor massage, aromatherapy and couples packages. Adventure seekers will enjoy the guided tours, led by Edgewater's own naturalist, who keeps guests on the lookout for wildlife such as white-tailed deer and great blue heron. If your first visit to this serene refuge isn't enough, come back for your next holiday, for Edgewater Resort is open year-round. Once you visit, you'll see why people keep coming back to this hidden jewel in Taylorsville, just 30 minutes from Louisville.

1238 Settlers Trace Road, Taylorsville KY
(866) 641-EDGE (3343)
www.etl-resort.com

Payne Bradford House

Once a meeting place for fugitive slaves traveling the Underground Railroad, the Payne Bradford House today stands as a relic of American history. Dr. John Bradford, a staunch abolitionist, purchased the property in 1854 following original owner General John Payne's death. From 1855 through the end of the Civil War, Bradford assisted slaves en route to freedom. The house remained occupied by the Bradford family into the 20th century, then sat vacant for 15 years until current owners Larry and Sharon Stamper began the restoration process. Without insulation, wiring or plumbing, the house had years of work ahead of it. Today the 215-year-old house is known as the oldest new house in the area. Retaining its original grandeur and Southern charm, it is a perfect place for a quiet weekend getaway. Sip lemonade on the preserved wrap-around porch, complete with wicker rocking chairs and a close view of the Ohio River. Each guest room has its own view of the river, along with ornate furniture and the personal touches that make it feel like home. Sharon and Larry believe that people don't come to the house just to have a place to lay their heads at the end of a busy sightseeing day—they come to experience the house as a part of their vacation. You can almost feel the ghosts of escaping slaves and their allies as you walk the halls. Stay at the Payne Bradford House to experience this treasure of American history.

102 Ferry Street, Augusta KY (606) 756-3762

First Farm Inn

Award-winning First Farm Inn is an elegantly updated 1870s farmhouse set on 20 acres just outside Cincinnati in the rolling hills where Indiana, Kentucky and Ohio join. White board fences south of I-275 make First Farm Inn the first farm you see upon entering Kentucky. The spacious rooms have queen-sized beds and private baths. The Treetops room with its cathedral ceiling is ideal for families or girlfriends' getaways. The 1870s room is nearly authentic to that time period with a vintage oak bedroom set that has been in the family for five generations. Bountiful homemade breakfast options vary from multi-grain pancakes to pasta carbonara or Swiss rosti. Enjoy in-room massages by licensed therapists, relax under the open sky in the whirlpool, fish, row or paddle around the pond, rock on the veranda or warm up beside the fireplace. Gift certificates. Perfect North Slopes ski packages. Mid-week, multi-day discounts. Guests as well as other horse-lovers may spend a two-hour session with the diverse, friendly and colorful herd of horses. As you groom and help tack up, you'll learn how to communicate with your horse. Riders work in the arena before touring the farm, returning to the historic tobacco barn to feed treats and do carrot stretches.

2510 Stevens Road, Petersburg KY
(859) 586-0199
www.firstfarminn.com

The Doolin House Gourmet Bed & Breakfast

Located in a reproduction 1850s house in the historic district of downtown Somerset, the Doolin House Gourmet Bed & Breakfast is owned and operated by two professional chefs. The husband-and-wife team of Charles and Allison Sobieck established the bed-and-breakfast as a more intimate way of entertaining. A five-year stint working in an upscale bed-and-breakfast in Louisville inspired Allison to dust off her business degree and create her own bed-and-breakfast in her native Somerset. The new, cream-colored Doolin House sprawls out onto a wide green lawn with welcoming porches filled with wicker furniture and pretty hanging baskets. Leather

chairs, tapestries, Oriental rugs and dark cherry wood accent the interior. All the rooms have 400-thread-count sheets, Crabtree & Evelyn toiletries, televisions and DVD players. Special rooms have whirlpools and fireplaces. The Sobiecks serve breakfast from 7 to 10, so you can wander down when you're ready. You'll find specialty omelettes, crêpes, stuffed French toast and such seasonal specials as gingerbread pancakes with lemon curd. To really take advantage of your visit, consider the chef's package, a two-night stay with dinner served each evening. Treat yourself to the unparalleled hospitality of professional chefs at the Doolin House Gourmet Bed & Breakfast.

502 N Main Street, Somerset KY
(606) 678-9494
www.doolinhouse.com

George Clarke House Bed & Breakfast

Lovingly restored to its original 1890 Victorian grandeur, the George Clarke House Bed & Breakfast offers guests the feel of a late 19th century upper-class home. The rooms are cast in the amber glow of gaslights, highlighting fine antique furnishings, elegant chandeliers and magnificent period wall coverings. Accommodations at the bed-and-breakfast feature carved mahogany king-size beds, period lighting with romantic tinted glass and coal/gas fireplaces with English grates. Some are quite large and include adjoining parlors. Each has a private bath with a specialty bath tub and warmed towels. Jeeves the butler is in service most weekends. Your hostess, owner Kathryn Bux, will greet you in Victorian costume each morning to show you to the breakfast table. Breakfast at the George Clarke House is a sumptuous affair, as it was

in George Clarke's time. Enjoy delicacies such as crème brûlée French toast or waffles with Grand Marnier strawberries served on delicate china with gleaming silver and sparkling crystal. Kathryn believes in the special touches that make outstanding service, so don't be surprised to find a handmade chocolate mouse on your pillow when you turn in at night. Live awhile in Kathryn's world of nostalgia and romance at the George Clarke House.

136 Woodland Avenue, Lexington KY
(859) 254-2500 or (866) 436-1890
www.georgeclarkehouse.com

Snug Hollow Farm Bed & Breakfast

Southern Living magazine has called it "one of our top most romantic getaways of the South." This secluded 300 acre organic farm offers guests a quiet and restful getaway with creeks, wildflowers, wooded mountainsides and abundant wildlife. Snug Hollow Farm is a favorite escape for artists and writers as well as vacationers. Frequent guest and author Gwen Rubio whose book *Icy Sparks* was chosen as an Oprah Winfrey Book Club selection, praises the peaceful, inspiring atmosphere of the farm and surroundings. Accommodations consist of a restored chestnut log cabin and a spacious two-story farmhouse with three comfortable bedrooms and private baths. Farmhouse guests may relax in the sun room, browse the library or sit by the fire with a book. The cozy cabin has fantastic views, handmade quilts and all the comforts of a genuine home in the mountains. Delicious vegetarian meals of fresh produce from the garden are a culinary delight. Proprietress and chef Barbara Napier serves up hearty breakfasts and elegant dinners including homemade pies, breads and gourmet pastas. Snug Hollow is very much a reflection of Napier, an artist in her own right. This is her canvas and with it she has created a masterpiece. *Taste of the South*, *Kentucky Living* and *National Geographic* have all praised it. The area is Appalachia at its best and a stay is an authentic experience in holler hospitality.

790 McSwain Branch, Irvine KY
(606) 723-4786
www.snughollow.com

Lake Cumberland
Photo by blueathena7

Lost Lodge Resort

Country living has never been so authentic. Lost Lodge Resort is located on 14 acres of lush Kentucky forest along the sparkling shores of Lake Cumberland. With 18 log cabins, RV hookups and camping facilities, you'll have your choice of accommodations in a quiet, secluded area close to shopping, restaurants and local attractions. The area offers a plethora of dazzling natural waterfalls, an old-fashioned train ride, and fun activities such as horseback riding, golfing and whitewater rafting. Each rustic cabin at Lost Lodge offers all the comforts of home. If you're looking for a relaxing afternoon, take a ride on the hill-o-vator to the boat dock and lakeshore. The hill-o-vator is an open air elevator that makes for a fun trip to a day of swimming, fishing or simply soaking up rays on the beach. If you're ready for some fast-paced adventure, boat and jet-ski rentals are available, too. Fishermen will delight in the guide services available from Lost Lodge, where they can charter a boat and skilled local fisherman to catch the large striper fish. For a relaxing getaway in a flourishing country setting and a fun-filled vacation on emerald waters, visit Lost Lodge Resort.

265 Lost Lodge Road, Somerset KY
(606) 561-4451 or (877) 562-4451
www.lostlodge.com

The Artist in You

Looking for something different to do with your family or friends? Visit The Artist In You, a paint your own pottery studio. It has all you need to create that one-of-a-kind keepsake. No experience or artistic ability is required. Lots of tools such as stamps, stencils, sponges and brushes are provided. The attentive staff can explain how the process works and point you towards idea books and sample pieces to help spark your creative side. It's a great way to spend an afternoon with a friend or with a child creating a gift for the person who has everything. Owned by Kim Alexander, The Artist In You has been open for over four years and is located in Louisville's open-air mall, the Summit Shopping center on Brownsboro Road/Hwy 22. The studio has about 48 seats with 16 outside. With over 400 different pieces of pottery to choose from, there is something for everyone. They have plates, bowls, mugs, tiles, goblets and many kid's items such as boxes and banks. After designing and painting your piece of pottery, leave it to be glazed and fired, which will make your item food and dishwasher safe. It's ready in about a week. No appointment is necessary. The Artist In You does birthday parties, scouts, summer camps, office parties and much more. Kid events included pizza nights, princess and boy's nights. These are drop-off parties, giving parents time to shop or have dinner. Check out ladies night and other monthly specials. Come in today and discover The Artist In You.

4015 Summit Plaza Drive, Louisville KY (502) 426-1266 *www.theartistinyou.net*

Warren A. May— Woodworker

Traditional Kentucky furniture is widely renowned for its uncompromising quality, graceful design and hand-rendered detail. Antique pieces are highly valued, yet no one seems to want to take the time to make new Kentucky furniture in the traditional manner. Warren A. May does. A native Kentuckian, Warren trained in classical woodworking at Eastern Kentucky University. He has spent more than 35 years making traditional Kentucky furniture and dulcimers. Using only solid native woods such as Black Walnut, Cherry and Poplar, he makes all his furniture in his shop on the farm where he lives with his wife, Frankye. She manages the gallery on the beautiful College Square of Berea College, where Warren will join her to do the small handwork on his pieces. You will often find Warren at work at the gallery on intricate inlays, moldings, keyhole diamonds or bellflower designs. These are the mark of his Kentucky pride-of-craftsmanship. His furniture is elegant yet has soft lines, and it is at home in any setting. It has been featured in *Popular Woodworking*, *Fine Woodworking* and *Woodwork* magazines. In addition to furniture, Warren has made more than 15,000 traditional Kentucky dulcimers. Kentucky dulcimers are characterized by a softer tone, a simpler design and of course, many ornamental wood features. Warren's dulcimers are as handsome as they are easy to play, with tuning keys of hand-carved rosewood, shaped sound holes and natural knotholes. See the work of one of the last Kentucky master woodworkers at the gallery of Warren A. May—Woodworker.

110 Center Street, Berea KY (859) 986-9293
www.warrenamay.com

David Appalachian Crafts

Members of the small community of David in the Kentucky Highlands have been making crafts for generations. Traditionally, they made baskets, pottery and wooden tools for practical purposes, and they made beautiful patchwork quilts, clothes and toys that were both serviceable and celebratory. Through David Appalachian Crafts, these beautiful handmade works are now available to the public. This nonprofit organization, founded in 1972, sells local crafts by consignment under the umbrella of the St. Vincent Mission. Members enjoy a 75 percent return that supplements their income while perpetuating a sense of self-sufficiency and pride in their heritage. Since the 1970s, when the local coal mines began to shut down, the nonprofit has been an important asset to a struggling economy. In addition to operating a permanent store, the cooperative tours regional craft shows and actively markets its wares. It is especially known for its one-of-a-kind patchwork quilts. In 1984, the U.S. Olympics Committee commissioned a quilt featuring the Olympic emblem to hang in the Olympic headquarters in California. You'll also find distinctive jewelry made of local coal, painted gourds and recordings by local folk musicians. Take home a piece of the Appalachians and support traditional communities when you shop at David Appalachian Crafts.

6369 Highway 404, David KY (606) 886-2377 *www.davidappalachiancrafts.com*

Hardin County History Museum

The Hardin County History Museum collects and preserves a mosaic of memorabilia that illustrates Hardin County history from the early Native American culture to modern times. The colorful founders and early inhabitants of the region come to life in exhibits and painted panels. They include future presidents Abraham Lincoln and James Buchanan, naturalist James John Audubon and General George Armstrong Custer. Union General William Tecumseh Sherman frequented two major civil war forts/staging areas in the county. The Secretary of War in Washington thought Sherman mad when he claimed that 200,000 troops would be necessary to hold the line for the Union in Kentucky, but Sherman was proved right. Carry Nation, vehement leader of the temperance movement, had a major altercation with local saloon proprietor, J.R. Neighbors, that left her bloodied in her own battle. The exhibits of artifacts, furnishings, documents, photographs, costumes and stories document highlights of the journey from early settlement through the organization of the county. Originally encompassing 4,000 square miles bounded by the Ohio, Salt, Rolling Fork and Green rivers, the county today spans 616 square miles. Its history is rich with the struggles involved in establishing a new frontier and fighting the Civil War. The museum offers a guided tour and dinner program that relives one of these stories, the 1862 dash across the countryside with Confederate General John Hunt Morgan. Track the rise of Fort Knox, local newspapers, public transportation and the modern way of life at the Hardin County History Museum.

201 W Dixie Avenue, Elizabethtown KY (270) 763-8339
www.hardinkyhistory.org

Belle of Louisville

The Belle of Louisville, built in 1914, is the oldest authentic Mississippi River-style steamboat still operating today. Docked at the Wharf in downtown Louisville, Kentucky, she serves as the westernmost anchor of the award-winning Waterfront Park. In 1989, the Belle earned the distinguished title of National Historic Landmark and continues to stand proudly as the icon of the city. Steamboat enthusiasts from all over the world flock to inspect the Belle's meticulously maintained engine room and visit with her crew. Each year, thousands of passengers board the Belle for a nostalgic trip on the beautiful Ohio River. The sound of the Belle's throaty whistle and the churning of her bright crimson paddlewheel, serve to announce yet another season is beginning. The Belle of Louisville offers public cruises Memorial Day to Labor Day and weekends in September and October. Delicious lunch and dinner buffets are regularly scheduled throughout the season. Mother's Day, Father's Day, and the Fourth of July are only a few of the special events planned for family entertainment. Try one of the Belle's romantic Sunset Dinner Cruises or a Friday Night Dinner Dance Cruise and experience an evening to remember. Year-round lunch and dinner cruises are available on the Belle's fleet companion, the Riverboat, Spirit of Jefferson, docked at the same downtown wharf.

401 W River Road, Louisville KY
(502) 574-2992 or (866) 832-0011
www.belleoflouisville.org

Kentucky Music Hall of Fame and Museum

Set in an elegant old barn-style building, the Kentucky Music Hall of Fame and Museum celebrates Kentucky music professionals. Honoring artists and others who have made contributions to Kentucky and the world, the Hall of Fame and Museum is a great destination for students and tour groups, as well as for anyone who wants to experience Kentucky's rich musical heritage. The site pays tribute to all genres of music. You can experience anything from opera and jazz to country and rap, and learn about the noteworthy people behind each musical

style. The museum exhibits centuries-old musical artifacts, memorabilia from today's best-known artists and everything in between. A display might speak of a musical culture gone by or convey a historical moment. An interactive room teaches visitors about tempo, tune and other musical concepts. The karaoke recording studio allows brave individuals to put their knowledge and skills to the test. The Kentucky Music Hall of Fame and Museum invites you to stop in and listen to the enriching sounds of Southern music.

2590 Richmond Road, Renfro Valley KY
(606) 256-1000 or (877) 356-3263
www.kentuckymusicmuseum.com

Waterway Adventures

Imagine waking up to a crisp summer morning as you drift lazily across a beautiful lake. Then spend a sunny afternoon sliding down the waterslide of your houseboat and splashing around in the sun. Let Waterway Adventures make your vacation dreams come true on the clear waters of Lake Cumberland and Lake Barkley. Rent a houseboat complete with hot tub, waterslide and a spacious cabin with all the amenities of home. With six varieties of boats, you can bring along a small group of friends for an intimate weekend or invite the extended family to comfortably sleep up to 12 people. While on board, enjoy a full size kitchen and dining area, living room with entertainment center and private bedrooms. Several of the boats offer top deck patio

seating, gas grills and a wet bar. If you're in the mood for a fast-paced ride, take advantage of Waterway's speed boat and jet ski rentals. For the best of both worlds, feel free to park your personal watercraft on your houseboat's private dock to relax after a fun-filled day of whitewater. For a completely different way to experience the lake, feel the wind in your face as you sail into the sunset with one of Waterway Adventures' sailboat vacations aboard a luxury yacht. Visit Waterway Adventures to begin a new summer vacation tradition.

680 W Lakeshore Drive, Burnside KY
(606) 561-0378 or (800) 844-8862
www.waterwayadventures.com

Kentucky Gateway Museum Center

The Kentucky Gateway Museum Center is so much more than a museum. The museum research library has been a resource for many biographical and historical works, including *Girl Singer* by Rosemary Clooney and *Beyond the River* by Ann Hagedorn. Photos from the Center's extensive collection have been exhibited at the Smithsonian and Monticello. A particular highlight of the museum is the Kathleen Savage Browning Miniatures Collection, a mesmerizing assortment of one-twelfth-scale reproductions of homes, furnishings, clothing and artwork collected

by Maysville native Kaye Browning. In the Regional History Museum, the past is illuminated through artifacts and award-winning dioramas. The temporary gallery hosts visiting exhibits that have included local art, the National Museum of Racing and Smithsonian exhibits. The new gift shop has books, local products, genealogical materials and gifts for everyone. The museum is in an original 1881 Italianate red brick building with a new three-story addition to the south and a heritage Siberian elm tree for shade. A new interior atrium features a balcony view. Behind the museum, a pioneer cemetery contains the graves of historical figures. Visit the Kentucky Gateway Museum Center for a beautiful view into history.

215 Sutton Street, Maysville KY (606) 564-5865
www.kygmc.org

Historic Locust Grove

Photo by Jason Meredith

Historic Locust Grove depicts Kentucky life in the early 1800s. William and Lucy Clark Croghan established the original farm in 1790. William's brother-in-law and surveying partner, George Rogers Clark, was the founder of Louisville and a Revolutionary War hero who spent the last years of his life at the estate. Visitors to Locust Grove learn the stories of the Clark family and the people surrounding them, including the enslaved African Americans who worked the property. Experience the challenges faced by the common people and the lives of the era's elite. Tour the beautifully restored Georgian-style home, or walk through woods and meadows dotted with rare and historic plants. The visitor center houses many fascinating exhibits, as well as merchandise made by local artists. Ongoing workshops provide educational opportunities for children and adults. More than 140 volunteers work together to preserve this slice of history and organize events such as the Revolutionary War-era reenactments. The formal gardens, manicured lawns and other picturesque settings provide idyllic backdrops for weddings, parties and conferences. Step back into a day in the life of a 19th century Kentuckian at Historic Locust Grove.

561 Blankenbaker Lane, Louisville KY
(502) 897-9845
www.locustgrove.org

Bluegrass Scenic Railroad Museum

Train lovers, history buffs and anyone looking for a fun family outing will enjoy the Bluegrass Scenic Railroad Museum, a tribute to the railroading history of Kentucky. The museum presents a collection of railroad memorabilia and offers entertaining and educational train rides in antique railroad cars through the thoroughbred horse fields of Central Kentucky, a scenic backdrop to the narrated history you'll hear along the way. "Our excursions are a new experience to our younger riders and a nostalgic trip for our older passengers," says executive director John Penfield. "I have never seen anyone get off the train who did not have a smile on their face." John leads a team of dedicated volunteers who operate every aspect of the museum, including actors who dress in period costume for specially dramatized rides, such as the Civil War Train Robbery and the Halloween haunted train ride. Back at the station,

you can see artifacts such as stones from the first railroad built in Kentucky in 1831 and interactive displays such as a working telegraph set that sends Morse code. Regular train rides leave the station at 2 pm every Saturday and Sunday, mid-May through October. You can discover the romance of riding the rails as it was in the days before air travel and interstate highways when you visit the Bluegrass Scenic Railroad Museum.

175 Beasley Road, Versailles KY
(859) 873-BGRM (2476) or (800) 755-2476
www.bgrm.org

Bobby Davis Museum and Park of Hazard and Perry County

In 1945, L.O. Davis lost his son, Bobby, in World War II. He channeled his grief into building a three-acre memorial park and urban forest that overlooks downtown Hazard. The Bobby Davis Museum and Park of Hazard and Perry County is dedicated to all the young men of Perry County who lost their lives in the war. The museum traces the history of Hazard and Perry County from the early 1800s to the middle 20th century. The facility also serves as an activity center for the community, hosting weddings, celebrations and events, inside and outside. The Heritage Herb Garden is another central focus in the park, planted and maintained by a

local committee that hosts an annual Herb Festival in June. Walkways offer visitors a tour of the trees and plants indigenous to Eastern Kentucky. A large, three-tiered fountain stands in front of the attractive building, both made of local sandstone. The Bobby Davis Museum and Park of Hazard and Perry County serves as a beautiful inspiration to local visitors and tourists. Come for history, sentiment or simply to walk the lovely grounds.

234 Walnut Street, Hazard KY
(606) 439-4325

Conrad-Caldwell House

A magnificent example of Richardsonian Romanesque architecture, the Conrad-Caldwell House is a pet project of the St. James Court Historic Foundation—in other words, of the neighborhood in which it is located. The Old Louisville district is famous for its Victorian mansions. It has the largest concentration of them in the country, according to the National Register of Historic Places, and the Conrad-Caldwell House is one the most impressive. When it went up for sale in 1987, the neighbors organized to buy, restore and refurnish the house. For the past 20 years, they have operated it as a museum representing the upper-class life of the early 20th century. Walk around the house and enjoy its gargoyles, swags, massive arches and fleurs-de-lis. Inside you will find breathtaking woodwork, stained glass and fixtures. Guided

tours point out the house's architectural details, fine art and original furnishings while recounting the story of its inhabitants. Theophilus Conrad, who built it, lived only 10 years in the house. After his death in 1895, his wife sold it to their neighbors, the Caldwells. The structure served as a boarding house during World War II before becoming the Rose Anna Hughes Presbyterian Retirement Home in 1947. You can retrace an era through a single, exceptional landmark when you tour the Conrad-Caldwell House.

1402 St. James Court, Louisville KY
(502) 636-5023
www.conradcaldwell.org

Kentucky Derby Museum

When you walk through the mock starting gates of the Kentucky Derby Museum, you'll feel instantly transported to the racetrack itself. The engaging museum not only presents the history of the famous Kentucky Derby horse race, but involves visitors in the experience. You can ride in your own simulated horse race atop a life-sized thoroughbred or test your derby IQ against the virtual race announcer. For the animal lover in you, the Life on the Farm exhibit gives a glimpse into the life and training a champion racehorse. Don't miss the jockey exhibit to witness the rigorous training a jockey goes through to prepare for a race. Rare artifacts and collectibles

from famous races at the derby will delight fans and educate the curious. The museum also features an award-winning Kentucky Derby film entitled The Greatest Race. A 360-degree high-definition screen places the viewer in the center of derby history. Located on the famous grounds of the Churchill Downs racetrack, the museum is your gateway to the derby itself. Take a tour of the track or millionaire's row or come early to watch the horses' morning workout. Stop by the Kentucky Derby Museum on your way to the race to experience the living history of this renowned American tradition.

Churchill Downs photo by Richard Hurt

704 Central Avenue, Louisville KY
(502) 637-7097
www.derbymuseum.org

Big South Fork Scenic Railway

Whether you've been witness to the age of the locomotive or not, when you ride the Kentucky & Tennessee Special on the Big South Fork Scenic Railway, you'll reminisce about the days when trains were the heart of transportation. This glimpse into America's rich industrial history is a tribute to the days when the journey was as exciting as the destination. The Route of the Painted Rocks begins in the historic district of Stearns, where the McCreary County Museum commemorates the lives of Native Americans and pioneers. From the train you can see spectacular vistas, lush vegetation and mountain streams as you descend 600 feet into the river gorge. A picture-perfect tunnel acts as a portal to the past. Riders are soon welcomed into a pristine realm beneath a canopy of sun-filtered foliage. Springtime visitors to this area are greeted along the way with roaring streams and a colorful abundance of wildflowers. The train stops at the Blue Heron Coal Mining Camp, an interpretive center where audio recordings housed in ghost structures tell tales of the people who worked and lived there. You can almost feel the spirits of the coal and lumber boom era. Experience the past first-hand when you visit Big South Fork Scenic Railway. Don't let this true American treasure pass you by.

100 Henderson Street, Stearns KY
(606) 376-5330 or (800) 462-5664
www.bsfsry.com

The Lincoln Museum

As the birthplace of President Lincoln, Hodgenville is chock-full of monuments in his honor. After visiting the house where he was born, the farm where he spent his early childhood and perhaps the origins of his parents, you'll want to complete your tour at the Lincoln Museum. Dedicated to the life of the 16th president, the museum puts these landmarks and episodes in context. You'll find it downtown in a national registered historic building marked by a Lincoln statue. The heart of the museum is a series of wax figure dioramas illustrating major periods in Lincoln's life. You'll see him as a child on Sinking Spring Farm, as young man splitting rails for the railroad, and as president drafting the Emancipation Proclamation and delivering the Gettysburg Address. Each scene is rendered with careful historical accuracy. Upstairs, you'll find a collection of rare newspaper clippings, campaign posters and memorabilia. There is also an art gallery dedicated to portraits of Lincoln and a short film about him. The museum is open daily year-round, but call ahead for the guided tour, which fills in details of 19th century culture, art and architecture. Get to know the 16th president at the Lincoln Museum.

66 Lincoln Square, Hodgenville KY
(270) 358-3163
www.noinkmedia.com/lincolnmuseum

Lexington Public Safety Museum

When the town of Lexington was established in 1795, the General Assembly of Kentucky ordained that a number of watchmen should be employed to prevent fires, robberies, murders and other civic disruptions. That was the beginning of the public safety office. Opened in 2004, the Lexington Public Safety museum chronicles the history of the police, firefighting and corrections offices in Fayette County from the 1800s through the 1970s. Located in the old Lexington courthouse, now the Lexington History Center, the museum spans five rooms, each designated by timeline. Exhibits in the first room date to the 1930s. You'll see 100-year-old badges, the first mug shot ever taken by Lexington police and the original camera that took it. A photograph of the last public hanging in the county dates to the 1920s. There's also an

authentic replica of a 19th century public safety officer's uniform. Several of the rooms are dedicated to photographs of old police departments, jails and fire stations. Another honors officers who fell in the line of duty. The museum offers collectible diecast police cars, badge pins, thematic polo shirts and blankets. A volunteer team of acting and retired public safety officers maintains the museum. Visit the Lexington Public Safety Museum, open Friday through Monday. Please call ahead for hours.

215 W Main Street, Lexington KY
(859) 225-6351

Kentucky Museum of Art and Craft

Named one of eight great craft museums by *American Style* magazine in 2006, the Kentucky Museum of Art and Craft is a must-see. Businesswoman and former Miss America Phyllis George founded the museum in 1981 as a nonprofit organization to promote the state's arts and crafts heritage. Indeed, Kentucky supplies 80 percent of the 200 or so artists whose work is regularly displayed in the Gallery Shop. The museum's exhibitions feature local, regional and national artists. Since 1984, it has presented over 175 exhibitions, reaching about 65,000

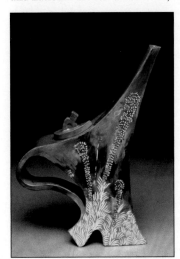

viewers annually. Three galleries feature two to three month exhibitions: the Mary and Al Shands Gallery, the Steve Wilson Gallery and the Lindy and Bill Street Gallery. An ongoing selection of works from the museum's permanent collection are shown in the Brown-Forman Gallery. In 2001, the museum was able to move into its current 27,000-square-foot facility, which it has beautifully renovated. The museum promotes art education for children and adults alike and houses an Education Center, which conducts workshops and artists' demonstrations. The Center also is responsible for the museum's *Traveling Suitcase* program that ships 20 varied collections of artworks to schools in Kentucky. Come to the Kentucky Museum of Art and Craft and support the great artists of Kentucky.

715 W Main Street, Louisville KY
(502) 589-0102
www.kentuckyarts.org

Louisville Visual Art Association

Since 1974, the headquarters of the 98-year-old Louisville Visual Art Association (LVAA) has been the Water Tower, a 19th century Greek Revival-style landmark on the bank of the Ohio River. More than 100,000 people a year now participate in the association's exhibitions, educational classes and special events. The LVAA enriches the community by showcasing local and regional art and sponsors the oldest art education program in the city. The association

began offering the Children's Free Art Classes in 1925. Since then, it has cultivated the talents and creativity of thousands of young people. The LVAA's annual DinnerWorks program is in its 21st year. At DinnerWorks, 15 artists create distinctive dinnerware while 15 designers interpret the work and present visually expressive tablescapes. The Kentucky Arts Council and the National Endowment for the Arts help support the association and its mission, expressed in the following words: "Because art nourishes the human spirit, we will enrich community life by educating people about the value and meaning of today's visual arts and by championing artists and the creative process." For inspiration and art you can take home, visit the Louisville Visual Art Association at the Water Tower.

3005 River Road, Louisville KY
(502) 896-2146
www.louisvillevisualart.org

Photo by Bob Hower

Riverside, the Farnsley-Moremen Landing

Riverside, the Farnsley-Moremen Landing, is an introduction to mid-1800s culture located about 25 minutes from downtown Louisville. Louisville-Jefferson County Metro Parks maintains the original appearance of this antebellum mansion and 300-acre farm. The Farnsley-Moremen house, a red brick Federal/Greek Revival building, dates to 1837. The ground floor reflects the Spartan décor favored by original owner Gabriel Farnsley. The second floor is filled with Victorian heirlooms of the Moremen family that owned Riverside from the 1860s to the 1980s. The county opened the house to the public in 1993, and it offers tours year-round. A 19th century-style detached kitchen has been added as an extension to the house, and costumed docents frequently give cooking demonstrations. You can volunteer to work in the kitchen

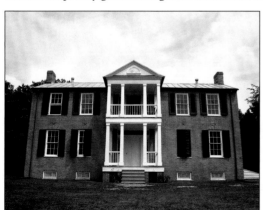

garden growing vegetables and herbs served in the 19th century. You can even participate in the archaeological dig next to the house, which has produced a wealth of artifacts. Modern additions to the site include a visitor's center with an auditorium, museum, modern riverboat landing and gift shop, plus a large picnic pavilion overlooking the river. Come visit historic Riverside, a gracious park and an experience of yesteryear.

7410 Moorman Road, Louisville KY
(502) 935-6809
www.riverside-landing.org

Old Fort Harrod State Park

In 1774, James Harrod established the first permanent settlement west of the Alleghenies in what would become Central Kentucky. Old Fort Harrod State Park preserves Kentucky's pioneer history with a lifelike reconstruction of the fort near its original site. Heavy stockade walls enclose cabins, blockhouses and a one-room schoolhouse. From April through October, visitors can see the fort come to life with costumed interpreters performing the daily tasks that made the settlement function. Woodworkers and weavers ply their craft, a blacksmith toils at the smithy and farmers tend live animals and gardens. The site encompasses several other historic attractions, including the original log cabin where Lincoln's parents were married and the oldest cemetery in Kentucky. Tours of the park and its many attractions are available year-round. From March through November, the Mansion Museum is open to visitors. Set in one of the oldest Greek Revival houses in Kentucky, the museum features a Civil War exhibit, Lincoln memorabilia, Native American artifacts and much more. A gift shop offers Kentucky handcrafts, books and souvenirs. The park hosts regular community events, including live music in its outdoor amphitheater and an annual Civil War reenactment. Bring the whole family to explore Kentucky history at Old Fort Harrod State Park.

100 College Street, Harrodsburg KY
(859) 734-9614

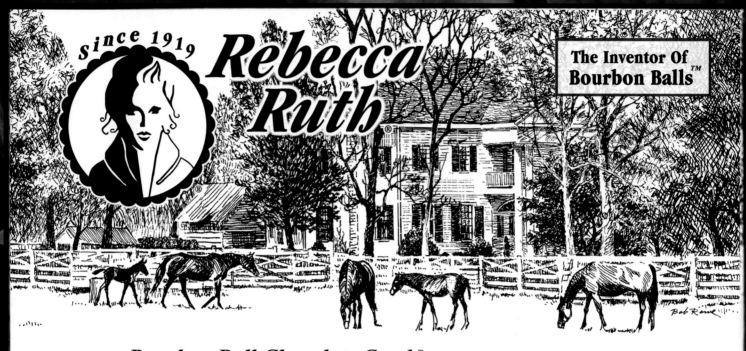

Rebecca Ruth Candy & Tours

Known worldwide as the inventor of Bourbon Ball Chocolates, Rebecca Ruth is a both a historic and gourmet landmark. For tourists, it's a fun, family friendly event. You will smell the wonderful chocolate aroma upon your first step into this world of chocolates and confectionery history. The factory is located in the beautiful South Frankfort district of Downtown Frankfort, Kentucky. Rebecca Ruth was founded in 1919 by two young women who had worked together as substitute school teachers. They felt their talents were better suited in other areas. At a time when it was virtually unheard of for women to go into business independently without a husband, Ruth and Rebecca believed in their talent and the possibility of providing for themselves. To prove the point, they used their first names to create the name of the candy company (maternal style) rather than using their last names (a paternal style of naming a company that implies masculine ownership as well as passing a company down through a line of male leadership). For the record, both women got married anyway. It was Ruth Booe who would continue to run the business into modern day—even though she suffered the tragic loss of her husband, was tested by the Great Depression, World War II sugar rationing, and even a fire that destroyed nearly everything. It was Ruth who invented the Bourbon Ball, a dark chocolate confection laced with a punch of real Bourbon Whiskey. Ruth's ideas and resolve were dynamic. Ruth preferred dark chocolate and always insisted that it was superior to milk chocolate. Her ideas continue to define the taste of Kentuckiana, where dark chocolate is the largest seller. In 1964, Ruth retired from active candy making and her only son, John Booe, took over and added other liquor-filled chocolates to the line, including rum, scotch, cognac and the Kentucky Irish coffee. John's son, Charles Booe, purchased the company in 1997, and today they are both active in every aspect of the business. The family run confectionery has four Frankfort locations, provides mail-order services via the Internet and provides guided tours. Check the website or call for more details.

112 E Second Street, Frankfort KY
(502) 223-7475 or (800) 444-3766
www.rebeccaruth.com

Rosemark Haven

A graciously restored 1848 antebellum Southern house, Rosemark Haven is worth a visit whether you stay overnight or simply stop for a meal, a glass at the wine bar or afternoon tea. The beautifully decorated interior features period antiques, 13-foot ceilings and a dazzling three-story oval staircase. You'll want to stay when you see the rooms, with their plush king beds, wood floors, fireplaces and large windows overlooking the park-like landscaping around the house. Guests enjoy a full breakfast in the dining room, including such classics as fluffy omelettes and French toast. You can also return to the dining room at dinner for gourmet Italian fare. The wine bar is in a handsome converted tobacco barn and serves a range of wines and beers from around the world in a semi-casual environment of tables with clusters of plush chairs and sofas. Aficionados of fine, loose leaf teas will want to visit the charming Rosemark Tea Room. Decorated in pastel colors, the shop serves such traditional nibbles as scones with Devonshire cream, lemon tarts, chicken salad puffs and tea sandwiches. Whether for tea, wine, dinner or vintage atmosphere, you won't want to miss stopping at Rosemark Haven, a *Country Living* featured Inn of the Month.

714 N 3rd Street, Bardstown KY
(502) 348-8218
www.rosemarkhaven.com

Sisters Tea Parlor & Boutique

An unabashedly girly place, Sisters Tea Parlor & Boutique is resplendent in pink, owner Connie Young's favorite color. She named it in honor of her three daughters and to celebrate the universal sisterhood of women. Her daughter, Lori, runs the tea shop today. As you enter the Paris Pink Dining Room, you'll encounter the Dress-up for Grown-ups Vanity, inviting you to indulge in complimentary hats, fur wraps, pearls and antique gloves before sitting down to tea. Tea at Sisters is a ceremonial affair, ordered as a complete table spread. The walk-in menu offers breakfast, lunch and dessert tea spreads and a Casual Tea for minimalists, served with

fresh-baked tender Southern scones, lemon curd and whipped cream. Those willing to plan ahead can partake of the Royal Teas menu, with spreads available to private parties by reservation only. Rally the gals for a Friendship Tea, which comes with a three-tiered tray of finger desserts, assorted tea sandwiches and savories. Afterwards, you'll have fun browsing the boutique, which offers loose teas and accoutrements, gourmet sweets and gifts for women. Sisters maintains a monthly calendar of events that includes a father-daughter tea and an integrated tea and etiquette class for children. Bring someone special to enjoy an intimate tea at Sisters Tea Parlor & Boutique.

4765 Fox Run Road, Buckner KY
(502) 222-6420
www.sistersteaparlor.com

The Sweet Tooth

The mother and daughter team of Cathy Strange and Sara Woodford know how to satisfy Louisville. They opened the Sweet Tooth in 2005 and have been Catering to Your Cravings ever since. Sara does the baking here, and her mother Cathy handles lunch. Armed with a degree in baking and pastry arts from Sullivan University, Sara uses her own recipes to create the treats here. "It's about learning the right techniques and having the right tools," she says. Her desserts feature large portions and focus on flavor. You will find everything from traditional chocolate cake to such Kentucky specialties as Pony pie, which features walnuts, chocolate and an ample amount of Kentucky bourbon. The bakery's lunch menu also emphasizes original takes on classics. Your children may never settle for regular peanut butter and jelly once they've tasted

the PB & Fruit sandwich with its filling of peanut butter, cranberries, raisins and Granny Smith apples. Cathy uses her own recipe for chicken salad. Soups, salads and corn muffins are all popular. A business lunch or party becomes extraordinary when it's catered by the Sweet Tooth. The atmosphere here is fun and friendly, and children are always welcome. For old-fashioned goodness that might remind you of treats from grandma's kitchen, bring your cravings to the Sweet Tooth.

3110 Frankfort Avenue, Louisville KY
(502) 895-4554

Bauer's Candies

It is unusual for a business to last 100 years, but Bauer's Candies has exceeded that mark and shows no signs of stopping. Currently, Bauer's is in the capable hands of the first female owner in the family, Anna Bauer Satterwhite. Anna is a fourth-generation owner. Chances are good that one or both of her sons will carry Bauer's Candies into the future. The first owner was Anna's great grandfather, who opened the first shop in 1889. While attending the play, *A Doll's House*, at the McCauley Theater in Louisville, the local makers were so enthralled by Madame Helena Modjeska's performance that when introduced to her, they asked for permission to name their recent confectionary invention after her. Permission was granted. Bauer's Candies still produces its famous Modjeska candy in the traditional way, using the very same original recipe and the finest ingredients. Rich and creamy caramel surrounds a fluffy, handmade marshmallow center like a velvety cloak of sugary heaven. Bauer's offers personalized greeting cards and gift wrapping to customize corporate or personal gifts. The candies are hand-wrapped and packaged. There are no shortcuts to perfection. You can still buy old-fashioned goodness every time you visit Bauer's Candies. Treat yourself and your loved ones to and old-fashioned confectionary delight. You can order Modjeska candies online, or get the full, aromatic, friendly experience by stopping by Bauer's Candies in person.

1103 Dylan Drive, Lawrenceburg KY
(502) 839-3700
www.bauerscandy.com

Root-A-Bakers

After 13 years honing her bakery skills at home, Lana Root finally took the advice of friends and family by opening her own bakery, Root-A-Bakers. It only took that first step, and soon the business had found a life of its own. Its secret was the simple sugar cookie. Lana makes an old-fashioned, pure butter, frosted cookie with no trans fat, and it's the best sugar cookie you could ever put in your mouth. Root-A-Bakers sells about 30 dozen on an average day, but during the Christmas season, that figure jumps to around 500 dozen per week. First time visitors get a free one. The bakery is also renowned for Lana's cinnamon rolls, pies, and cakes covered with world-renowned buttercream frosting. The bakery café offers lunches and a total of seven salads, including chicken salad and fruit salad. Pick up some fresh-baked sourdough bread for later while you're there. Root-A-Bakers ships to 50 states and as far as Iraq and Afghanistan. Enjoy warm, friendly hospitality and the best sugar cookie around when you visit Root-A-Bakers in Morehead.

313 Flemingsburg Road, Morehead KY
(606) 780-4282

Sheltowee Farm

A fully-functional, family-owned and operated farm in the heart of the Daniel Boone National Forrest, Sheltowee Farm produces and delivers certified-organic, gourmet-quality mushrooms across the mid-eastern United States. The name has become so respected, both for quality and for its farming practices, that many of the restaurants that use Sheltowee Farm mushrooms credit the source on their menus. Bill and Rebecca Webb, he a retired Naval officer and she a Ph.D. candidate, both left traditional jobs to start the farm. Bill was a state economic development coordinator and Rebecca was a university research associate. Today, their children help sell the mushrooms at the farmer's market. Rebecca's parents help with delivery and Bill's father lives on the farm and tends it after hours. Bill and Rebecca have collected exotic mushroom spawn from all over the world to grow at the farm, especially shiitake and oyster mushrooms—up to 16 varieties. The farm operates 365 days a year with both indoor and outdoor operations. The Webbs have received several grants to further develop the ever-growing market for value-added products. They also offer classes on shiitake and oyster mushroom cultivation and lead foraging expeditions into the forest that teach how to identify edible mushrooms. Take yourself on a mushroom hunt at Sheltowee Farm.

1327 Sheltowee Lane, Salt Lick KY
(859) 219-3400
www.sheltoweefarm.com

The Corders presenting Bernice Dalton (center) with a Simon G.Jewelers diamond pendant for her 25-plus years of service to the store.

Corder's Jewelry

In business since 1935, Corder's Jewelry is one of the few independently owned and family-operated jewelry stores still running strong in Kentucky. Harold and his wife, Gerema, credit the store's success to a combination of old-fashioned values, quality staff and leading-edge technology. Clients from eight counties shop Corder's almost every week for its handpicked selection and individualized service. But Corder's also offers the advanced services that would otherwise draw customers away to larger companies, such as plating, laser-welding and computerized diamond analysis. Corder's screens all of its diamonds for artificial color-enhancement and synthetics using the latest technology from around the world. In addition to diamonds, the 3400-square-foot store stocks a vast selection of colored gemstones, with lesser-known varieties well-represented. Three jewelers, including Harold, are on staff to help you create your original design. Harold, who grew up in the business his dad started 72 years ago, knows jewelry inside and out and has continued to update his knowledge of gemology. He and his wife handpick the jewelry in the store to serve the middle-to-upper classes in this eight-county area. His criterion is simple: "You want to look at it and say, 'wow'," he says, referring to both the quality and the originality of the design. The store has been at its present location for 40 years and has just undergone a floor-to-ceiling remodeling. Come by and see what is showing today at Corder's Jewelry.

**370 S Highway 27, Suite 17, Somerset KY
(606) 678-8144**

Charles W. Traxel Co.

In 1909, Charles W. Traxel opened a jewelry store with partner Miles Brown that became a family tradition. When Charles died, his nephew, William, took his place. Eventually William bought Brown's share and with his wife, Clara, worked until retirement. Next, their son Charles and his wife, Libby, took the helm. In time, their son Drew and his wife, Michele took their place as the fourth generation at Traxel's, and moved it to a shopping district a mile away. The old store was formerly owned by Andrew Clooney (Nick and Rosemary Clooney's great-grandfather) and Dan Perrine. The second Charlie still works at the store half of each year. In the new location, the same antique jewelry showcases that were used in the original downtown location sparkle with the fine jewelry that Traxel's is known for. The old clock outside of the old store stayed behind, but a tall clock stands in the center of the new showroom in deference to the former icon. The store retains the ambience befitting a prominent fine jeweler. The showroom displays exclusive giftware such as fine crystal, pewter, sterling and china. Distinct gifts and a bridal registry service make it easy to shop for that special event, and all gifts are wrapped in the signature mint green box with a gold, handmade bow. Jewelry and watch repair, as well as engraving, are done on-site by specialists. Charles W. Traxel Co. provides some of the best in the jewelry world, and does it with style.

1120 US Highway 68, Maysville KY
(606) 564-3220

Karina's Jewelers

Alicia Garcia and her husband opened Karina's Jewelers together in 1996, the same year their daughter, Karina, was born. Alicia worked for five years behind the scenes, but in 2002 she was faced with running the whole show by herself. She had to learn a few things about business, but Karina's loyal clientele stuck with her and today numbers 5,000. Quality remains standard at Karina's, with such fail-proof names as Raico, Daring Diamonds and the Jacqueline Kennedy Collection in the mix, but Alicia has also made the shop distinctly her own. She hunts down distinctive pieces at design shows when only a few samples have been made. Are you in the market for a fine belly button ring valued at $500? Karina's is your place. Alicia also collects unusual gems such as yellow diamonds, green garnets and black opals, and especially enjoys making custom-designed jewelry. If you're shopping for a wedding ring, Alicia won't just hand you what's in the case. After you find the design you like, she'll bring together four or five diamonds to compare side by side, and you can have your favorite one used in your order. You'll find a wide variety of wedding rings for men, a market often ignored by larger jewelry stores. Go to Karina's Jewelers for quality jewelry and watches that will stand out from the crowd.

4025 Summit Plaza Drive, Louisville KY
(502) 394-9122

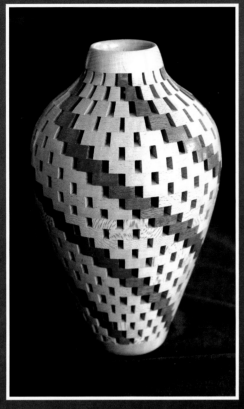

Appalachian Artisan Center

The Appalachian Artisan Center opened its doors in 2001, kicking off the transformation of downtown Hindman into a community rich in celebrating Appalachian heritage and supportive of local artistic endeavors. The Appalachian Artisan Center is comprised of multiple facilities, programs and services for the visiting public and art community. The shop sells artwork by over 100 eastern Kentucky artists. The artwork is diverse and creative, ranging from jewelry and walking sticks to furniture and paintings. An ever-changing inventory of handcrafted art is on display and for purchase. A featured artist display rotates every two months promoting the premiere work of local artists. The Appalachian Artisan Center studios help small arts-based businesses flourish by giving artists access to professional-quality machinery, affordable studio space and a marketplace for their work. The café provides indoor or patio dining where guests can enjoy a meal or snack while seated on hickory chairs handcrafted by well-known Kentucky artist Mike Angel. Executive Director Stuart Burrill notes that the café, studios and shop are integrated parts of the Center, "really just different facets of the same diamond." The Center provides a place to meet and observe true artists at work, as well as enjoy the rich art forms come to life. The Appalachian Artisan Center has become a national model for arts and heritage-based economic development, and has enhanced the Hindman community and the Appalachian region. Enjoy the art, artists and rich heritage of eastern Kentucky at the Appalachian Artisan Center.

16 W Main Street, Hindman, KY
(606) 785-9855
www.artisancenter.net

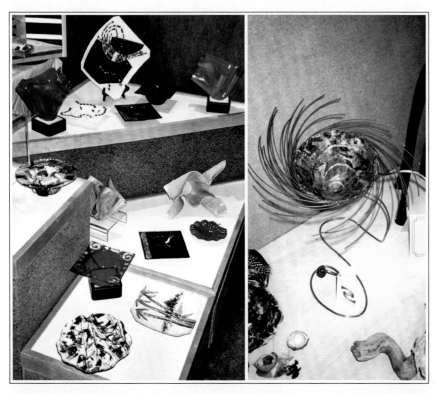

Art of Healing Gallery

The Art of Healing Gallery is a place where can you rouse your inner muse while getting a therapeutic massage. Located within the tranquil walls of the Art of Healing massage office, this gallery is the perfect setting for a healing experience. The gallery features the creative works of owner and massage therapist Debbie Cherie Joplin. Exquisite glasswork and vibrantly colored sculptures adorn the shop, making an inviting environment for art lovers and novice admirers. For more than 20 years, Debbie has been creating beautiful pieces that are both functional and decorative. When you see the elegant displays of distinctively designed sculptures, you'll see why Debbie has won many awards for her art. What began as a hobby in her youth developed into a special form of expression. Debbie's fiber-fused glass, oil paintings, watercolors and silk wall hangings encompass her love of color and ability to produce truly original artwork that speaks to the observer. In addition, the Art of Healing Gallery displays Debbie's funky jewelry in the form of earrings, necklaces and bracelets. Handmade glass beads are the perfect addition to Debbie's dolphin and dragonfly pendants. Come in for the annual Art of Healing Gallery's open house or look around before your healing massage and see this alluring art for yourself.

4217 W Highway 146, Buckner KY
(502) 225-0800
www.artofhealingky.com

Brook Forrest White, Jr. in action in the Hotshop

Flame Run

Watch as molten glass transforms into breathtaking works of art at Flame Run, the region's largest glassblowing studio. Walk from the roaring fires of the hot shop into the gallery featuring works by Flame Run artists as well as national talents. Gallery items range from paperweights and ornaments to large one-of-a-kind artworks. Flame Run artists often create special commission pieces, including light fixtures and sculptures. The Flame Run Gallery is a great place to find a handmade glass treasure to suit anyone's price range. Brook and Susie White, originally business partners and now husband and wife, have designed an atmosphere of creativity and teamwork within their 13,000 square foot facility. At Flame Run, experience the endless possibilities of glass through studio and gallery tours, hot glass demonstrations, community classes, private lessons, visiting artist workshops, special events, teambuilding seminars and studio rental. Be a part of the excitement that is sweeping the Louisville art community by visiting Flame Run.

828 E Market Street, Louisville KY
(502) 584-5353 or (888) 584-5353
www.flamerun.com

The Chestnut Tree Gallery & Still Waters Studio

Visitors to Central Kentucky needing to quench a thirst for original art will find their cup running over at this delightful art gallery and studio. Located in the heart of downtown Richmond, a small, historic, university community, Chestnut Tree Gallery & Still Waters Studio offers more original art than many galleries in larger cities. The works of more than 50 Kentucky artists can be found in the gallery. It features over 150 original paintings and drawings, including watercolor, oil, pastel, acrylic, pen and ink, and pencil. You will also find signed and numbered limited-edition prints, raku and Bybee pottery, knives, stained glass, wood carvings, canes, wood-turned items, baskets, Christmas ornaments, folk art and more. The gallery is owned by the Rollins family, and they are always willing to give visitors a personal informative tour, allow you to browse at your own pace, or just sit and contemplate one of the many R.M. Rollins abstracts or special exhibits. Art classes and calligraphy services are offered by studio artist Jonathan Rollins, who creates unbelievably detailed pen and ink drawings based on Bible scriptures. Whether you want to add to your art collection, look for your first original or purchase a gift handmade in Kentucky, don't miss the Chestnut Tree Gallery & Still Waters Studio experience. Please call for regular and special event hours.

102 E Main Street, Richmond KY (859) 623-2144 *www.thechestnuttreegallery.com*

Mad About Art

If you like an eclectic array of talent represented in an uncluttered, charming space, then Mad About Art is worth the visit. The gallery, which opened in 2005, is truly one of Louisville's best kept secrets. The spacious viewing area possesses ample light and an open, modern feel that changes each time you visit. Mad About Art features fine crafts that are handcrafted in traditional, modern and contemporary styles by a number of award-winning artists from the United States, Canada and as far away as Israel and Bulgaria. As a weaver, proprietor Mary Simione understands the needs of the artisans she represents and works to give them the confidence to promote their own work and the recognition each one deserves. Every two months, the marigold-colored walls play host to a fresh new exhibit by local and regional artists. These 2-D works can include black and white photographs from a local dentist's travels, latex skin body paintings by a mixed media artist, watercolors, vibrant stained glass and felted fiber wall hangings, to name a few. Mad About Art also offers a wide selection of glass, wood and metal art as well as handwoven scarves, pottery and jewelry, jewelry and more jewelry. On the second Friday at the start of each new exhibit, Mary hosts an open house where repeat patrons and new customers can mingle with the artists and enjoy original and distinctive creations. Next time you're in the neighborhood, stop by Mad About Art and see what's new.

625 Baxter Avenue, Louisville KY
(502) 568-4916

Pat Banks Watercolor

Pat Banks uses her watercolor and acrylic painting as a lens through which she explores and interprets her world, especially her home in Eastern Kentucky. From landscapes and florals to animals and portraits, Pat's uses skillfully rendered realism to paint a beautiful view of life. Inspired by her architect father, she began painting as a child. Watercolor is now her primary medium. She imparts her environmental and social concerns, spontaneity and passion into each work. For her efforts, she has received numerous TIP and AIR grants from the Kentucky Arts Council and she is a roster artist with the Kentucky Arts Council. Pat has conducted an extensive list of workshops and has illustrated several children's books. She is also involved in integrating visual arts into school curriculums. Pat's work is in many regional galleries, juried

events and shows, and has been purchased for many corporate and private collections. She has been a visiting artist in Ecuador, Japan and France. Her studio overlooks the beautiful Kentucky River Valley featured in many of her works. This studio home was built by Pat and her husband and is surrounded by forest and fields. The artist's collection, portfolio and recent works are available for viewing upon request, and patrons may visit the studio and meet the artist by special appointment.

952 High Reeves Road, Richmond KY
(859) 527-3334

EAT Gallery

Simon and Laurie Watt came to Mason County with their family about 15 years ago from Los Angeles, drawn by the friendly community and well-preserved history. When they decided to open a natural art gallery in historic downtown Maysville, nothing would do but to rescue what was known in town as the EATS building. About 60 years ago, the building had been home to Morgan's Restaurant, and a large neon sign reading "EAT" was hung over the door. "I'll meet you at EATS" became a common saying in town. The sign, which remains to this day, now stands for Exquisite Art Treasures. EAT Gallery specializes in naturally formed minerals, stone carvings, fossils and artisan jewelry. Simon and Laurie, longtime gemstone dealers, are the owners and buyers for the gallery while their daughter, Erin, manages the business. They travel to India, Sri Lanka and many other corners of the globe in pursuit of rare specimens.

Some of the cathedral geodes that grace the shop stand as tall as six feet. You'll also see fossils dating back hundreds of millions of years and sculptures carved in jasper, quartz and lapis. The jewelry at the gallery is sophisticated and artistic, with an emphasis on the purity of the stones. Browse natural wonders and award-winning jewelry designs by world-renowned goldsmiths at Maysville's EAT Gallery.

46 W 2nd Street, Maysville KY
(606) 564-5578
www.eatgallery.com

Irish Acres Gallery of Antiques and the Glitz Restaurant

It's no accident that Irish Acres Gallery of Antiques is called a gallery. Housed in a remarkable, 32,000-square-foot building dating to 1936, the store displays rare antiques in beautifully-laid out, themed rooms for a captivating experience. American and European furniture, linens, rugs and decorative accessories outfit the rooms while glassware, china, crystal, silver, dolls and jewelry spill from the shelves, drawers and tabletops. There's something for every budget, starting with cookware priced at three dollars and extending to a 250-year-old, hand-painted Venetian bedroom suite priced at $72,000. Your sensory delight doesn't stop in the gallery. After browsing, head down to the lower level for a three-course, Southern-gourmet luncheon Tuesday through Saturday in the Glitz Restaurant. Named for its glitzy mauve and black interior, the restaurant is decorated with tangled grapevines and atmospheric, cellophane-covered bulbs. Family-owned and operated since 1970, Irish Acres was the original vision of Arch and Bonnie Hannigan. Arch spent two years remodeling the former elementary school that houses the gallery. His daughters, Jane and Emilie, went to design school to follow in the family business. Today, Jane handles the interior design while Emilie is the executive chef of the restaurant, serving recipes her mother taught her. Enjoy entrées such as salmon soufflé with dill hollandaise sauce followed by the Glitz signature dessert, a mocha ice cream hot fudge sundae in a baked shell called the Nonesuch Kiss. You'll be stimulated on every level when you visit the Irish Acres Gallery of Antiques and the Glitz Restaurant.

4205 Fords Mill Road, Versailles KY (859) 873-7235
www.irishacresgallery.com

Glassworks

Photo by Kelly Cookson

Glassworking has been the Von Roenn family business for generations, and with Glassworks, Ken Von Roenn is putting Louisville on the map as an important center for fine glass art. Glassworks encompasses open studios, classrooms and a gallery that showcases works by local and national artists. The original Architectural Glass Studio has been in continuous operation by the Von Roenn family since 1892. Six years ago, Ken went looking for a larger space and found Glassworks, where you'll find studios for glassblowing and flameworking as well as architectural glass. The public-friendly Glassworks puts on a good show for all ages. Flameworkers soften and mold small rods of glass in an open flame, while glass blowers breathe life into molten glass. The Architectural Glass Studio produces large-scale two-dimensional and three-dimensional works that are integrated into building designs. You can see as many as 50 artists at work in the studios on any given day. Saturdays feature guided tours. The artists also host periodic workshops. In the gallery, you'll see jewelry, baubles and ornaments for as little as $10 and fine glass vases and sculptures that run up to $800. A second gallery now in preparation will showcase the finest in glass art, ranging from $800 to $3,000. Prepare to be dazzled when you visit Glassworks.

815 W Market Street, Louisville KY
(502) 584-4510
www.louisvilleglassworks.com

Hawksview Gallery and Café

With its imaginative café setting, the Hawksview Gallery is a fun way for parties and even families to experience magnificent Kentucky-made glass art. The Hawksview Café is integrated with the Hawksview Glass Blowing Studio and Gallery to give diners an up-close and personal view of the art and art-making process. Choose from seating at glass counters along the glassblower observation windows or at tables throughout the gallery, where a large fountain provides ambiance. The main dining area offers a fireplace and live video of the glassblowers on a widescreen television. You'll marvel at the many forms glass art can take, from flowing seascapes to towering freeform masterpieces. Those looking for a keepsake or gift will find beautiful blown-glass angel fish and conch shells, twisting glass taper holders and picture frames trimmed with glass flowers. Chef Scotty serves homemade soups and pastas, salads

and sandwiches for lunch six days a week and dinner on Fridays and Saturdays by reservation. The Hawksview team sets an elegant table with glass napkin rings and wine bottle stoppers. Birthday parties feature blown-glass balloons and cupcakes. Berni North is the visionary owner and head designer of the glass blowing team. She invites you to enjoy a dining experience like no other at the Hawksview Gallery and Café.

170 Carter Avenue, Louisville KY
(502) 955-1010
www.hawksviewgallery.com

Kaviar Forge and Gallery

Transubstantiation takes place every day at Kaviar Forge and Gallery, Craig Kavair's studio. Here, cold, hard steel is transformed into warm, mesmeric works of art, war machines become implements for making art and vegetable oil turns from biological waste into a vital energy source. Kavair recycles vegetable oil from a local restaurant to fuel his forge and his diesel truck. A 200-pound Chambersburg Air hammer built during World War II for a battleship has become a tool of creation. Kavair's work is a dynamic combination of old and new. "I try to create cool, classical sculptural work from the inferno of the forge," he says. From Holocaust memorials to bed frames and architectural railings, all of Kavair's pieces embody his dedication to craftsmanship. Much of the art is solid and monumental, but visible forged marks provide a sense of movement and connection. Many pieces are in the collections of major corporations

and celebrities. In 2005, Kaviar was co-curator of the largest forged metal exhibition ever assembled, shown at the Kentucky Museum of Art and Craft. He has taught more than 60 artists, and many of them have gone on to successful careers. Feast your eyes on the outdoor sculpture garden and exhibits when you visit Kaviar Forge and Gallery, and consider gracing your own surroundings with a Kavair original.

1718 Frankfort Avenue, Louisville KY
(502) 561-0377
www.craigkaviar.com

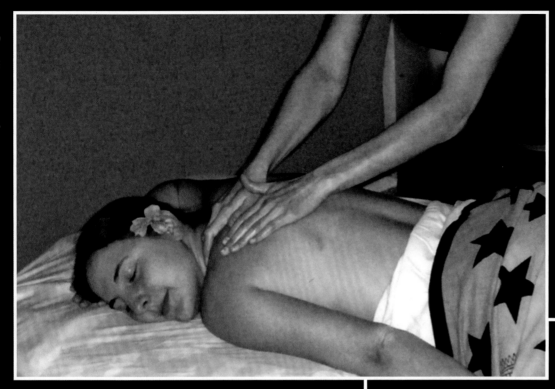

Art of Healing

Debbie Cherie Joplin tells people that anything you do well, you can think of as an art form. Debbie combines her passion for helping people through massage therapy and her love of art in an artistic setting at the Art of Healing. Debbie, a licensed massage therapist who is also on staff at the Louisville School of Massage, uses many techniques to help her clients conquer a variety of ailments. The Art of Healing offers Swedish massage, acupressure, deep muscle massage and energy work. Local doctors and chiropractors frequently refer patients to Debbie for her abilities with medical rehabilitation work, such as relieving pain after an automobile accident or on-the-job injury. Debbie is also nationally certified to work with special needs clients. In addition to Debbie's talent and skills, the Art of Healing offers three other specialists. Sarah Flick specializes in cranio-sacral work as well as massage. Collette Wilson specializes in deep tissue massage. Registered nurse Judy Revell is a clinical hypnotherapist and is a Ph.D. candidate in behavioral science. After your massage session, the Art of Healing will teach you stretches and maintenance you can do at home to keep you feeling great. Just stepping inside the Art of Healing provides an element of calm, with cozy touches such as an antique copper tub in the body treatment room. Original art and jewelry made by Debbie and her daughter decorate the space. Your body is a priceless piece of work and deserves to be kept in top condition with treatments from the Art of Healing.

4217 W Highway 146, Buckner KY (502) 225-0800

Plant Kingdom

Recognized leaders in Kentucky horticulture, Shelly and Tony Nold bring 28 years of experience to Plant Kingdom, where they manage a colorful, inspiring garden center and offer expert gardening services and advice. The Nolds consider plants to be integral components of our urban lives and encourage gardening as a hobby that's good for the heart in more ways than one. They pride themselves on offering the best plant collection around, ranging from natives to exotics, houseplants to trees. A service-oriented garden center, Plant Kingdom is dedicated to helping you put the right plant in the right place. Plant Kingdom's Personal Gardeners can assist you with everything from landscaping to maintenance. Plant Kingdom has designed and developed the local Valhalla golf course, the Six Flags Kentucky Kingdom and the Bernheim Arboretum. Shelly is a regular columnist who writes "At Home in the Garden" in *Kentucky Living* magazine, the largest-circulating publication in the state. Staff member Angie McManus writes the "Ask the Gardener" segment. For an hourly rate, they offer straightforward advice, problem diagnosis, environmental tips, plant recommendations and even sketches to keep. Visit the experts at Plant Kingdom to add a little green to your life.

4101 Westport Road, St. Matthews KY
(502) 893-7333
www.plantkingdom.net

Charlotte's Web

Charlotte's Web is the original and one of the largest furniture consignment shops in St. Matthews, Louisville, Kentucky. Established in 1998, owner Kathleen Sandman combines an interest in home décor with an interest in serious recycling. The 11,000-square-foot store offers an affordable alternative to buying new furnishings for your home. This results-oriented

shop can help you downsize to a new dwelling, change your style or add decorative elements to your existing décor. Its fairly priced furniture and accessories can provide your home with character and style. Previously owned furniture is usually less expensive than new and often contains features, such as all-wood joinery, that are missing from modern pieces. Charlotte's Web keeps a mixed inventory of antique, vintage and new items to satisfy every taste. Paintings, lamps and brightly colored accessories add personality to your rooms. You'll even find jewelry, and the unexpected. Find that unique item for yourself or a friend at Charlotte's Web. Many customers come in to browse, and enjoy the fun and peaceful atmosphere. As the merchandise changes daily, Kathleen suggests that you stop by weekly to see what's new.

4175 Lyndon Way, St. Matthews, Louisville KY
(502) 719-4444

Walnut Creek Rustic Living

Janet and Marvin O'Koon believe in the simple pleasures of a rustic lifestyle. Their love of spending time fly fishing and relaxing at their cabin on the Barren River Lake inspired Walnut Creek Rustic Living, their home décor and furnishings store. You'll find rough-hewn aspen log beds, tables and chairs made from bent willow, and handcrafted hickory furniture at the store to outfit log cabins, lake houses and other rustic homes. The store is a trendsetter in Kentucky, where the lodge lifestyle is just beginning to catch on with the kind of fervor it has traditionally enjoyed in other mountain and stream areas. Wildlife-themed textiles, art and accessories help bring the outdoors in. Add a vintage campground welcome sign to your wall or an antler lamp to your room. Tonight, unplug the noise makers, light a candle and spend an evening with friends or family in the comfort of furniture and décor from Walnut Creek Rustic Living.

1860 Mellwood Avenue, Louisville KY
(502) 238-7318
www.walnutcreekrusticliving.com

Woodhouse Day Spa

Somerset, Kentucky is tucked between Lake Cumberland and the Daniel Boone National Forest. It is a beautiful environment, but even in Somerset the hectic pace of life can wear you down. That's when the Woodhouse Day Spa comes to the rescue. With a choice of more than 70 invigorating treatments, Woodhouse pampers you head to toe, from the Shirodhara scalp massage to reflexology and pedicures. Whether you have a little time to spare or a whole day, there is a treatment custom-made for the occasion. The Minkyti Facial is a favorite of clients. Intensive treatments include the Secret of Victoria Package, beginning with a detoxifying seaweed wrap or aromatherapy bath and followed by an aromatherapy massage, facial, pedicure and Spritzer manicure. The Executive Workout is a treatment plan for gentlemen that includes sports massage, reflexology, hot towel facial, manicure and foam sea soak pedicure. Owners Tyler and Cindy Jasper lovingly refurbished a circa 1908 home for the spa, painstakingly restoring the original woodwork and stairs to their former splendor. Leave your troubles at the door and let the professional, licensed staff at the Woodhouse Day Spa take you on a journey of integrated health and total relaxation.

400 W Columbia Street, Somerset KY
(606) 676-0400
www.woodhousespas.com

Indian Ridge Campground

Constance and Rocky Kelly began camping together almost 10 years ago. Their first time out, they stayed at a campground owned and operated by a couple about their age. "We thought, 'This looks like fun,'" said Constance. They kept their dream alive while they finished raising their son, and recently they proudly opened Indian Ridge Campground. The Kellys completely renovated the former KOA site, gutting and rebuilding the bathrooms and swimming pool and adding such facilities as a laundry room, basketball and volleyball courts. The recreation room got a major upgrade that included separate game rooms for kids and adults. Now kids can enjoy video arcade games, pool tables and a jukebox while the adults enjoy foosball, ping pong, darts and a big screen television tuned to the sports channel. A live band plays regularly at the recreation hall. Located just a mile out from Green River Lake, the campground is a popular spot for locals who come out to enjoy the fishing, boating and swimming. Its rolling, shady 46 acres host six cabins and 94 campsites with water and electricity, 21 of them with sewer. The campground sits on a ridge overlooking Ted's Bend on the Green River, where the historic Battle of Green River is still commemorated with kiosks and a Confederate graveyard. Find a perfect blend of atmosphere and amenities at Indian Ridge Campground.

300 Campground Road, Campbellsville KY
(270) 465-7697

Canoe Kentucky

Whether you're looking for an adrenaline-boosting whitewater rafting adventure or a lazy sightseeing cruise along the river, Canoe Kentucky can make it happen. Located on the swift Elkhorn Creek, Canoe Kentucky can send you or guide you through waters tame or furious on trips ranging from six to 19 miles. Seasonal trips journey to other local rivers to feature special scenery such as fall foliage or spring flowers. Family-owned and operated since 1981, Canoe Kentucky is Kentucky's premiere resource for paddlesports, rentals, purchases and instruction. Founders Ed and Bess Councill passed the business to their daughter and son-in-law, Allison and Nathan Depenbrock, five years ago. They offer classes in canoeing and kayaking for every age and skill level, including specialty classes for women and children. In the paddle sports shop, they sell top-of-the-line boats such as you won't find in generic sporting stores, including canoes by Wenonah and kayaks by Hurricane. "We sell the models that we can guarantee," explained Nathan. "We know the owners of these companies personally, so we know that if any problems crop up, they'll take care of their product." Best of all, you can test drive your new boat on the Elkhorn Creek before purchase. Come to Canoe Kentucky for serious paddlesports products and instruction—and serious fun.

7323 Peaks Mill Road, Frankfort KY
(888) CANOE-KY (226-6359)
www.canoeky.com

Battlefield Golf Club

The Battlefield Golf Club commemorates an important but often overlooked victory for the Confederate Army—the Battle of Richmond. On August 29 and 30, 1862—the same two days as General Robert E. Lee's victory at Second Manassas—the Confederate Army won its most decisive victory at Richmond, allowing the army to occupy central Kentucky, a valuable piece of territory. Citizens of Richmond have continued to preserve the history of the battle and honor those who sacrificed their lives in both the Union and Confederate armies. In 2003, the Madison County Fiscal Court purchased the site, now a golf course, with the intent to improve the facilities while preserving the historic value of the land. Visitors will find a beautiful, links-style course of 5,993 yards and 18 holes. The greens and approaches are Bent grass and the rough areas blend Kentucky Blue Grass and Fescue. The clubhouse operates out of the historic Palmer House, which once served as a hospital for Union and Confederate soldiers. Also on the property are the historic Mount Zion Church and Herndon House. Both are about 200 years old and now serve as museums. Feel the depth of history as you stroll the walking trails on the property or play a pleasant game of golf on the very fields where the Battle of Richmond was fought.

524 General Cruft Drive, Richmond KY (859) 624-8005
www.madisoncountyky.us/golf

Hole 14

Raven Rock Golf Course

Undulating greens, water hazards and links-style rough make for a challenging experience for golfers of all levels at Raven Rock Golf Course. The signature hole is number 14, a 125-yard par 3 surrounded by water. Designed by Jack Sykes in 1995, the 18-hole course stretches over 6,500 yards of beautifully varied Kentucky landscape. Winter rye ripples on the fairways, an image reminiscent of Kentucky's grazing pastures, while the hilltops offer amazing views of neighboring Pine Mountain. The mountain is home to the real Raven Rock, an extraordinary 290-foot monolith that juts into the air at a 90-degree angle. Raven Rock Golf Course shares with its namesake a feeling of elevation and exhilarating surroundings. A community of homes is also located on the site. Brett Richards manages the course as the resident golf professional. You'll find an attractive clubhouse and upscale dining is a casual environment at the in-house restaurant. Enjoy a scenic round at Raven Rock Golf Course in Jenkins.

586 Golf Course Lane, Jenkins KY
(606) 832-2955

Head Figure Skating Coach, KY Special Olympic; Lorene Caudill
Roger Kappesser 4th place
Jeannie Luerson 1st place
At Special Olympics World Games, Nagano Japan 2005

Moms on Ice

You don't have to be a mom to belong to the Moms on Ice team, but you do need to be dedicated to an active lifestyle and have a big heart. You also need to be a competent skater, capable of meeting the standards of membership in the Ice Skating Institute. The organization, affectionately referred to as Moms on Ice, gives adults an opportunity to perform on skates and enjoy the camaraderie of like-minded folks. For the last 39 years, its members have also donated time as a group to raising thousands of dollars for the Kentucky Special Olympics Ice Skating Program. Erika Amundsen founded Moms on Ice in 1966 at the Alpine Ice Arena in Louisville, and the team still meets there today, under the leadership of head coach Lorene Caudill. Team members range in age from 33 to 80; you'll find mothers and professionals from assorted fields coming together to demonstrate the beauty and creativity that can be a part of an active lifestyle. The team takes part in skating competitions and exhibitions; it has performed at the opening ceremonies of the Cincinnati Riverfront Coliseum, Pittsburg's Mt. Lebanon Arena and the Lexington Ice Arena. The team has traveled as far as Japan and Hong Kong to promote adult skating as a challenging and enjoyable form of exercise. To find out how you can be part of the Moms on Ice team, contact Lorene Caudill.

1825 Gardiner Lane, Louisville KY (Alpine Ice Arena)
651 Veech Road, Fisherville KY
(502) 592-3795
www.alpineicearena.com

Dinner at Wingspan Gallery

Located in an historical building at the corner of Second and Jefferson Street in Lexington, Kentucky, Wingspan Gallery is the only art gallery to serve gourmet meals. The fixed-price, fixed-menu, four-course dinners take place each Thursday evening by reservation only. The comfortable gallery provides a relaxing atmosphere for patrons to meet and enjoy art. Wingspan diners arrive after 7 pm and begin by exploring the main gallery and three smaller galleries. Dinner is served in the main gallery as each group is ready to sit. Weekly menus are published on the Wingspan Gallery website at the beginning of each month. The Gallery is also available for private functions. Newly married and merging their households, Livia Theodoli and Carleton Wing redefined Wingspan Gallery to include both of their passions: art and great food. Carleton is an artist and manages the gallery. Livia, who grew up in Italy, is an excellent chef; she spearheads Dinner at Wingspan. Most of her recipes reflect the Mediterranean influence of good, fresh, and whenever possible, local ingredients. Carleton and Livia agree that it is rewarding to offer dinners for people who enjoy excellent art, skillfully prepared food and a good time that combines both. Many patrons have expressed their gratitude for this very special event. Call to reserve your space.

191 Jefferson Street, Lexington KY
(859) 225-5765
www.wingspangallery.com

KingFish Restaurants

Since 1948, great seafood and KingFish Restaurants have been synonymous. KingFish has built a proud reputation for excellence by offering abundant variety, friendly service and reasonable prices. You can start with a shrimp cocktail, Louisville's own Rolled Oyster or crab cakes, among other choices. Salads are a good beginning as well. Platters and sandwiches star seafood that has been grilled, broiled, baked or hand-breaded and gently fried. Tilapa, North Atlantic whitefish and lobster are all delicious possibilities. For variety, try the frog legs. On Derby Day 1948, Russell Austin and Henry Burns opened the first KingFish Restaurant in a building they built with their own hands in downtown Louisville. The partners sold their company to Charles A. Brown, Jr. and Norman V. Noltemeyer in 1989. These two added a location on the Jeffersonville, Indiana riverfront in 1998. With the River Road location in Louisville, and the Jeffersonville location, KingFish now has two destination spots on the Ohio River with outside dining, entertainment and even miniature golf. Planning a celebration or gathering? Sit down with KingFish's professional banquet staff and plan your dream wedding or your company party. KingFish's river locations offer beautiful indoor and outdoor settings. The Riverwatch Terrace at the River Road location, with a spectacular view of the Louisville skyline, is perfect for receptions, parties and dinners. The elaborate ironwork and covered walkway to the main building create a romantic corridor for a wedding procession. Whenever you're in the mood for great seafood, make your way to one of the three KingFish Restaurants in the Kentuckiana area.

3021 Upper River Road, Louisville KY (502) 895-0544
1610 Kentucky Mills Drive, Louisville KY (502) 240-0700
601 W Riverside Drive, Jeffersonville IN (812) 284-3474
www.kingfishrestaurants.com

Opal's Restaurant

When Opal's Restaurant opened more than 20 years ago, Opal's daughter, Kathy Carpenter, landed a job there. A few years ago, Carpenter bought the restaurant from her mother, continuing her tradition of great food and service that treats every customer like family. Opal's is renowned for its burgers and pies. The cream pies are made fresh daily, flavored with chocolate, butterscotch, coconut or lemon. Daily specials include such wholesome, traditional favorites as chicken and dumplings and pork chops with soup beans. The buffet bar is open every day but Saturday, offering the comfort foods you grew up with: meat loaf, fried chicken, country-fried steaks and fish on Fridays. Drinks are free with the buffet. There is also a salad bar. The menu offers a variety of sandwiches. Try the tenderloin or the Philly steak. You'll also find homemade chili and soups and the hearty T-bone or rib-eye you've been craving. No matter what you order, it is going to be good at Opal's Restaurant.

89th Street & Water Street, McKee KY
(606) 287-1530
www.kaht.com/places/opal_res.htm

Vincenzo's Italian Restaurant

Brothers Agostino and Vincenzo Gabriele inherited their taste for fine dining from their father, a captain in the Italian merchant marine. His duties frequently included luxury cruises in the Mediterranean Sea, which made fine dining a part of family life. The senior Gabriele was fond of saying, *"La cosa piu importante dell'òspitalita é la sincerita"* . . . "The most important thing about hospitality is sincerity." The brothers never forgot it. At Vincenzo's Italian Restaurant, Vincenzo manages the dining room with the same dedication that Agostino displays in the kitchen. "Ultimately, we are in the people business," Vincenzo says. Agostino's menu reflects his European heritage with delicate combinations of meats and vegetables, fresh seafood, handmade pastas and specialty soufflés. Start with an appetizer of baked artichoke hearts stuffed with crab meat and scallops and glazed in a lime Hollandaise. Entrées range from meat-filled crepes to New York strip with Jack Daniels sauce. The wine list draws from all over the world. Vincenzo's has won 22 awards in its 21 years in business, most recently the 2007 Best of Louisville Readers Choice award from *Louisville* magazine. The brothers credit their success to their attentive preparation and service. Be their guest at Vincenzo's Italian Restaurant and experience genuine Italian hospitality.

150 S 5th Street, Louisville KY
(502) 580-1350
www.vincenzositalianrestaurant.com

The Engine House Deli

Whoever says time travel doesn't exist obviously hasn't been to the Engine House Deli. Bob Tabor is the man with the plan, bringing that old-fashioned feeling back in style in downtown Winchester. Once you walk through the door of Winchester's firehouse, originally built in 1885, you'll want to stay a while. The décor of this firehouse-turned-deli may be the closest you'll ever get to riding in a time machine, furnished as it is with antiquities such as a potbelly stove and a claw foot bathtub converted into a couch. Bob takes phone orders on an authentic rotary dial phone, and the soda fountain, booths and chairs actually come from old Kentucky restaurants and honkytonks. Kids and adults take pleasure in the friendly, casual setting and are entertained by the tunes playing on the old jukebox. Bob is practically a celebrity for his River Rat Beer Cheese, made at the deli. Each year, he makes over 10,000 pounds of this bluegrass specialty, inspired by the legendary Johnny Allman's original beer cheese recipe. Spicy and garlicky, the cheese itself is worth a trip. The Engine House Deli has been a staple of downtown Winchester since 1984. Come on in and let the old-fashioned theme and good food entertain you.

9 W Lexington Avenue, Winchester KY (859) 737-0560
www.riverratbeercheese.com

Park Place on Main

Kentucky flavors come to life with Chef Jay Denham's regional contemporary cuisine. Denham works with local farmers and producers to ensure he has the freshest and finest ingredients for his exquisite dishes. "It is all about the quality and the origin of the food," remarks Denham. The bar is stocked with a variety of top-shelf spirits, including fine Kentucky whiskey and more than 50 types of bourbon. Try the special barrel Woodford Reserve, which is bottled exclusively for Park Place on Main. Creative bar plates with treats like herb and truffle popcorn are available along with a line of signature cocktails. Park Place on Main's décor is alive with colors reminiscent of Denham's lovely dishes. Sage and green apple colored walls are accented with chocolate fixtures and furniture. Soft pendulum lights blend with the natural light pouring in from the floor-to-ceiling windows. Artwork of local produce is displayed, reflecting the chef's passion for regional ingredients. The wine room is separated from the restaurant with a glass wall, so guests can see the 300-plus fine wines available. The restaurant seats 110 people with a private room, which seats up to 30 people. Groups are always welcome and off-site catering is available. To book a culinary experience at Park Place on Main, located at Louisville Slugger Field, call for reservations.

401 E Main Street, Louisville KY
(502) 515-0172
www.diningonmain.com

Goose Creek Diner

Goose Creek Diner has the best fried green tomatoes in Louisville. The home-cooked dish is served with the restaurant's specialty Creek Sauce, a spicy Ranch dipping sauce. Locals Chris and Anne Mike own the colorful, cozy diner that features classic American cuisine. You'll find such Kentucky favorites as the Hot Brown, a sandwich created in 1926 by Chef Fred K. Schmidt for the Brown Hotel that went on to become a regional staple. Other good choices include a traditional country-fried steak or flavorful grilled salmon. Goose Creek makes its own pastas in house—all eight of them. A feast of a Sunday brunch is accompanied by live music. Customers can always expect to find good food served by a friendly staff when they step into the Goose Creek Diner. Look for it on the east end of town.

2923 Goose Creek Road, Louisville KY
(502) 339-8070
www.gcdiner.com

Chat-N-Nibble Restaurant

Chat-N-Nibble Restaurant has been a community icon in Eminence since opening in 1932. Customers instantly feel welcome when they walk into the family-style setting, where the friendly staff makes it a priority to make you feel at home. Owner Alice Ferguson takes pride in Chat-N-Nibble's down-home atmosphere and is happy to know that she has employees who genuinely enjoy coming to work. Upon entering, you might smell the enticing aroma of simmering roast beef or fresh-baked pies. The time-perfected menu includes such folksy

American recipes as mashed potatoes and gravy, mouth-watering burgers and whole catfish, a hard-to-find classic that repeat customers swear by. Locals also favor the homemade cream pie. After you've ordered, take a look around the restaurant to see the pieces of local history that adorn the walls. Antiques from previous owners and customer memorabilia such as old teapots, kettles and dishes highlight the restaurant's community heritage. If you're looking for a real down-home Kentucky experience, visit Chat-N-Nibble Restaurant.

28 S Penn Avenue, Eminence KY
(502) 845-9109

Southern Hospitality Antiques and Gifts

Rural Kentucky is steeped in heritage, infusing partly isolated communities with vibrant local culture, lively history and tradition. Prestonsburg is no exception, and in this town Southern Hospitality Antiques and Gifts has a beautiful display of regional wares. The store is the fulfillment of a lifetime dream for owner Lane Dutton. Set against the foothills of the Appalachian Mountains, the store is on the second floor of an old gas station beside the Big Sandy River. Dutton used the old gas station canopy for a sign and placed containers of colorful flowers outside. The interior was completely renovated and fitted with partitions. The new space is filled with exotic Oriental rugs covering tile floors and three sections of goods. One is full of antiques and elegant items, another is filled with primitives and the last has a little bit of everything. From furniture to oil paintings and prints, Southern Hospitality has something for everyone and in every price range. It even has a floral department with a talented florist who lends her talented touch throughout the store. Southern Hospitality has a wedding and shower registry, and will deliver the gifts. The three powerhouses responsible for this shop are Lane Dutton, Bobbie Wells (manager, artist and floral talent) and Eileen Campbell (bookkeeper and everything else). This trio graciously fed and entertained visitors at the grand opening without anyone guessing they had been up all night getting ready—a true demonstration of Southern Hospitality. Stop by and see the enchanting merchandise at Southern Hospitality Antiques and Gifts.

5459 Kentucky Route 321, Prestonsburg KY
(606) 886-9995

English Garden

Photo by Rogers Photography Somerset

Growing up on a farm in Western Kentucky, Annetta Matthews nurtured a lifelong passion for growing flowers. At English Garden, Somerset's newest floral and gift shop, customers find a new twist to Annetta's designs. "Very trend-setting and avant garde," commented one customer on FlowershopNetwork.com. "English Garden is a very sophisticated little treasure." Come to Annetta for wedding flowers, funeral flowers and exotic arrangements using imported tropical blossoms. Annetta also makes balloon bouquets, fruit and gourmet food baskets and silk arrangements. She takes orders from all over the country and even internationally. English Garden is set in a charming Victorian house in the heart of town with a wraparound porch, stained glass and hardwood floors setting the scene for the charming assortment of gifts. Fine chocolates and candies, scented candles, home décor items and baby gifts are available to compliment your flowers. As with a real English garden, flower lovers can't help but feel drawn to visit. Even Annetta's husband, Dr. Clifford Matthews, stops by to lend a hand when he has a spare moment from his busy nephrologist practice. Annetta and Clifford share a passion for healing and flowers. "Flowers are just another way of nursing people back to health," Annetta says. Get flower therapy for yourself or your loved one at English Garden.

111 N Main Street, Somerset KY
(606) 679-2332 or (866) 730-4240
www.myfsn.com/englishgarden

Mom & Me Candles

Who knew that a small crockpot and a little candle wax could lead to such success? This is exactly how mother-daughter duo Vicki Dillow and Sherry Stephens started their candle business. Mom and Me Candles opened in 1995, after months of experimentation with different candle-making techniques. Once Vicki and Sherry discovered the perfect candle recipe, they opened their shop and haven't looked back. Customers travel from all over the country to get their candles from a selection of over 165 different wax creations in all shapes, sizes and scents.

Vicki and Sherry regularly ship large orders to crafters, restaurants and beauty salons all over the United States and overseas. The shop focuses on originality, and customers can find fun-shaped candles with scents such as Grandma's Kitchen, Passionate Kisses or even Candied Chestnuts. Vicki and Sherry have definitely discovered the secret to candle-making and offer customized candles for weddings, showers and banquets. Besides candles, Mom and Me Candles also carries a selection of other fine gifts such as lotions and hand soaps. Though it quickly outgrew the crockpot, Mom and Me Candles remains committed to maintaining their high standards and quality products and is guaranteed to be a magnet for candle lovers.

6510 S Highway 27, Somerset KY
(606) 561-0548
www.momandmecandles.net

Pine Cone Primitives

Step into a quaint country cottage built in the early 1900s and inhale the aroma of lavender while you browse through this full-line gift shop. Owned by sisters Linda Spanier and Dale Crockett, Pine Cone Primitives features both Dale and Linda's art as well as jewelry, candles, gourmet foods, place mats and napkins, cookbooks, pottery, seasonal décor, Crabtree & Evelyn bath and body products and fine dinnerware from Vietri. Browse the baby corner for blankets,

toys and picture frames. Linda creates hand-painted monogrammed and floral lavender sachets, guest towels, napkins and pillows. Dale's hand-painted glassware, gourds and folk art are exquisitely detailed and feature a variety of original designs. Both women are juried Sheltowee Artisans. Pine Cone Primitives has evolved from two rooms to this large old home over the past 13 years, and has an atmosphere radiating warmth and imagination. Dale and Linda welcome you to Pine Cone Primitives, a place to find one-of-a-kind items that stir the creative soul.

409 Monticello Street, Somerset KY
(606) 677-1228

Goodall's Pearcy House Antiques

You will find Goodall's Pearcy House Antiques on Middletown's historic Main Street, a charming stretch of brick-lined sidewalks, old-fashioned street lamps, restaurants and antique shops. The revival is recent, but between 1929 and 1962, Louisville was the center where Consider H. Willett furniture, a premium antique brand, was made. Barry and Diane Goodall were among the first to notice the rising popularity of Willett several years ago. Today, they are among the most recognized purveyors in the country of the highly-coveted brand. They travel within a six-state radius to acquire pieces directly from estates and at auctions, cutting out the middle man. Their collection and their expertise have been widely publicized on the internet and in regional newspapers, bringing visitors from far and wide to survey the cherry hardwood furniture with the Willett label. Visitors also find other high quality furniture, such as Romweber. chandeliers and Roseville and Shawnee pottery. Barry and Diane moved the shop into the Pearcy House, an 1867 Victorian, four years ago when the original family put it up for sale. The glassed-in front porch makes a classy display window, while a converted garage in back serves as Diane's personal vintage record shop. Young and old alike find treasures at Goodall's Pearcy House Antiques, where the pride of historic Middletown thrives.

11611 Main Street, Middletown KY
(502) 244-4409

2023 Antiques

Fans of 1950s furniture and fashion will find much to love at 2023 Antiques. Owner Judy Champion started this Louisville store in 1996 after having sold 1950s collectibles through an antique mall for five years. Her shop runs the gamut from mid-century modern classics like Nelson Bubble Lamps and Eames shell chairs to kitschy television lamps and dinette sets. Vintage art glass, dinnerware, prints and paintings line the shelves. The clothing is classic 1940s and 50s styling from stores around the country. Remember those glittering Lucite handbags? Judy always has a good selection of these, along with hats and gloves. The large cases of brilliant costume jewelry, all vintage, will dazzle you with their color and variety. Come into 2023 Antiques and let Judy take you back 50 years while sharing her love and knowledge of one of the most defining eras in American design history.

2023 Frankfort Avenue, Louisville KY
(502) 899-9872

A Mother's Touch

Cenia Wedekind has been creating gifts with the tender warmth of a mother's hug for seven years. For an once-in-a-lifetime occasion such as a First Communion, a milestone anniversary or a wedding, A Mother's Touch provides a shopping experience like none other. You can use the comprehensive selection of beads in her Louisville shop to create mother's bracelets and personalized jewelry for any occasion. The shop's inventory includes sterling silver, gold fill, Swarovski crystal and pearl beads. You create your gift using birthstones, sterling silver blocks or engravable pendants. A Mother's Touch carries thousands of charms and engravables, including intricate Chamilia charms and whimsical beads by Trollbeads and Zoppini. Savvy hostesses also take advantage of the Tea Party Room to celebrate birthdays and hold fundraisers. Your next bridal shower or Mother's Day will be unforgettable in the homespun atmosphere. This shop has the close-knit warmth of a sewing circle. A visit to A Mother's Touch is an exceptional way to give something special to someone you love.

12312 B Shelbyville Road, Louisville KY
(502) 253-9477
www.amotherstouchjewelry.com

Derby City Antique Mall

If you love antiques and don't have the time to travel the world in search of them, why not let someone do it for you? At Derby City Antique Mall, 170 of the areas finest dealers do just that. The mall is full of antique furniture, primitives, silver, glassware and jewelry. Discover local and worldwide advertising, Derby memorabilia and other treasures. Five siblings put together this extraordinary mall in 1998 in the old Hikes Grade School, after updating it with air conditioning, an elevator and good lighting. The 30,000-square-foot building sits on the sight of the original one-room schoolhouse (circa 1875). The family also transformed the old school cafeteria into a quaint Victorian eatery called the Bluegrass Bistro, where expert chefs prepare foods using local produce. Choose a chicken salad with walnuts and Granny Smith apples or

smoked kielbasa sausage with Bavarian sauerkraut and homemade spätzle dumplings. How does a Reuben pizza sound, or maybe a side of sweet-fried apples? The menu changes seasonally. The siblings will go to great lengths to find what you need. Come to Derby City Antique Mall and prepare to be spoiled by the family—Kay Peak, Lauri Knabel, Kim Neuner, Debbie Owens and Billy Kinman—or just visit the website.

3819 Bardstown Road, Louisville KY
(502) 459-5151
www.derbycityantiquemall.com

European Antique Market

Like many people who have visited the magical cities of Paris or Marsilles, Shawn Stucker fell in love with France and its beautifully crafted furniture and architecture. In 1999, she turned her passion for French furnishings and décor into a full-time career, opening the European Antique Market. The market caters to interior designers, boutique owners, antique dealers and homeowners with 17th and 18th century furniture, chandeliers and garden fixtures you

won't find anywhere else. You may find an antique buffet table in the style of Louis XV or an antique bridge side transformed into wall décor at the market. The merchandise continually changes, and Shawn travels to France several times each year to find new pieces for the store. Because she serves as the direct importer and does all of her own buying throughout Europe, the shop operates on a smaller markup, which results in lower prices for the customer. Find the exceptional antiques and accessories that will set your home or business apart at the European Antique Market.

933 Barret Avenue, Louisville KY
(502) 585-3111
www.euroantiquemarket.com

Hardin's Jewelry & Gifts

A family business since 1949, Hardin's Jewelry & Gifts is Springfield's source for quality jewelry and gifts at small-town prices. Owner Carolyn Hardin inherited her eye for well-made jewelry and unusual designs from her father, who ran the store until his death in 1981. Carolyn and her sister, Phyllis, had helped out in the store since they could walk, but when it came time to make a decision about the store's future, they hesitated. "When you grow up in an industry, it's in your blood, but you usually don't know it," Carolyn explained. The sisters decided to give running the store a try for their father's sake—and never looked back. Today, the stock is a little different than it was 50 years ago, but the store retains its mid-century flavor. It's only Carolyn and a phone running the business since Phyllis married. Carolyn adheres to the maxims she learned

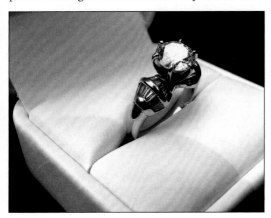

early on—for instance, the customer is always right—and stocks her shelves with handcrafted jewelry from the Ronaldo Collection, Pulsar watches and other individual finds. She has expanded the gift section significantly over the years to accommodate a range of budgets. You'll find picture frames, pewter figures and silver charms along with fine crystal, Seth Thomas antique clocks and Louisville Stoneware. Visit Hardin's Jewelry & Gifts for quality items with a personal touch.

114 W Main Street, Springfield KY
(859) 336-9425

Keepsake Treasures

You'll find great shopping at Keepsake Treasures, a friendly store that stocks unusual and delightful items. The store is in a striking early 1900s house in the Old Washington village on the edge of Maysville. Keepsake Treasures offers a variety of antiques, collectibles and new gifts. The range of vintage jewelry, especially necklaces, is impressive. Much of it is from estate sales. The shop has books on the Civil War, the Underground Railroad and the state of Kentucky, plus many cookbooks. You'll find antique furniture, which might include a dresser, a marble-topped table, a wicker couch or a crib complete with handmade quilt. Glassware, china, linens and baskets are everywhere. Old Washington is a 1700s complex of shops, six museums, tours and fine Kentucky dining. Marsha Jones, owner of Keepsake Treasures, is past president of

Old Washington Inc. and has helped organize festivals such as the Simon Kenton Frontier Festival and the Civil War Living History Weekend. She's also on two museum boards. Marsha got into the antiques business years ago while living in Kansas and Germany with her military husband. After gaining much experience, she was able to open her own shop in 1999 in her native Kentucky. Visit Keepsake Treasures—you'll be surprised at the reasonable prices.

2116 Old Main Street, Washington KY
(606) 759-0505

Just Creations

Customers at Just Creations take home beautiful items created by artisans from around the globe. At the same time, they enjoy knowing that the artisans were treated with respect and fairly compensated. This not-for-profit store offers pieces from more than 35 countries throughout Asia, Africa and Central and South America. You'll find handcrafted ceramics and jewelry, musical instruments, baskets and many other crafts. Among the more unusual items are elephant dung paper products from Sri Lanka, exquisite beaded jewelry from Guatemala and Shona stone carvings from Zimbabwe. The difference between shopping at Just Creations and other import stores is that Just Creations purchases exclusively from Fair Trade organizations including Ten Thousand Villages, A Greater Gift and Equal Exchange. The goals of the Fair Trade movement are to provide a fair wage and marketing assistance for producers in developing countries. This allows the artisans who supply Just Creations to pay for necessities including food, health care and housing. Come to Just Creations and shop for a beautiful handcrafted gift or a treasure for your home and know that your purchase is making a difference in the lives of people around the world.

2722 Frankfort Avenue, Louisville KY
(502) 897-7319
www.justcreations.org

Old Capital Antiques

Old Capital Antiques was established about 20 years ago in a restored pre-Civil War building that still has the original punched tin ceiling. The name was inspired by the compelling old Capitol building, just across the street. Located in an antique mall that is part of the historic, renovated downtown community, Old Capital Antiques has 15 dealers supplying the store with everything a historic antique shop should have. The store specializes in Kentucky Derby memorabilia, collectibles, vintage clothing and jewelry and Kentucky antiques. From furniture to fishing lures, it carries a select sampling of treasures from the past. Linen collectors will enjoy the vintage aprons from the 1920s and 1930s, along with other linen products. If you need an appraisal of your own antiques, Old Capital Antiques is qualified to provide that service as well. The shop is near the Kentucky History Center, the Kentucky River and the monument to frontiersman Daniel Boone in the Frankfort Cemetery. Don't leave Frankfort without doing some exploration of your own in Old Capital Antiques.

231 W Broadway, Frankfort KY
(502) 223-3879

The Leroy Galleries, Inc.

Put on your kilt and come into the Leroy Galleries, a gift shop specializing in Celtic gifts from Scotland, Ireland and Wales. Founded by William Leroy in 2004, this one-of-a-kind store offers a variety of accessories, collectors items and home décor. When you visit the Leroy Galleries you will find items expressing the proud and mystical Celtic legacy characterized by ornate works of art. William is proud to carry on the Scottish tradition by offering items such as day and evening coats and traditional kilts, which can be special ordered in the tartan colors of your choice or rented for special occasions. In addition, an assortment of fine silk and wool scarves and hats are available, as well as purses and kilt accessories. Clan heritage jewelry, books, pins and badges are available, each piece distinctly original and detailed. Also, don't forget to check out the exclusive

Belleek China, some of Ireland's oldest pottery, usually inscribed with Irish proverbs or wisdom and painted intricately with clovers. The Leroy Galleries also carries such food items as Welsh cookies, Scottish shortbread, Irish Blarney Scones mix, Licorice Scottie Dogs and more. Enjoy yourself as you peruse the Celtic collections and authentic Scottish souvenirs at the Leroy Galleries.

333 W Broadway Street, Frankfort KY
(502) 223-9946
www.leroygalleries.com

Luna Boutique

From the outside, Luna Boutique looks like a sturdy old wood home with snazzy modern accents. In this case, appearances don't deceive. Owner Mary Beth O'Bryan strives to create a contemporary feel with a down-home flair in her store, which stocks feminine accessories, home décor and art. Mary Beth seeks out top designers from Los Angeles and New York to offer her Louisville clientele a selection they won't find elsewhere in the city. Locally-made merchandise is well-represented too. Shoppers can browse racks of evening bags and shelves of glass work and stylistic table and barware. Hats are big sellers, and Mary Beth will even have her milliner custom-make one and have it finished in about a week. A dozen people might be in the store at the same time, and it's likely that no two are shopping for the same kind of thing. Luna Boutique stays open late, so the dinner crowd can shop. Check out the fresh and fashionable Luna Boutique.

1310 Bardstown Road, Louisville KY
(502) 454-7620
www.lunaboutique.net

Two Chicks and Co.
Jewelry & Gifts

College friends Alison Meyer and Ashley Backer created Two Chicks and Co. Jewelry & Gifts. As the popularity of Two Chicks grew, Barbara Sparrow, Paula Jackson and Karen Mayes joined the company. With two locations, in Louisville and Lexington, Two Chicks and Co. creates a fun and exciting shopping atmosphere that captivates customers with its colors, presentation and distinct gift items. At Two Chicks and Co. you will find designer-inspired and fashion jewelry, one-of-a-kind handbags, hats, wraps and comfortable shoes. The featured children's lines are just too adorable for words. You will also find accessories to accent your home, including exclusive table-top designs, lamps, mirrors and wall hangings. You can dress up your garden with a variety of topiaries, garden art and plants. Two Chicks and Co. is committed to its customers and the community. It has become one of the most called upon businesses for fundraising by offering organizations a variety of opportunities to earn money, with an emphasis on the non-traditional, easy and fun. It will host benefits in-house or set up mini-stores in corporate lobbies with a percentage of all sales benefiting charity. Treat yourself to a fun shopping experience at Two Chicks and Co. Jewelry & Gifts, the business that knows how to give back.

124 Southland Drive, Lexington KY (859) 276-0756
12121 Shelbyville Road #102, Louisville KY (502) 254-0400
www.twochicksandcompany.com

Woodford Landing Miniatures

At Woodford Landing Miniatures, customers will find everything they need to furnish a house—a dollhouse, that is. Open for more than 30 years, this Louisville shop started out as a general antiques shop, and you'll still find fine antique dolls from as far back as the early 1800s here. But it's dollhouses rather than dolls that are in the spotlight here. Barbara Fort and Pat Norwood own the store and stock it with handcrafted dollhouses of many shapes and sizes. Some of these doll dwellings date back to the 1940s, while others hail from more modern eras. From tiny tables to itsy bitsy beds, this store stocks every piece of furniture it takes to make a dollhouse a doll home. You'll also find an array of lighting kits here to make the houses glow. Woodford Landing offers other miniature buildings, too, including barns, churches, lighthouses and fire stations. You can also find miniature representations of such wonders as the Sphinx and the ancient Egyptian pyramids. The old-style warmth and charm of this store sets it apart other businesses in this part of the city, such as the ultra-hip coffee cafés. In fact, it's the only dollhouse-centered store in Louisville and exudes a Santa's workshop feel in keeping with its inventory. Whether you are a toy collector or just looking to give your child a special gift, enter a doll-size world of delights at Woodford Landing Miniatures.

2632 Frankfort Avenue, Louisville KY
(502) 893-7442

Oopsie Daisies

Boutique comes from the French word for *shop*, and it generally means a specialty store with select merchandise. Oopsie Daisies is a boutique for children, and *oopsie daisies* translates into hours of fun for the adults who do the shopping. Clothing sizes run from newborn to 8 for boys and 14 for girls. You'll find quality brands such as Letop, Kate Mack, Sweet Potatoes and Mis-Tee-Vus. Gift possibilities include frames, jewelry, plush animals, first birthday and baptismal items. Robeez, Ragg and L'Amour are just a few of the shoe brands that Oopsie Daisies offers for boys and girls. A baby registry makes it easy for friends and family to discover what the new mother wants and avoid duplicate gifts. Monogramming is available on-site to personalize gift purchases. Melissa and Doug puzzles and gift items are a regular part of the inventory, as are Especially For Me accessories and backpacks. Oopsie Daisies' small town prices and big town selection attract attention, but it is the customer service and the selection that have made the difference to loyal customers. The owner, Tracy Shrout, is pleased to make special orders if you don't see what you are looking for, but chances are good that you'll find everything you need already on the rack at Oopsie Daisies.

20 E Main Street, Mt. Sterling KY
(859) 499-0098

Quilt Box

Down a winding rural road and nestled in the peaceful countryside away from the bustle of town is the Quilt Box, named one of the 10 Best Quilt Shops in America by *Better Homes and Gardens*. The shop offers as many as 5,500 bolts of fabric, modern and traditional patterns and the down-home friendly atmosphere you'd expect from a cottage quilt shop set on a farm. The antique quilt trunk and ornate quilts hung for display contribute to a pastoral, nostalgic feeling. Owner Natalie Lahner has been in the quilting business for over 24 years. She credits her success to her grandmother, who taught her quilting, and a happy childhood spent quilting with her. The atmosphere at the Quilt Box is as warm as the quilts created here, and you can't help but pat Fergus the orange tabby cat, as he suns himself on the windowsill. Among the

fabrics, you'll find all the popular calico prints, flannels, plaids and pastels, as well as a rare jacquard imported from Japan. Natalie also offers craft kits and sewing projects and has a special room set aside for quilting lessons and workshops. Make a trip to the romantic Quilt Box. Whether you're a seasoned quilter or simply drawn to the atmosphere, you may find a piece of your heart resides in this tranquil country store.

490 E Flynn Road, Dry Ridge KY
(859) 824-4007

Shaving Horse Antiques

A primitive country antique shop that feels like an old-time country home, Shaving Horse Antiques offers visitors a glimpse into Linda William's fondest childhood memories. Growing up, Linda spent a lot of time with her grandmothers in their quaint homes with no electricity and all-handmade quilts, pottery and baskets. She went on to learn basket weaving and began collecting primitive antiques until she finally had too many to keep. That's when she decided to open a shop, naming it after the horse-shaped tool she used to shave wood for basket weaving. Linda's husband, Leo, hand-built the yellow poplar log cabin that houses the shop, modeling it after one that he saw on a trip out West. He went on to build log homes for a living, but is now retired. The

shop has two levels, and the stair rail that joins them is made from one long poplar log that is as smooth as glass. Inside, the shop is arranged like a house, with Johnston Benchworks furniture draped with hand-stitched throws and quilts, handmade jugs and crockery on the shelves and baskets hanging from the beams. You'll often find Leo watching Westerns on the couch while Linda runs the shop. Be sure to stop by and visit them and look over Linda's charming collection at Shaving Horse Antiques.

733 Old U.S. Highway 60 W, Farmers KY
(606) 784-2806
www.caverun.org/go/shavinghorseantiques.htm

E. Stephen Hein Florist & Party Productions

Expect high style and originality when E. Stephen Hein puts his name on a business. Now on his third career in Lexington, Stephen boasts loyal followers dating back to his days as an antiques and home accessories shop owner and even as an ice skating instructor. Since 1987, E. Stephen Hein Florist & Party Productions has been the go-to place in town for hotel concierges, wedding coordinators and community leaders looking for a new twist on the big bash. Stephen consults with clients personally before setting his design staff to work on dramatic centerpieces that incorporate such striking features as curly willow, witch hazel or theme-based props. For a recent wedding rehearsal dinner with a South Seas theme, Stephen placed flowers in sea shells and artfully scattered sand around. One of his specialties is the Monet Garden, a fresh flower arrangement made to look like a piece of a growing garden, complete with clumps of Spanish moss, bird's nests and critters such as butterflies and frogs. He also makes artful

gift baskets combing fruit, flowers and other goodies. What you won't get from Stephen is carnations, baby's breath, leather leaf or plastic baskets. With thousands of regular customers, he takes his reputation seriously. When you're serious about getting something special in floral design, rely on E. Stephen Hein Florist & Party Productions.

Lexington KY
(859) 255-6249 or (800) 755-6249
www.estephenheinflorist.com

Photo by Angela Anderson Photography

Fassler Florist & Gift Shop

Fresh cut flowers line the walls and shelves of this fragrant modern-day Eden. Fassler Florist & Gift Shop is a family-owned floral design shop. President Celeste Mackey and her daughter, vice president Destiny Mackey, love what they do and it shows. Destiny has been a part of the floral world her entire life. From the playpen to designing her own arrangements, Destiny is proud to follow in her mother and grandmother's footsteps as a third generation florist. Celeste and Destiny's aromatic creations include custom arrangements, home décor and exotic floral gifts. With hundreds of bridal bouquets, wedding hairpieces and corsages, Fassler is also one of the most sought-after wedding florists in the area. Featured in *Cincinnati Wedding* magazine

and with national recognition by industry organizations such as the Society of American Florists and the Kentucky Florists Association, Fassler has been cultivating its reputation for more than 35 years. If you're not in the Covington area, Fassler is happy to meet your needs by phone or web order, and is a proud member of the Teleflora wire service that can send a bouquet across the world. Stop in to browse the colorful displays or set up a private consultation to see what Fassler Florist & Gift Shop can do.

1892 Ashwood Circle, Fort Wright KY
(859) 331-ROSE (7673) or (800) 252-9902
www.fasslerworldwideflst.com

Grace Creations

Grace Creations is a friendly local florist with a lovely variety of fresh flowers, live plants and creative gift choices to suit any style or budget. The shop is located in a historic red brick building that dates to 1900, with beautiful wood work and high ceilings. Planning a wedding, a party or a corporate event? Grace Creations can add the beauty of flowers to all your festive occasions, large or small. When you need to send flowers to a funeral, the courteous staff will design and deliver a funeral arrangement that serves as a lovely tribute to the deceased. The shop can open on Sunday or at night as needed for funerals and other special concerns. Grace Creations has gift ideas for all ages and occasions—silk flowers, fruit and gourmet baskets, candy and chocolates, greeting cards, wax-covered teddy bears, quilts, scented candles, plush stuffed animals, balloons and more. Peg Williams, owner of the shop, named it after her late mother who taught her flower arranging. The name also refers to the Lord's blessing, which Peg believes she has experienced. Grace Creations gives back to churches and to individuals in need. Of late, Peg has been able to add interior decorating to the shop's other activities. For an arrangement that inspires the senses, visit Grace Creations.

200 West Main Street, Grayson KY
(606) 475-9070 or (877) 975-9070
www.myfsn.com/gracecreations

White Lily Florist

When in need of wedding flowers, permanent silk designs or emergency deliveries, discerning citizens of London turn to White Lily Florist. Again and again, reader polls in the *Sentinel Echo* have elected White Lily as the Best Florist in town. Maybe it's the stellar reputation of owner and head designer Donna Fields, who has won many honors since opening the shop in 1995. She was named a Kentucky Master Florist in 2000 and Designer of the Year by the Kentucky Florist Association in 1999. Most recently, she won the 2007 Kentucky Cup for floral design. Overseeing three other designers at the shop, Donna specializes in distinctive, contemporary designs. Frequent referrals and repeat business keep her busy. Customers often request custom silk designs to complement their interiors. They also come to White Lily Florist for speedy international deliveries. The shop is a member of Teleflora, an international network of florists who collaborate to make sure anything can be delivered or picked up anywhere. When flowers alone won't do, you can browse the elegant selection of gifts, including wedding cake cutting sets, baby gifts and luxury bath and beauty products. Stop by White Lily Florist for inspiring floral designs and gifts you'll feel proud to give.

1257 S Main Street, London KY
(606) 864-0693 and (800) 874-4352
www.thewhitelily.com

Tingle's Riverview Florist

Tingle's Riverview Florist is the source for a great selection of fresh and silk flowers, plants, greeting cards and treasures to warm your heart. Owned by Jodey and Margaret Tingle and managed by their son, Ronnie, Tingle's Riverview Florist also serves as an example of exemplary customer service. The full-service florist delivers to Frankfort and Franklin County personally, with worldwide delivery available through FTD and Teleflora, satisfaction guaranteed. Tingle's Riverview Florist can create custom gift baskets for any occasion. Pick up supplies for your celebration from their selection of balloons, candies, greeting cards and wedding invitations. Items such as stuffed animals, breathtaking quilts, baby gifts and angels make it easy to put

together a memorable package. The Tingles also offer machine quilting for your quilt tops and make custom quilts through Quiltmakers. They specialize in T-shirt and memory quilts. Tingle's Riverview Florist has been voted Best of Franklin Florists by the public each time the Frankfort/Franklin County Chamber of Commerce has offered the award. It also is one of the top 500 florists in the nation through FTD. When ordinary is not enough, visit Tingle's Riverview Florist and let flowers whisper what words can never say.

610 E Main Street, Frankfort KY
(502) 875-4037 or (888) 875-4037

Wildflowers Florist

Wildflowers Florist creates vibrant, professional flower arrangements for all occasions or just to add splashes of color to your home or office. Order custom corsages, wedding flowers or reception garlands to match your event, or browse the website too see examples of oft-requested designs. Wildflowers Florist specializes in exotic tropicals, including elegant orchids, birds of

paradise and red ginger, in minimalist designs that make the most of the shapely, vibrant flowers. In addition to flowers, the Wildflowers designers specialize in creative gift baskets filled with gourmet treats and keepsakes. Treat the movie buff in your life to a collectible movie tin filled with candy and popcorn and finished with a filmstrip-printed bow. Golfers will love the reusable golf bag cooler packed with duffer favorites. The Taste of Tuscany basket is decorated with grapevines and filled with dipping oils, vinegars, sauces and herbs. The Ultimate Coffee Break comes on a coffee tray, including Starbucks coffee, Tazo tea, a mug and accompanying sweets. Wildflowers Florist makes it easy to deliver a thoughtful gift, even if it's as simple as a candy bouquet or a cake inscribed with congratulations. When you're looking for that special touch for your special occasion, contact Wildflowers Florist.

2406 S Preston Street, Louisville KY
(502) 584-3412
www.wildflowersfloristlouisville.com

Talon Winery

Talon Winery and Vineyards sit on 300 acres of picturesque farmland adorned by sparkling ponds and bold red-roofed barns. The original 18th century farmhouse contains the tasting room and a gift shop filled with Talon souvenirs and a lavish supply of wine-related gifts and accessories. At the corking complex, visitors can view the entire bottling process. Every Talon wine is a medal winner. The vintages have won medals at competitions including the International Eastern Wines, Lonestar International Wines, Wines of the South and Indy International Wines. In line with its spirit of celebration, the winery provides a variety of venues for guest events. Covered porches on the landscaped grounds, a private tasting room, a pavilion and a party barn are available for all types of occasions. Talon employs an event planner to help with special events. Full-service catering is also available. Visitors can enjoy picnics and self-guided tours of the vineyards, the processing center and the Kentucky oak barrels. The winery holds a weekly drawing from the business cards left at the Homestead Tasting Room. Join the wine club for quarterly wine shipments with wine notes and free goodies. Other benefits include discounts on wine and on admission to shows presented by the Talon Summer Concert Series and admittance to a members-only annual club event. If you like fine wine, you'll love Talon Winery.

7086 Tates Creek Road, Lexington KY (859) 971-3214
www.talonwine.com

Chrisman Mill Vineyards & Winery

Chris and Denise Nelson have shared a lifelong love of Tuscany, its charming scenery, festive cuisine and relaxed way of life. With Chrisman Mill Vineyards, they have brought a little piece of Tuscany to Kentucky. The winery is made in the Old World image, with soft colors, French doors, cobblestone trails and herb gardens. Many of the herbs show up in the homemade breads, sauces and dressings in the gift shop. Denise is a professional chef who specializes in authentic Tuscan cuisine. She offers a full-service luncheon Thursday through Saturday at the winery's Tuscan Café and an authentic Tuscan dinner once a month by reservation only. Chris is a master winemaker whose nationally acclaimed wines have won numerous awards. Try the First Vineyard Reserve, a gold medal winning wine made from all locally grown Chambourcin. Chrisman Mill Vineyards specializes in working with Kentucky grown fruit like Vidal Blanc, Chambourcin, Norton and Seyval Blanc. Chris and Denise host a variety of special events throughout the year to help celebrate life, food and wine, including vineyard concerts, themed dinners and a chance for guests to be a winemaker for a day. Come share the passion for Kentucky excellence handcrafted one bottle at a time.

2385 Chrisman Mill Road, Nicholasville KY
(859) 881-5007
store: 2300 Sir Barton Way #175,
Lexington KY
(859) 264-WINE (9463)
www.chrismanmill.com